BORN *in* BLOOD *and* FIRE

# BORN in BLOOD and FIRE

## A Concise History of Latin America

### THIRD EDITION

John Charles Chasteen

UNIVERSITY OF NORTH CAROLINA
AT CHAPEL HILL

W. W. NORTON & COMPANY
New York   London

W. W. Norton & Company has been independent since its founding in 1923, when William Warder Norton and Mary D. Herter Norton first published lectures delivered at the People's Institute, the adult education division of New York City's Cooper Union. The firm soon expanded its program beyond the Institute, publishing books by celebrated academics from America and abroad. By midcentury, the two major pillars of Norton's publishing program—trade books and college texts—were firmly established. In the 1950s, the Norton family transferred control of the company to its employees, and today—with a staff of four hundred and a comparable number of trade, college, and professional titles published each year—W. W. Norton & Company stands as the largest and oldest publishing house owned wholly by its employees.

Nicolás Guillén, "Balada de los dos abuelos," *Obra Poetica 1920–1958, Vol. 1* (1972), pp. 137–139. Reprinted by permission of Fundación Nicolás Guillén.

Manufacturing by Maple-Vail Book Manufacturing Group
Book design by Charlotte Staub
Composition by Westchester Book Group
Project editor: Justin Hoffman
Production manager: Eric Pier-Hocking

Library of Congress Cataloging-in-Publication Data

Chasteen, John Charles, 1955–
    Born in blood and fire : a concise history of Latin America / John Charles Chasteen.—3rd ed.
        p.   cm.
    Includes bibliographical references and index.
    ISBN 978-0-393-91154-1 (pbk.)
    1. Latin America—History.   I. Title.
    F1410.C4397 2011
    980—dc22

                                                                2010045642
ISBN 978-0-393-91154-1 (pbk.)

W. W. Norton & Company, Inc., 500 Fifth Avenue, New York, N.Y. 10110
www.wwnorton.com

W. W. Norton & Company Ltd., Castle House, 75/76 Wells Street, London
WIT 3QT

1   2   3   4   5   6   7   8   9   0

*To my children,*
  *Ana and Erwin Chasteen,*
    *two among so many Latin American immigrants*
    *who are making the United States a better place*
                            *in the new millennium*

# CONTENTS

# MAPS

# Acknowledgment

At least one hundred of my students at the University of North Carolina read this book before it was published. To them, my grateful acknowledgment. Their enthusiasm encouraged me to keep it informal, vivid, and short. "I feel like this book *wants* me to understand it," said one of them.

When the first edition appeared, several professors and graduate students helpfully set me straight on factual errors. Much appreciated! I also got, and still get, e-mails from undergraduate readers who write just to say "I like your book." Thanks for those e-mails. It's really *your* book.

# Time Line

| | |
|---|---|
| **ENCOUNTER** 1492–1600 | The fully sedentary Mexicas, who built the Aztec Empire, were conquered and their empire was taken over by the Spaniards, but Mexican blood still runs in Mexican veins. |
| **COLONIAL CRUCIBLE** 1600–1810 | Because of its dense indigenous population and its rich silver mines, Mexico (or much of it) became a core area of Spanish colonization. |
| **INDEPENDENCE** 1810–1825 | The large peasant uprisings led by Hidalgo and Morelos frightened Mexican Creoles into a conservative stance on independence, which they embraced only in 1821. |
| **POSTCOLONIAL BLUES** 1825–1850 | The national government was frequently overthrown as liberals and conservatives struggled for control. The career of the caudillo Santa Anna represents the turmoil. |
| **PROGRESS** 1850–1880 | The great liberal Reform of the 1850s provoked the conservatives to support a foreign prince, Maximilian. The liberals, led by Juárez, emerged triumphant by the late 1860s. |
| **NEOCOLONIALISM** 1880–1930 | The dictatorship of Porfirio Díaz, called the Porfiriato (1876–1911), embodied neocolonialism in Mexico. Díaz invited international investment and used it to consolidate the Mexican state. |
| **NATIONALISM** 1910–1945 | The Mexican Revolution led Latin America's nationalist trend in 1910. The presidency of Lázaro Cárdenas (1934–40) marked the high point of its accomplishments. |
| **REVOLUTION** 1945–1960 | Mexico's revolution became more conservative and institutionalized (in the PRI) even as radical change accelerated elsewhere. |
| **REACTION** 1960–1990 | Overall, the PRI used its revolutionary imagery to absorb challenges from the left—except when it used bullets, as in the 1968 Tlatelolco massacre. |

| BRAZIL | ARGENTINA |
|---|---|
| The semisedentary Tupi people of the Brazilian forests were destroyed and their labor replaced by African slaves whom the Portuguese brought to grow sugarcane. | The nonsedentary, plains-dwelling Pampas people were eventually wiped out. Much later, European immigrants took their place on the land. |
| Profitable sugar plantations made the northeastern coast a core area of Portuguese colonization, but much of Brazil remained a poorer fringe. | Most of Argentina remained on the fringe of Spanish colonization until 1776, when Buenos Aires became the capital of a new Spanish viceroyalty. |
| The Portuguese royal family's presence kept Brazil relatively quiet as war raged elsewhere. Prince Pedro declared Brazilian independence himself in 1822. | Without massive populations of oppressed indigenous people or slaves to fear, Buenos Aires Creoles quickly embraced the May Revolution (1810). |
| The stormy reign of Pedro I (1822–31) was followed by the even stormier Regency (1831–40). But the Brazilian Empire gained stability in the 1840s as coffee exports rose. | The conservative dictator Rosas dominated Buenos Aires (and therefore, much of Argentina) for most of these years, exiling the liberal opposition. |
| Pedro II (1840–89) cautiously promoted liberal-style progress while maintaining a strongly hierarchical system. Brazil ended slavery only in 1888. | Liberals took over after the fall of Rosas (1852), but not until the 1860s did they manage to unite all Argentina under one national government. |
| Brazil's First Republic (1889–1930) was a highly decentralized oligarchy built, above all, on coffee exports. The leading coffee-growing state, São Paulo, became dominant. | Buenos Aires and the surrounding areas underwent an agricultural and immigration boom of vast proportions. Various regional oligarchies ruled until the election of 1916. |
| Getúlio Vargas, president 1930–35, defined Brazilian nationalism in this period. In 1937, Vargas dissolved Congress and formed the authoritarian Estado Novo. | Argentina's Radical Party was driven by the ballot box. It displaced the landowning oligarchy but remained mired in traditional patronage politics. |
| Populism and the electoral clout of organized labor (led first by Vargas, then by his heirs) energized Brazilian politics after World War II. | Juan and Evita Perón (1946–55) made the working class a leading force in Argentine politics. Perón's followers remained loyal long after his exile. |
| The Brazilian military overthrew the populist president Goulart in 1964 and ruled for twenty years in the name of efficiency and anticommunism. | Taking control in 1966, the Argentine military won its "dirty war" against Peronist guerrillas but bowed out in 1983 after losing to Britain in the Falklands war. |

BORN *in* BLOOD *and* FIRE

**PABLO.** Pablo was a little boy who lived at a Colombian boardinghouse in 1978, when I lived there, too. On hot afternoons, Pablo sometimes took a bath in the back patio of the house, the *patio de ropas,* where several women washed the boarders' clothes by hand. He was having a wonderful time on this particular afternoon, as happy as any little boy anywhere, despite the modest character of our dollar-a-day accommodations. *Snapshot taken by the author at the age of twenty-two.*

# INTRODUCTION

Latin America was born in blood and fire, in conquest and slavery. So that is where to begin a brief introduction to Latin American history, cutting straight to the heart of the matter, identifying central conflicts, and not mincing words. It is precisely conquest and its sequel, colonization, that created the central conflict of Latin American history. Conquest and colonization form the unified starting place of a single story, told here with illustrative examples from many countries. We need a single story. Rapid panoramas of twenty national histories would merely produce dizziness. But, before beginning the story, we must ask whether so many countries can really share a single history. At first blush, one might doubt it. Consider everything that story would have to encompass. Consider the contrasts and paradoxes of contemporary Latin America.

Latin America is young—the average age is in the teens in many countries—with all the innovative dynamism that youth implies. And it is old—a land of ancient ruins, of whitewashed walls and red-tile-roofed hamlets continuously inhabited for a thousand years. Some Latin Americans still grow corn or manioc on small plots hidden among banana trees, carrying on fairly traditional rural ways of life. These days, however, most Latin Americans live in noisy, restless cities that make their societies far more urbanized than those of developing countries in Asia or Africa. Megacities like Buenos Aires, São Paulo, and Mexico City have far outstripped the ten-million mark, and many other capitals of the region are not far behind. Latin America is the developing world and also the West, a place where more than nine out of ten people speak a European language and practice a European religion. Most of the world's Roman Catholics are Latin Americans. And Latin America has deep roots in indigenous cultures, too. Most of the world's native Americans, by far, live south of the Rio Grande.

Today many Latin Americans live and work in circumstances not so different from those of middle-class people in the United States. The resemblance seems to have grown in recent years, as government after government throughout the region has liberalized its trade policies, facilitating the importation of cars, videocassette recorders, and fax machines. But the vast majority of Latin Americans are far from being able to afford such things. A family that owns any sort of car is much better off than most, but the great majority do have some access to a TV, if only at the house of a neighbor. So Brazilians and Chileans and Colombians who cannot have a car nevertheless live thoroughly immersed in Western consumer culture and, night after night, watch bright television commercials tailored to those able to emulate the lifestyle of the US middle class. It is for this reason, and not just because of proximity and poverty, that so many Latin Americans come to the United States.

Consider next the contrasts among countries. Brazil occupies half the South American continent, its population surging toward two hundred million. Most countries in Latin America are quite small, however. The populations of Panama, Puerto Rico, Paraguay, Nicaragua, Honduras, and El Salvador *added together* could fit in Mexico City or, for that matter, in Brazil's urban giant, São Paulo. Contrasts in other social indicators are also vast. Argentina and Uruguay have adult literacy rates comparable to those in the United States and Canada, whereas 30 percent of the adult population in Guatemala cannot read. Costa Ricans live to a ripe old average age of seventy-seven, Bolivians to only sixty-three.

Now ponder the incredible ethnic complexity of Latin America. Most Mexicans are descended from indigenous people and from the Spanish who colonized Mexico. The Mexican celebration of the Day of the Dead—with its candy skulls, inviting people to "eat their own death"—embodies a mood so unfamiliar to people from the United States precisely because its intimate inspirations are largely non-Western. The capital of Argentina, on the other hand, is ethnically more European than is Washington DC. Not only does a larger percentage of the population descend exclusively from European immigrants, but they also maintain more European contacts, such as dual Argentine-Spanish citizenship and relatives born or still living in Italy or England. The modern cityscape of Buenos Aires is very self-consciously modeled on Paris, and French movies enjoy a popularity there unheard of in the United States.

The experience of racial diversity has been central to Latin American history. Latin America was the main destination of the millions of people enslaved and taken out of Africa between 1500 and 1850. Whereas the United States received about 523,000 enslaved immigrants, Cuba alone got more. All Spanish America absorbed around 1.5 million slaves, and Brazil by itself at least 3.5 million. From the Caribbean, down both coasts of South America, African slaves performed a thousand tasks, but most especially they cultivated sugarcane. Today their descendants form large parts of the population—about half, overall—in the two greatest historical centers of sugar production, Brazil and the Caribbean region.

Latin American countries are highly multiethnic, and all sorts of racial combinations occur. Costa Rica, Uruguay, and Southern Brazil, like Argentina, have populations of mostly

European extraction. Some countries, such as Mexico, Paraguay, El Salvador, and Chile, have very mixed, or *mestizo* populations of blended indigenous and European heritage. Other
countries, such as Peru, Guatemala, Ecuador, and Bolivia, have
large populations of indigenous people who remain separate
from the mestizos, speak indigenous languages such as Quechua or Aymara, and follow distinctive customs in clothing and
food. In many countries, black and white populations live in the
coastal lowlands, with a more indigenous and white mix in the
mountainous interior regions. Cuba, Puerto Rico, Nicaragua,
Costa Rica, Honduras, Colombia, Ecuador, Peru, and Venezuela all follow this pattern. Brazil, the fifth largest country in the
world, shows regional demographic variations on a grand scale—
whiter in the south, blacker on the north coast, with indigenous
influence still visible only in the large but sparsely populated
Amazon basin.

To repeat the question, then, do these twenty countries, in
all their startling variety, really have a single history? No, in the
sense that a single story cannot encompass their diversity. Yes,
in the sense that all have much in common. They experienced
a similar process of European conquest and colonization. They
became independent more or less at the same time. They have
struggled with similar problems in a series of similar ways. Since
independence, other clearly defined political trends have washed
over Latin America, giving its history a unified ebb and flow.

In 1980, most governments of the region were dictatorships of
various descriptions. In 2010, elected governments rule almost
everywhere. The globalizing energies of the 1990s helped Latin
America leave behind its 1980s "Lost Decade" of debt, inflation,
and stagnation. Economic recovery gave prestige to the "neoliberal" (basically free-market) policies pursued by practically all
governments in the region. But, as in much of the world, current
free-market growth seemed to make the rich richer, the middle
class more middle-class, and the poor comparatively poorer. In

Latin America, with a poor majority, that kind of growth can produce more losers than winners, and a strong reaction to free markets has now set in.

Winners and losers. Rich and poor. Conquerors and conquered. Masters and slaves. That is the old, old conflict at the heart of Latin American history. The conflict remains alive and well. To protest the implementation of the North American Free Trade Agreement (NAFTA) between the United States and Mexico in the 1990s, Mayan rebels began an uprising that lasted years. These Mayan rebels took the name Zapatistas in memory of earlier rebels, many of them indigenous, who fought for land reform in the early 1900s. Middle-class Mexicans found that NAFTA reduced prices and increased the availability of urban consumer goods. The Zapatistas continued to protest, but the Mexican government kept NAFTA in place. Meanwhile, Bolivians elected their first indigenous president in 2006, but he faced angry defiance from the less indigenous parts of the country.

Aspects of this confrontation can be traced straight back to 1492, which is the purpose of this book. Here, in a nutshell, is the story: In the 1500s, Spanish and Portuguese colonizers imposed their language, their religion, and their social institutions on the indigenous Americans and enslaved Africans, people who labored for them in mines and fields and who served them, too, at table and in bed. After three centuries of this, however, things began to change (at least partly) with the introduction of two new political forces.

The first force was *liberalism*. Students should carefully separate this international meaning of liberalism from narrow US uses of the word. Liberalism, in this larger sense, comprises the core principles of the US constitution, principles shared by Republicans and Democrats alike. Historically, liberalism is a complex of values and practices that developed in the 1600s and 1700s, largely in France and England. Both 1776 and 1789 (marking the American and French Revolutions) are landmark dates in world liberalism. Liberalism favors progress over tradition, reason over faith, universal over local values, and the free market over government control. Liberalism also advocates equal citizenship over entrenched privilege and representative democracy over all other forms of government. Unfortunately, these last elements have sometimes been treated as icing on the cake, a finishing touch too often put off. Overall, the US experience with liberalism has produced prosperity. The Latin American experience with liberalism, on the other hand, has been more mixed.

*Nationalism*, the second new political force, eventually became liberalism's rough opposite. Liberalism and nationalism emerged together in the struggle for Latin American independence. Latin American nationalism—different in different countries but always built on similar themes—is deeply embedded in the region's historical experience. A portrait of nationalism will emerge gradually over the course of this book. One initial observation: People in the United States often regard nationalism (nationalism *elsewhere*, anyway) as negative. But Latin American nationalism has often provided an ideological self-defense against imperialism, a positive force for social equality, and an antidote to white supremacy.

At the turn of the twenty-first century, Europeans no longer ride on the backs of indigenous porters or in sedan chairs carried by African slaves. But everywhere, wealthier people still have lighter skin and poorer people still have darker skin—a sweeping but sadly accurate generalization that does have exceptions, and lots of them, but only of the kind that prove the rule. The conclusion is inescapable: The descendants of the Spanish, the Portuguese, and later European immigrants to Latin America still hold power, and the people who descend from slaves and subjugated indigenous people still work for them. Half a millennium later, this is clearly the enduring legacy, rippling across the centuries, of the fact that African, European, and indigenous

American people did not come together on neutral terms, like various pedestrians arriving simultaneously at a bus stop. Just how they did come together will be our concern in the next chapter. (Get ready for the blood and fire.)

This quick introduction is for US readers who are encountering Latin American history for the first time. Such readers need to know something about past US thinking on Latin America, because examples of it float freely in our popular culture and still influence our ideas.

Until roughly the 1930s, the interpreters of Latin America focused largely on race and culture, considering the Latin American varieties defective goods. "Hot-blooded Latins" with too much "nonwhite blood," according to this outmoded idea, simply lacked the self-discipline and the brains to make stable, democratic, prosperous societies. As Catholics, they lacked a "Protestant work ethic" (to make work not just a necessity, but a virtue), and their tropical climates further discouraged economic activity with debilitating heat and too many sensuous satisfactions—mangoes, papayas, and passion fruit—literally, as well as figuratively, growing on trees. In this version, Latin American history was racially, culturally, or environmentally "determined," and more or less inescapably so.

Between 1940 and 1970, racial and environmental determinism went out of style intellectually. US historians of Latin America replaced the former villains of the region's history (those pesky indigenous or African genes) with new bad guys: backward mentalities and traditional social structures that had to be "modernized" so that Latin America could advance along the developmental trail blazed by other countries. While "modernization theory" was an advance over racial and environmental determinism, it maintained existing stereotypes. Greedy landowners and backward rulers took over from congenital laziness and tropical heat as explanations for Latin American

Modern
Latin America

problems. One thing remained the same: US explanations for the region's problems always began and ended with Latin America itself.

During the 1960s, however, most historians of Latin America inside and outside the region became convinced that earlier interpretations of its problems were a convenient way to blame the victim. Instead, they argued that Latin American economies stood in a permanently dependent position relative to the world's industrial powers, which were always at least one step ahead of them developmentally. "Dependency theory" thus located the origin of Latin American problems outside the region, partly in the action of colonizing powers, partly in the forces of economic globalization—although "globalization" was not yet the common term.

Dependency theory still provides useful insights, but it has lost its central place in Latin American studies. In the United States, interest in Latin America now focuses on matters that also preoccupy us at home. For example, as US citizens explore new ways of thinking about race, they are interested to learn that Latin Americans long ago embraced multiracial identities. People concerned with multiculturalism and "identity politics" in the United States find a valuable comparative perspective in Latin America. By the 1990s, both the humanities and the social sciences gave new prominence to the study of culture and, more specifically, to the way race, gender, class, and national identities are "constructed" in people's minds. To be male or female is a matter of genes, of biology, but the definition of a "real man" or a "real woman," for example, differs greatly from culture to culture. In matters of cultural and racial complexity, the world has much to learn from the Latin American experience.

Let us begin our story.

**COLUMBUS AND THE ARAWAKS.** Until recently, we spoke of the "Discovery" of America, which means telling the story from the European point of view. Today, in memory of the people already here in 1492, we use a more neutral term—the "Encounter." This 1594 engraving by Theodore de Bry helped Europeans imagine Columbus (with a jaunty hat) encountering the Arawaks of the Caribbean for the first time. (Yes, those are the gift-bearing Arawaks looking more like figures from European art history than like indigenous Americans.) *Courtesy of Bettmann/Corbis.*

| 1400s | 1492–1500 | 1500–20 | 1520s–30s | 1548 |
|---|---|---|---|---|
| Aztec and Inca Empires rise | Columbus and Cabral voyages | Slave trade under way | Defeat of the Aztecs and Incas | Royal government established in Brazil |

# I.

# ENCOUNTER

Indigenous peoples inhabited almost every inch of the Americas when the Europeans and Africans arrived. Deserts and forests were less densely populated than fertile valleys, but no part of the continent lacked people who lived off the land and considered themselves part of it. The Encounter between native Americans and Europeans constitutes a defining moment in world history. Neither the Europeans' "Old World" nor the "New World," as they called the Americas, would ever be the same afterward. For Latin America, conquest and colonization by the Spanish and Portuguese created patterns of social domination that became eternal givens, like the deep and lasting marks of an original sin.*

The Iberian invaders of America were personally no more sinful than most. They came to America seeking success in the terms dictated by their society: riches, the privilege of being served by others, and a claim to religious righteousness. It makes little sense for us to judge their moral quality as human beings because they merely lived the logic of the world as they understood it, just as we do. The original sin lay in the logic, justified

---

*In Christian belief, Adam and Eve committed the original sin in the Garden of Eden, and all their descendants later inherited that sin.

in religious terms, that assumed a right to conquer and colonize. One way or another, the European logic of conquest and colonization soured the Encounter everywhere from Mexico to Argentina. The basic scenario varied according to the natural environment and the indigenous peoples' way of life when the European invaders arrived.

## PATTERNS OF INDIGENOUS LIFE

The indigenous peoples of the Americas had adapted themselves to the land in many ways. Some were *nonsedentary*, an adaptation to difficult environments such as the northern deserts of Mexico, the territory of the Chichimecas. Nonsedentary people led a mobile existence as hunters and gatherers, and movement kept their groups small and their social organization relatively simple. Often they roamed open plains. Arid plains occupy a wide swath of the interior of South America, then inhabited by tribes of hunters and gatherers. Not forests, neither were these exactly grasslands at the time of the Encounter. Instead, they bristled with various kinds of scrub that, as in the northeastern Brazilian area called the *sertão*, might be thorny and drop its leaves in the dry season. The Pampas peoples who gave their name to the Argentine grasslands were also nonsedentary.

Other indigenous Americans were forest dwellers. Hunting was important to them, too, but the abundant rainfall characterizing most forest environments allowed them to depend on agriculture in a way that the nonsedentary people could not, and so forest peoples were often *semisedentary*. Their agricultural practices were adapted to thin tropical soils. Thin soils? Yes: The exuberant vegetation of tropical forests produces a misleading impression. Outsiders think of these forests as "jungles," a word that suggests overpowering, unstoppable fertility.

Thus, a 1949 geography text* speaks of "the relentless fecundity and savagery of the jungle." In fact, the breathtaking vitality of tropical forests resides not in the soil, but in living things, such as insects, trees, and the various tree-dwelling epiphytes that have no roots in the ground. Particularly in the great rain forest of the Amazon basin, the soils are of marginal fertility. Once cleared for agriculture, tropical forest soils produce disappointing yields after only a few years. Therefore, forest-dwelling indigenous peoples practiced "shifting cultivation," sometimes called "slash and burn" because of the way they cleared their garden plots. Semisedentary people built villages but moved them frequently, allowing old garden plots to be reabsorbed into the forest and opening new ones elsewhere. Shifting cultivation was thus a successful adaptation to one of the world's most challenging natural environments. Semisedentary societies, like the forest-dwelling Tupi, the best-known indigenous people of Brazilian history, organized themselves by tribes and by gender roles, but not by social class. Nor did they build empires.

Finally, some indigenous people were *fully sedentary*. Permanent settlement, usually on high plateaus rather than in forests, made their societies more complex, and some constructed great empires, especially the fabled Aztec, Inca, and Maya empires. Not all sedentaries had empires, however. What all had in common were stationary, permanently sustainable forms of agriculture. For example, the capital of the Aztec Empire—more populous than Madrid or Lisbon—was fed by quite an ingenious method. Tenochtitlan was surrounded by lake waters on all sides, and in these waters the inhabitants of the city constructed garden platforms called *chinampas*. Alluvial deposits

*William Lytle Schurz, *Latin America: A Descriptive Survey* (New York: E. P. Dutton, 1949), 28.

periodically renewed their fertility. The builders of the Inca Empire had their own elaborate form of sustainable agriculture involving terraced slopes, irrigation, and the use of nitrate-rich bird droppings, called *guano*, for fertilizer. A permanent agricultural base allowed the growth of larger, denser conglomerations of people, the construction of cities, greater labor specialization—all sorts of things. Not all were good things. Whereas the non- or semisedentary people tended toward fairly egalitarian societies, in which outstanding individuals became leaders thanks to their personal qualities, fully sedentary groups were strongly stratified by class. Aztecs, Incas, and Mayas all had hereditary nobilities that specialized in war.

Note that the names Aztec and Inca refer to *empires* and not, strictly speaking, to their inhabitants at all. The rulers of the Aztec Empire were a people called the Mexicas, who gave their name to Mexico. The warlike Mexicas were relative newcomers to the fertile valley where they built their amazing city, Tenochtitlan, on a lake in the shadow of great volcanoes, but they inherited a civilization that had developed in Mexico's central highlands over thousands of years. For example, the gargantuan Pyramid of the Sun, the largest pyramid on earth, was built long before the Mexicas arrived. In the early 1400s, the Mexicas were only one among many groups who spoke Nahuatl, the common language of city-states in the region. But they conquered much of central Mexico during the next one hundred years. Tenochtitlan, the imperial capital, was a vast and teeming complex of towers, palaces, and pyramids that, according to the flabbergasted Spanish adventurer Bernal Díaz, rose like a mirage from the waters of the surrounding lake, linked to the shore by a series of perfectly straight and level causeways. "We were astonished and said these things appeared enchantments from a book of chivalry," wrote Díaz, describing the Spaniards' first sight of Tenochtitlan.

**The Great Temple of Tenochtitlan.** The site of human sacrifice was part of a walled ceremonial complex, 300 meters square, at the heart of the Aztec capital, later the location of the cathedral of Mexico City. *The Granger Collection, New York.*

From an imposing capital city in a high Andean valley far to the south, the even larger Inca Empire had grown just as rapidly and recently as had the Aztec Empire. The Inca capital was called Cuzco, meaning "the navel of the universe." Today one speaks of "the Incas," but the name Inca actually referred only to the emperor and his empire. Ethnically, the people of Cuzco were Quechua speakers, and they, too, drew on a long history of previous cultural evolution in the Andes. Cuzco's architectural marvels—earthquake-resistant masonry walls with interlocking stones—were an old trick among Andean builders. Heirs to ancient civilizations, the Aztec and Inca Empires were newer and more fragile than they appeared. The Mayas were less imperially inclined. Beginning much earlier than Tenochtitlan and Cuzco, various Maya city-states with imposing ceremonial centers held sway in Central America: Tikal, Copán, Tulum, Uxmal. In cultural attainments, such as art, architecture, and astronomy, the Mayas were second to none in America. But the Mayas did not create an empire to rival the Inca or Aztec empires. And since the high point of the Maya Empire, if such a term really applies, was many centuries before the Europeans arrived, it plays little part in our story.

At the moment of the Encounter, then, most of Latin America was inhabited by nonsedentary or semisedentary people, such as the Pampas of Argentina or the Tupis of Brazil. Today, few of their descendants remain. Instead, the large indigenous populations of Latin America descend from the sedentary farmers, many of whom lived under Aztec, Maya, or Inca rule until the Europeans arrived. Why did they survive when the others perished? The answer is complex, but it explains much about Latin America. It requires, first, some background about Spain and Portugal, joined under the geographical name *Iberia*.

## ORIGINS OF A CRUSADING MENTALITY

In the 1490s, when Europeans clambered out of their cramped sailing vessels to face indigenous Americans for the first time, the greatest question was how each would react to the other. This was truly a cultural encounter, a clash of values and attitudes. The Spanish and Portuguese outlook, along with their crusader rhetoric, had been shaped by the history of the Iberian Peninsula.

Iberia is a rugged, mountainous land. Parts of it are as green as Ireland (very green, indeed), but most of it is dry. On pictures taken from space, southern Spain appears the same color as nearby northern Africa. Historically, Iberia had been a bridge between Europe and Africa, and the narrow straits of Gibraltar separating the two continents had often been crossed, in both directions, by migrants and invaders. In the year 711, Muslims from northern Africa, called Moors, began to cross heading north and seized most of the peninsula from its Christian kings (whose predecessors, generations earlier, had taken it from the Romans, who, in turn, had seized it from the Carthaginians, and so on). For most of the next eight hundred years, Iberia contained multiethnic societies that intermingled but also fought one another. Both activities left their mark.

Along with the practical skills of the Islamic world, the Moors brought with them the learning of the Greeks and Romans, better preserved in the Middle East during Europe's Dark Ages. Christians who lived under Moorish rule or who traded with Moorish neighbors from the remaining Christian kingdoms learned a healthy respect for the cultural achievements of Islam. The Moors were better physicians, better engineers, and better farmers than the Iberian Christians, whose languages gradually filled with Arabic words for new crops (such as basil, artichokes, and almonds), new processes and substances (such as distillation and alcohol), new furnishings (such as carpeting), and new

*Moors = dark skinned*
*Did not look european*

sciences (such as algebra and chemistry)—eventually totaling about a quarter of all modern Spanish and Portuguese words. Although speakers of Arabic, the Moors were darker than Arabs. Shakespeare's "black" character Othello, for example, is a Moor. So the Christians of Iberia had long exposure to a sophisticated and powerful people who did not look European. In addition, on the eve of the Encounter, Iberia had one of the largest Jewish minorities in Europe, and Lisbon and Seville were already home to thousands of enslaved Africans. Not sympathetic to cultural and racial difference, the Iberians were nevertheless well acquainted with it. Spanish and Portuguese attitudes toward other people ranged from scorn to grudging admiration to sexual curiosity—dusky Moorish maidens figure erotically in Iberian folktales. The reign of Alfonso the Wise (1252–84), a noted lawgiver, represents a high point in this tense, multicultural Iberian world. In the end, however, the peninsula's eight hundred years of multicultural experience dissolved in an intolerant drive for religious purity.

The Christian reconquest of Iberia powerfully shaped the institutions and mentality of the Spanish and Portuguese. Iberian Christians believed that they had found the tomb of Santiago, Saint James the Apostle, in the remote northwestern corner of the peninsula never conquered by the Moors. The Moor-slaying Santiago, pictured as a sword-swinging knight, became the patron saint of reconquest, and his tomb in Santiago de Compostela became Europe's greatest shrine. Reconquest brought the repeated challenges of annexing new territory and subjugating infidel populations. As they pushed the Moors south toward Africa over thirty generations, the reconquering Christians founded new urban centers as bastions of their advancing territorial claims, and individual warlords took responsibility for Christianizing groups of defeated Moors, receiving tribute and service from them in return. The same challenges and the same procedures would be repeated in America. Another effect of the reconquest was to perpetuate the knightly renown and influence of the Christian nobility. For this reason, the values of the nobles (fighting prowess, leisure, display of wealth) lost ground only slowly to the values of the commercial middle class (moneymaking, industry, thrift). In addition, the requirements of warfare led to a concentration of political power to facilitate decisive, unified command. Two of the peninsula's many small Christian kingdoms gradually emerged as leaders of the reconquest. The most important by far was centrally located Castile, whose dominions eventually engulfed much of Iberia and, when united with the kingdoms of Aragon, León, and Navarre, laid the political basis for modern Spain. On the Atlantic coast, the king of Portugal led a parallel advance south and managed to maintain independence from Spain. Portugal was the first to complete its reconquest, reaching the southern coast of Iberia in the mid-1200s. On the Spanish side, the Moorish kingdom of Granada held out for two more centuries before finally succumbing to Castilian military power in 1492.

When Queen Isabel of Castile decided to bankroll the explorations of Christopher Columbus in the 1490s, she did so in hopes of enriching her kingdom, true enough. By sailing west, Columbus proposed to outflank a profitable Venetian-Arab monopoly on trade routes to Asia. But we should not underestimate the religious mystique that also surrounded the Spanish and Portuguese monarchs. Isabel was above all a Catholic monarch. Centuries of reconquest had created a true crusading mentality in Iberia, and the monarchies used this fervor to justify their increasingly absolute power. Moors who had accepted Christian rule, Jews whose families had lived in Iberia for close to a thousand years, and anyone suspected of religious infidelity found themselves objects of a purge. Moors and Jews were forced to convert or emigrate. In fact, in the very year of the surrender of Granada, Isabel expelled tens of thousands of people from Spain because they refused to renounce the Jewish

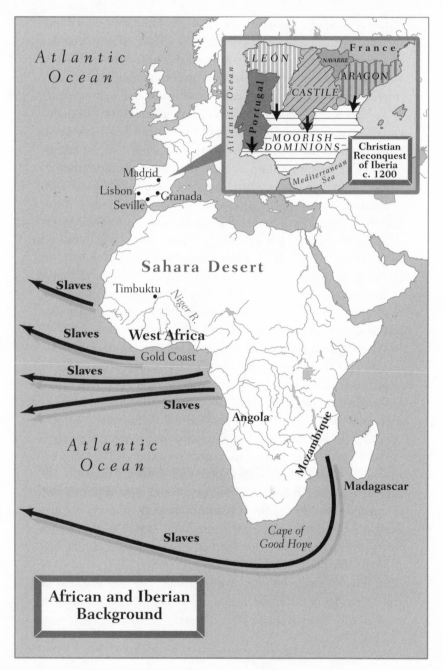

African and Iberian Background

faith. And Moors and Jews who did convert remained subject to discrimination as "New Christians." The famous Spanish Inquisition was established to impose religious purity.

During the 1500s, Catholics and Protestants began fighting bitterly in western Europe, and the monarchs of a unified Spain led the Catholic side, pouring prodigious resources into the war effort. Recall that in 1588 the Spanish Armada attempted to invade Protestant England. Overseas exploration also took on religious significance. The earlier Christian reconquest in Portugal allowed the Portuguese to extend their crusading activities into Africa ahead of Spain. As Portuguese ships edged down the coast of Africa during the 1400s, bringing back gold and slaves, they found religious justification in tales of a lost Christian kingdom that supposedly lay beyond the Sahara, waiting to be reunited with the rest of Christendom. Isabel's decision to fund the voyages of Columbus was Spain's bid to catch up with Portugal. Thus, the two Iberian monarchies, strengthened politically by the reconquest, became the first in Europe to sponsor major overseas exploration, and they arrived in the Western Hemisphere neck and neck.

Although the Spanish-sponsored expedition of Columbus arrived in America first, the difference was less than a decade. Let us start with the Portuguese, who had pioneered the navigational skills and naval technology needed to get there. The Portuguese colonization of Brazil exemplifies what happened when the Europeans encountered indigenous people who were not fully sedentary. An initial look at Brazil will help us appreciate the unique qualities of the very different, and far more famous, encounter of the Spanish with the fully sedentary peoples of indigenous Mexico and Peru.

## THE BRAZILIAN COUNTEREXAMPLE

The first Portuguese fleet arrived in Brazil in 1500. Like Columbus a few years earlier, the Portuguese commander Pedro Alvares Cabral was bound for India, but in contrast to Columbus, he actually did get there. Cabral had no intention of sailing around the world. Instead, he was sailing from Portugal down the west coast of Africa and around its southern tip into the Indian Ocean. To catch the best winds, he had swung far out into the South Atlantic on his southward voyage—so far out, in fact, that before turning back east he bumped into Brazil. Like Columbus, Cabral did not know exactly what he had found, but he knew that it was not India. After naming Brazil the "Island of the True Cross," Cabral hurried on to his original destination.

Brazil seemed unimportant to the Portuguese at the time. Just a few years earlier, they had succeeded in establishing a practical route to the fabled riches of South Asia—which Columbus had failed to do. For the rest of the 1500s, the Portuguese concentrated on exploiting their early advantage in the Far Eastern trade. Portuguese outposts elsewhere reached from Africa to Arabia, India, Indonesia, China, and Japan. Portuguese ships returned to Europe perilously overloaded with silks and porcelain, precious spices (pepper, nutmeg, cloves, and cinnamon), and Persian horses, not to mention gold and silver. Monopoly access to these riches made Portugal, for a time, a major player in world history. Brazil offered nothing comparable to India in the eyes of Cabral or his chronicler, Pero Vaz de Caminha. Caminha's curious description of what he saw on Brazilian shores presented a vision of a new Garden of Eden, paying particular attention to the fact that the indigenous people there wore no clothes: "They go around naked, without any covering at all. They worry no more about showing their private parts than their faces." The Portuguese sailors plainly found indigenous women attractive and inviting, but the only thing that seemed to have potential for sale in Europe was a red dye made from the "brazilwood" tree.

The name of this export product quickly replaced the original name of "Island of the True Cross," just as economics upstaged religion, overall, in the colonization of Brazil and Spanish America. Still, religious ideas must not be discounted. "Fathers, pray that God make me chaste and zealous enough to expand our Faith throughout the world," implored the young Portuguese prince Sebastian, with unquestionable sincerity, to his Jesuit tutors. Europeans of the 1500s believed in the teachings of their religion as a matter of course, and some Portuguese and Spanish men, especially those in holy orders such as the Jesuits, undertook quite perilous voyages around the world primarily to save souls. In sum, however, the vast majority of people had a mundane mix of motivations, and the lure of worldly success was constantly evident in their actions. The idea of spreading Christianity provided, above all, a compelling rationale for laying claim to huge chunks of the "undiscovered" world. Consequently, religious ideas became particularly influential at the level of formal rationalization. Whenever the invaders of America had to explain and justify their actions, they invoked religious goals for reasons no more sinister than the common human wish to present oneself in the best light.

Aside from their immortal souls, forest dwellers like the Tupi did not have very much that the Europeans wanted, so they were left more or less alone at first. Along the Brazilian coast, some mutually advantageous trade developed when Tupi men were willing to fell the brazilwood and float the logs to trading stations in return for useful items such as steel axes. Occasionally, Portuguese castaways or exiles "went native," to live among the indigenous people, and found a different kind of worldly success, becoming influential figures in their localities and, in a manner foreshadowed by the chronicle of Pero Vaz de Caminha, fathering dozens and dozens of children—the beginnings of a process of racial mixing that has characterized the history of Brazil. The king of Portugal was too preoccupied with his Asian empire to think much about Brazil until the 1530s, when the appearance of French ships along the Brazilian coast made him fear for his claims there. To secure them, he finally sent Portuguese settlers to Brazil. Suddenly, the Portuguese did want something that the Tupi possessed—their land. Now everything would change.

To the Portuguese, settling the land meant clearing the forest and planting crops, and sugarcane was the only crop with major export potential. It could be milled and boiled down into concentrated, imperishable blocks packed in wooden chests that fit easily into the small sailing ships of the day, and it brought a high price in Europe, where sugarcane did not grow. These qualities made sugarcane the cash crop of choice for centuries, first in Brazil and later in the Caribbean and throughout the lowlands of tropical America—anywhere landowners measured their success according to what they could buy in Europe. And that was more or less everywhere in the Iberian colonies. Sugar was a plantation crop, requiring plenty of capital investment and a large labor force, a crop where the profits of the planter were partly a function of cheap labor. But no Portuguese settlers wanted to provide cheap agricultural labor. Indeed, Iberians in America were typically loathe to do any manual work at all, because it contradicted their model of wordly success. As for Tupi men, they traditionally hunted and fished and regarded farming as women's work. Why should indigenous men or women hoe weeds and chop cane for meager wages under the burning sun when the forest gave them everything they wanted? In any event, their semisedentary way of life involved periodic movement incompatible with the plantation's need for a fixed labor force.

To gain the land and the labor of forest people like the Tupi, the Portuguese resorted to force of arms. This meant attacking and enslaving each tribal group of a few hundred, one by one, in bloody skirmishes, an activity quite taxing to the limited manpower of the Portuguese. Here were no decisive battles that put large defeated populations at the victors' disposal. Other factors made the task even harder. American forest dwellers used the bow and the blowgun with deadly effect. The invaders' horses—elsewhere something like a secret weapon for the Europeans, because they did not exist in America before the Encounter—could hardly move amid hanging vines, fallen trunks, and tangled roots. To those who know it, the forest provides countless opportunities to hide, to escape, and to ambush pursuers. Even after they were defeated, native Brazilians would melt into the limitless woodland beyond the plantations if not supervised constantly. In other words, extracting land and labor from semisedentary forest dwellers meant totally destroying their society and enslaving them. Most were likely to die in the process.

This is exactly what happened all along the coast of Brazil once the Portuguese began to establish sugar plantations. The king of Portugal, who viewed the indigenous people as potentially loyal subjects, did not approve of this wholesale annihilation, but his power in Brazil was surprisingly limited. In an attempt to settle two thousand miles of coastline on the cheap, the king had parceled out enormous slices to wealthy individuals, called captains, who promised to colonize and rule in his name. Significantly, the most successful were those who minimized conflict with the indigenous people. Pernambuco, on the very northeastern tip of Brazil, became the model sugar captaincy, partly because the family of its captain established an alliance by marriage with a local chief. Most of the captaincies failed, however. By the mid-1540s, indigenous rebellions threatened to erupt up and down the coast. On the splendid Bay of All Saints, the Tupinambá, a subgroup of the Tupi, had demolished one of the most promising settlements. So, in 1548, the Portuguese king stepped up the colonization of Brazil by

**A Tupinambá Warrior.** The warrior in this 1643 painting belonged to a subgroup of the Tupi, among the most widespread of the many semisedentary indigenous people in what is today Brazil. *The Granger Collection, New York.*

appointing a royal governor and building a capital city, Salvador (also called Bahia), on that site.

Over the next half century, between the planters' efforts to enslave the Tupinambá people and certain disastrous efforts to protect them, the Tupinambá vanished from the area of the sugar plantations. Particularly lethal were European diseases, against which indigenous people had no natural resistance; contagion ran rampant among Tupinambá slaves in the close quarters of plantations. Any gathering of native populations facilitated this "demographic catastrophe." The same ship that brought the first royal governor also brought the first black-robed Jesuit missionaries to Brazil. Famous for their intelligence and zeal, the Jesuits moved quickly to establish special villages where they gathered their indigenous flock to teach them Christianity and defend them from enslavement. Despite all good intentions, however, epidemic European diseases decimated the indigenous inhabitants of the Jesuit villages. On the plantations, too, indigenous slaves were fast disappearing because of disease and despair. To replace them, the Portuguese bought slaves in Africa and crowded them into the holds of Brazilian-bound ships. By 1600, Africans were rapidly replacing indigenous people as the enslaved workforce of Brazilian sugar plantations. The surviving Tupinambá either fled into the interior or intermarried and gradually disappeared as a distinct group. This pattern was to be repeated throughout Brazil as sugar cultivation spread.

## Africa and the Slave Trade

In several parts of Latin America, Africans totally replaced indigenous laborers in the 1600s. How were so many people enslaved and taken out of Africa? Why did they survive to populate Brazil and the Caribbean while people like the Tupi died? Now that Africans have entered our story—never to leave it— we should consider the part they played in the Encounter.

The Encounter brought together people from three continents to create new societies, but as we have seen, the Africans
and the Iberians were not total strangers. In fact, the first slaves
to arrive in America were Africans who had already spent time
as slaves in Iberia itself. Europeans and Africans had more in
common with each other than with indigenous Americans.
Along with Europe and Asia, Africa formed a part of what Europeans called the Old World. For tens of thousands of years, the
indigenous people of the New World had been isolated, and
thus protected, from the diseases circulating in the Old World.
Hence their utter vulnerability to European diseases. Africans,
on the other hand, were not so susceptible. Old World trade
routes and migrations had already exposed them to these
microbes. Similarly, indigenous Americans had never seen the
horses, cattle, sheep, pigs, chickens, and other domestic animals
brought by the Iberians, but Africans already raised the same
animals, and some Africans were skilled horsemen. Although
indigenous people fashioned intricate jewelry out of gold and
silver, they did nothing with iron. Africans, on the other hand,
were experienced ironworkers and even produced high-quality
steel. Then too, most Africans were fully sedentary agricultur-
ists and therefore closer than the semisedentary Tupi to the
pattern of Iberian rural life. Finally, indigenous people like the
Tupi had every reason to expect the worst when captured and
enslaved, because among the Tupi, slaves were frequently sac-
rificed and sometimes eaten. Africans brought a different set of
expectations to the experience of slavery.

Slavery was everywhere in African societies, a social institution basic to economic life. In Africa, as in Iberia and indigenous America, slaves were most often war captives, but with
an important difference. In Africa, captives did not necessarily remain eternally degraded servants, and often their children were not born slaves. Eventually, African forms of slavery
allowed full social integration of the slaves' descendants. In some

Africans v. Americans

African societies, slaves might even attain high status and elite privileges as administrators. Buying and selling slaves at markets, on the other hand, was a European tradition. The African slave *trade* per se began to take on massive proportions only after the Portuguese arrived in the 1400s.

Along the African coast, the Portuguese established trading centers stocked with silks, linens, brass kettles, and eventually rum, tobacco, guns, and gunpowder, but most especially with bars of iron for metalworking. African traders brought long lines of slaves, chained together at the neck, to these embarkation centers. Most had been captured in wars between African states, and eventually the profits of the trade of war captives provided a new stimulus to warfare. Slaving vessels might also stop anywhere along the coast to buy captives from local traders. Meanwhile, the Portuguese sought ideological justification in the notion that buying such captives to Christianize them was actually doing them a favor. The Board of Conscience in Lisbon cleared the procedure as long as the Portuguese slavers were supposedly "rescuing" the captives of cannibals, or enslaving certified practitioners of human sacrifice, or engaging in some form of certified "just war." In practice, however, such legal distinctions mattered little to slave traders. They bought whoever was for sale, willy-nilly, with a special preference for healthy young men, and then packed them into the holds of slave ships where 15 to 20 percent on average would die on the voyage. Probably more than a million people died in the passage across the Atlantic alone. Early exploration of the African coast led to about a century of Portuguese dominance in the slave trade. Portuguese slavers supplied human cargo to Spanish American, as well as Brazilian, buyers.

We have few firsthand accounts of what being human cargo was like, although around twelve million people over four centuries had the experience. One exception is the account of Olaudah Equiano, written in the 1700s, after the trade had been

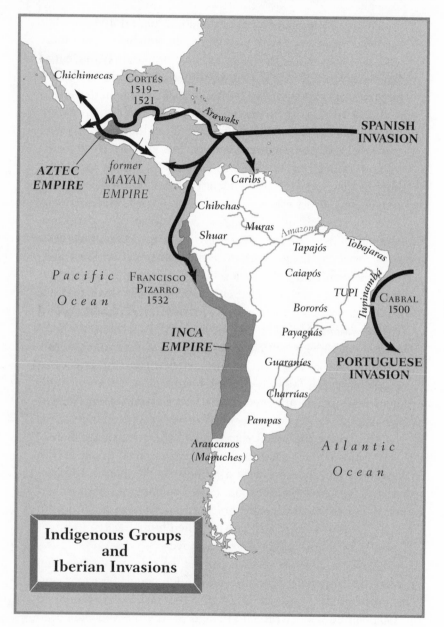

Chichimecas  CORTÉS
1519–
1521

Arawaks

SPANISH
INVASION

AZTEC
EMPIRE

former
MAYAN
EMPIRE

Caribs

Chibchas

Muras  *Amazon*

Shuar              Tapajós

Tobajaras

Caiapós

TUPI

Pacific   FRANCISCO
          PIZARRO
Ocean      1532

CABRAL
1500

Bororós

INCA
EMPIRE

Payaguás

PORTUGUESE
INVASION

Guaraníes

Charrúas

Atlantic

Pampas

Ocean

Araucanos
(Mapuches)

**Indigenous Groups
and
Iberian Invasions**

underway for more than two centuries. Equiano describes his confusion and despair when arriving aboard ship to encounter the claustrophobic horror of the dark, foul, and narrow cargo spaces. Not until he found a few other people who spoke his language did Equiano learn that he was being taken to work in the white man's land. Enslaved Africans came to Latin America in diverse groups, speaking many different languages, originating in three widely separated areas of Africa.

The first area to be affected by the slave trade was West Africa, from Senegal to Nigeria. Here a coastal belt of tropical forest gives way, farther inland, to savanna (the Sudanic belt) and eventually to the beginnings of the Sahara desert. This is a special part of Africa, traversed in a great arc by the Niger River, the cradle of many cultural developments. Beginning about five thousand years ago, Bantu-speaking people set out from the area around the mouth of the Niger River in great migrations, spreading their culture east and south over much of the continent. Along the course of the Niger, a thousand years ago, arose kingdoms famous in Europe for their wealth in gold. Enough of that gold had trickled north across the Sahara in camel caravans to excite the interest of medieval Europeans, and the Portuguese undertook their exploration of the African coast partly to find the source of the precious flow. Communication across the Sahara also brought Islam to West Africa. Before the slave trade, the most powerful kingdoms arose inland on the upper Niger, where stood the fabulous walled city of Timbuktu, with its bustling markets and university. In 1324, when Mansa Musa, king of Mali, made a pilgrimage to Mecca (as devout Muslims try to do at least once in their lives), his caravan carried enough gold to cause oscillations in currency values in the areas it crossed. The fatal attraction of precious metals first brought the Portuguese to "the Gold Coast" (modern Ghana), but the value of human cargoes from this region eventually far outstripped the golden ones. The British, the French, and the

Dutch eventually established their own trading stations, finally breaking the Portuguese monopoly on the West African coast.

Two other areas of Africa remained more or less monopolized by the Portuguese: Angola and Mozambique, where coastal stretches of grassy, open land allowed the Portuguese to penetrate far inland and actively colonize, in contrast to their more limited West African trading strategy. As a result, Portuguese remains the language of government in Angola and Mozambique today. These regions became chief sources for the slave trade only after the Portuguese were edged out of West Africa by competition from other European countries. But that gets ahead of our story.

For now, having observed how Portugal's exploration of the African coast and its clash with the semisedentary Tupi laid the ethnic and demographic foundations for a black-and-white Brazil, let us return to the sedentary societies of Mexico and Peru, where Aztec and Inca rulers boasted astonishing golden treasures.

## The Fall of the Aztec and Inca Empires

While Brazil remained a backwater in the 1500s, Mexico and Peru drew the Spaniards like powerful magnets, becoming the two great poles of Spanish colonization. For three centuries, Mexico and Peru would remain the richest and most populous places in the Americas, but first their indigenous rulers had to be defeated. The Aztec and Inca emperors commanded tens of thousands of warriors and vast material resources. Their precipitous defeat at the hands of a few hundred Spanish adventurers is unparalleled in world history. Several circumstances conspired to make it possible.

In 1519, when they first set foot in Mexico, the Spaniards already knew a lot about America. After all, a full generation had passed since they began settling the Caribbean islands where Columbus made landfall: Hispaniola (today divided between Haiti and the Dominican Republic) and Cuba. The initial Spanish experience there with the semisedentary Arawak people, who were not so different from the Tupi, had begun with trading but rapidly degenerated into slaving. The outcome was similar to what had transpired on the Brazilian coast. Disease and abuse decimated the Caribbean's indigenous people within a generation. Soon they would cease to exist altogether, to be replaced by African slaves.

The Spanish invaders were not soldiers but undisciplined adventurers seeking private fortunes. The first to arrive laid claim to the indigenous inhabitants and, eventually, the land, leaving little for the next wave of adventurers. These had to conquer somewhere else. Operating from the Caribbean bases, Spanish newcomers began to explore the coast of Central and South America, crossed Panama, and found the Pacific Ocean, making contact with many different indigenous groups and beginning to hear rumors of glittering, mysterious empires in the mountains beyond the Caribbean. So it was that, by the time he found the Aztec Empire, the Spanish leader Hernán Cortés had already been dealing with indigenous Americans for fifteen years.

In the conquest of Mexico, no other single Spanish advantage outweighed the simple fact that Cortés more or less knew what was happening, whereas Mexica leaders, including Moctezuma, the Aztec emperor, had no earthly idea who, or what, the Spaniards might be. For centuries the story has circulated that Moctezuma suspected the Spaniards were gods from Aztec mythology, that Cortés himself could be Quetzalcoatl, a white-skinned deity whose coming had been foretold in prophecy. That story now appears to be incorrect, however, because it originated several decades after the arrival of the Spaniards. Although repeated a thousand times, it should now be corrected. On the other hand, the list of never-before-seen things that the Spanish brought was long and intimidating: tall-masted sailing ships, ferocious attack dogs, horses of monstrous size, cannon belching fire and thunder, steel blades, and body armor. The Mexica had never seen Europeans or Africans (who were always present among the conquistadors), and had no prior clue that such strange-looking people even existed. Logically, they regarded these outlandish invaders as beings from outside the world they knew. Searching for a name to call the Spaniards, the Mexica used the Nahuatl word *teul*, which at the time was routinely translated into Spanish as *dios*, or "god." Since the word *teul* could be used for a spirit or demon, it did not imply adoration, but it clearly implied supernatural power. The Spaniards' humanity, vulnerability, and hostile intentions did not become clear until Cortés and his expedition had been welcomed into Tenochtitlan, where they took Moctezuma hostage. By the middle of 1521, smallpox and indigenous allies had helped Cortés annihilate Tenochtitlan, and the Aztec Empire as a whole quickly collapsed.

It took more fighting to overthrow the Inca Empire. Still, the stunningly rapid and complete Spanish triumph in both cases calls for explanation. Once again, experience was on the Spanish side. The leader of the Peruvian expedition, Francisco Pizarro, was another seasoned conquistador who, like Cortés (his distant relative), employed a tried-and-true maneuver, something the Spanish had been practicing since their first Caribbean encounters with indigenous people, when he treacherously took the Inca ruler Atahualpa hostage in 1532. Then, too, the Spanish advantage in military technology must be recalled. Horses, steel, and (less importantly) gunpowder gave the invaders a devastating superiority of force, man for man, against warriors armed only with bravery and stone-edged weapons. Spanish weaponry produced staggering death tolls. At one point, the Spanish under Cortés massacred ten times their number in a few hours at the Aztec tributary city of Cholula. Spanish military advantages came from their Old World heritage, which included

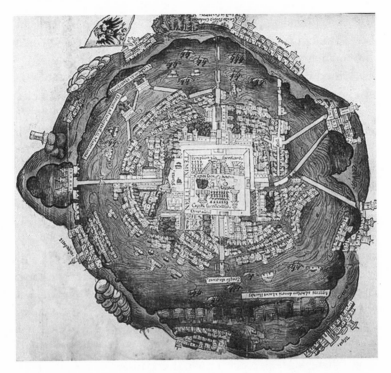

**TENOCHTITLAN AND ITS SURROUNDING LAKE.** The Aztec capital was linked to the lake shore by causeways and was crosscut, like Venice, by a series of canals. Note the square ceremonial complex at the city center. Smaller cities and installations are visible around the edge of the lake in this 1524 map. *Newberry Library, Chicago.*

gunpowder from China and horses from Asia. Old World microbes were Spanish allies, too.

Imagine the horror of the Incas when Pizarro captured the Inca emperor, Atahualpa. Atahualpa had arrived with an army numbering in the tens of thousands; Pizarro had only 168 Spaniards. Atahualpa had reason to be overconfident, and he walked into an ambush. Pizarro's only hope was a smashing psychological victory, so he drew on another tried-and-true Spanish tactic, one repeatedly used in Mexico: the surprise slaughter of indigenous nobles within an enclosed space. At Pizarro's invitation, Atahualpa's multitude of followers entered a square where the Spaniards had hidden cannons. Without warning, the cannons fired into the crowd at close range, creating gruesome carnage. Then Spaniards on horses charged into the mass of bodies, swinging their long steel blades in bloody arcs, sending heads and arms flying, as no indigenous American weapon could do. Meanwhile, surprise and armor protected Pizarro's men. Not one of them died that day, yet they succeeded in taking Atahualpa prisoner, killing and maiming thousands of his men in the process. Atahualpa's people brought mountains of gold to ransom him, but Pizarro had him executed anyway. Depriving the indigenous defenders of leadership was part of the "divide-and-conquer" strategy.

Neither the Incas nor the Aztecs could have been defeated without the aid of the Spaniards' indigenous allies. In Mexico, Aztec taxes and tributes had weighed heavily on the shoulders of other Nahuatl-speaking city-states. Tributary city-states had furnished sacrificial victims for the Aztec state religion, the ideology that glorified Aztec imperial expansion and bathed the pyramids of Tenochtitlan in the blood of hundreds of thousands. As a result, Cortés found ready alliances, most notably with the nearby indigenous city of Tlaxcala, an old rival of Tenochtitlan. Eager to end Aztec rule, rival cities sent thousands of warriors to help Cortés.

Pizarro, too, used indigenous allies to topple the Inca Empire. Unlike the Aztecs, the Incas had imposed a centralized power that broke up rival city-states and resettled their populations. While the Aztecs had merely imposed tributes, the Incas administered, building roads and storage facilities and garrisons. Like the Aztecs, and like the Spanish and Portuguese, too, the Incas had a state religion that provided an ideological justification for empire. Unfortunately for the Incas, however, both the reigning emperor and his successor had died suddenly in the epidemic that, advancing along trade routes ahead of Pizarro, ravaged the Inca ruling family, creating a succession crisis just before the Spanish arrival. Disastrously, an Inca civil war had begun. Atahualpa led one side and his brother Huascar the other. The wily Pizarro was able to play the two sides against each other, achieving the ultimate victory for himself. Each side in the Inca civil war saw the other as the greatest threat. How could they know that Pizarro's tiny expedition was only the entering wedge of vast colonizing forces beyond the Atlantic?

Aztec and Inca treasures soon attracted Spaniards by the thousands. The defeat of Aztec and Inca power was only the first step in establishing Spanish dominion over the mainland. Now the Spanish had to colonize, to assert effective control over large populations and sprawling territories, over the civilizations that underlay the Aztec and Inca empires and that remained in place after their destruction. This was a gradual process, requiring several generations and contrasting markedly with the pattern of colonization on the Brazilian coast.

## THE BIRTH OF SPANISH AMERICA

Even before the dust of imperial collapse had settled in Mexico and Peru, the Spanish began to parcel out the plunder of conquest. Some was treasure captured from indigenous royalty, but most took a form called *encomienda*, whereby the conquerors were rewarded with people. In this system, indigenous people were "entrusted" (the meaning of the word *encomienda*) to each conqueror, who had the responsibility of Christianizing them and the privilege of making them work for him. Encomiendas of conquered Moors had been awarded aplenty during the Christian reconquest of Iberia, so it was a familiar system to the Spaniards. Conquerors who received encomiendas became much like European nobles, able to live from the labor of serflike farmers who delivered part of their crops as regular tribute.

For indigenous farmers accustomed to paying tribute to imperial masters, the situation was familiar, too. Most often, the same city-states, villages, and clans that had once paid tribute to the Aztecs or Incas now paid tribute to the new Spanish overlords instead. Calamitous, repeated epidemics during the 1500s, comparable in severity to the Black Death of medieval Europe, reduced native populations to a fraction of their former size. But, unlike what occurred in the Caribbean or along the Brazilian coast, indigenous villages did not disappear from Mexico and Peru.

Whereas Tupi society was swept away by disease and replaced by Brazilian sugar plantations, the sedentary farming societies of central Mexico and the Andes survived, shaken but intact, for the Spanish to take over. The Spanish normally created encomiendas out of already existing communities with their own indigenous nobles, whom the Spanish called *caciques*.* The Spanish conquerors cultivated relations with these nobles, sometimes marrying into their families. Gradually, however, Spanish conquest undercut the defeated warrior nobility of Aztec and Inca days, and indigenous people adopted Spanish-style village governments. In Mexico, village officials with Spanish titles conducted their business and kept written records in Nahuatl. Hundreds of Spanish words came into Nahuatl, of course, indicating the powerful impact of conquest, but the basic structure of the language survived, preserving a distinctly indigenous worldview.

Mexico officially became "New Spain," but it was really two societies being grafted together, mostly by Spanish men and indigenous women. Spanish women, like Portuguese women in Brazil, were few. In the early years of the Encounter, Spanish

---

*Cacique* is actually an Arawak word that the Spanish adopted in the Caribbean and later applied elsewhere.

men in America outnumbered Spanish women roughly nine to one. So, within a few years, indigenous women and Spanish men became the parents of a legion of mestizo children, exactly as anticipated by Pero Vaz de Caminha's letter from Brazil. Malinche had Cortés's baby soon after the fall of Tenochtitlan.

What an intriguing figure is Malinche, a Spanish deformation of her indigenous name, Malintzin. She was one of twenty female slaves given to Cortés as he sailed up the Mexican coast seeking the Aztec Empire in 1519. She already spoke Maya and Nahuatl, and she learned Spanish in months. This astoundingly quick-witted and self-possessed sixteen-year-old girl became inseparable from Cortés and was instrumental in the capture of Moctezuma. Understandably, her life has been read as a romantic novel, but also as a betrayal of Mexico. It was neither. As for romance, Cortés summoned his Spanish wife, who was waiting in Cuba, then gave Malinche a bit of property and turned her away. As for betraying Mexico, that country did not yet exist, unless one refers to the Aztec Empire, and Malinche had good reason to hate the Aztecs. Although Nahuatl was her first language, her own family had sold her into slavery to Mayas, which is how she learned that language. Malinche was more betrayed than betrayer. Cortés married her to one of his men, with whom she had a second child. She died, not yet twenty-five, only a few years later.

The Aztec princess Techichpotzín, baptized Isabel, was the daughter of Moctezuma. She became "Isabel Moctezuma," exemplifying the woman of indigenous nobility who could attract a Spanish husband because of her wealth. As the legitimate heiress of Moctezuma's personal fortune and the recipient of a desirable encomienda, Isabel attracted more than her share of husbands. Before her three Spanish husbands, she was married to two different leaders of the Aztec resistance in the last days of Tenochtitlan. She outlived four of her spouses, bore seven mestizo children, adapted to her new life, and became a model of Catholic devotion and a benefactor of religious charities. She lived to the respectable age of forty.

As the Aztec and Inca nobility declined and the number of Spanish women increased, fewer and fewer Spanish men married indigenous women. Although Spanish men continued fathering unnumbered mestizo children, most were illegitimate and inherited little or nothing from their Spanish fathers. These children were "people-in-between": not Europeans or Africans or indigenous Americans. Mestizo children were second-class people in the Spanish world, poor relations, if recognized at all. Malinche's son by Cortés, Martín, became virtually a servant of his half-brother, also named Martín, Cortés's son by his second Spanish wife.

Spanish women usually arrived after the fighting was over, but that was not always the case. A woman named Isabel de Guevara helped conquer Argentina and Paraguay in the 1530s and 1540s. Years later, in an attempt to gain an encomienda for her part in the conquest, she wrote a letter to the Spanish Crown, describing how the women of the expedition took over when famine killed two-thirds of their party. As the men fainted from hunger, wrote Guevara, the women began "standing guard, patrolling the fires, loading the crossbows . . . arousing the soldiers who were capable of fighting, shouting the alarm through the camp, acting as sergeants, and putting the soldiers in order."

The most famous "conquistadora" of all was Inés Suárez, a woman of thirty when she came to America in 1537, alone, looking for her husband. She searched first in Venezuela, then in Peru, where she found her husband already dead. Suárez then became the mistress of the conqueror of Chile, legendary for her actions during an indigenous attack there. Her plan was to terrorize the attackers by throwing them the heads of seven captured chiefs, and her most famous deed was to cut off the first captive's head herself. Despite (what was regarded as) her heroism, the conqueror of Chile, who had a wife in Spain, put Inés Suárez aside when he became governor of the new territory.

Favorable marriages outweighed even extraordinary ability in the lives of women. The marriage contract was a pillar of the Spanish social structure, crucial to the distribution of property. Marriage was a religious sacrament, and religious conformity was serious business in the Spanish Empire.

Spanish conquest had meant an earthly and a spiritual conquest, the defeat of the old gods. Spanish churchmen arrived to teach Catholic doctrine. They searched insistently for sacred objects that the indigenous people still preserved, hidden away, from their old religions—"idols," in Catholic eyes. The priest and the holder of the encomienda stood side by side in many areas, as the only two representatives of Spanish authority. As had occurred during the Christianization of Europe centuries earlier, the conversion of kings (or, in America, caciques) brought whole communities into the church at once. In their haste to baptize, missionaries perfunctorily sprinkled holy water on indigenous people in mass ceremonies that did little to teach them Christianity. Still, the baptized could remember the imposition of other imperial state religions, for that was a pattern familiar from before the Encounter. Among sedentary peoples, the Spanish made a habit of erecting churches on sites already sacred to indigenous deities. The people of Tenochtitlan cannot have been surprised to see Spanish conquerors level the Aztec Great Temple and construct their cathedral on practically the same spot.

The fully sedentary people of central Mexico and Peru survived the Encounter infinitely better than did semisedentary people such as the Tupi. Still, the Encounter had a dire impact on settled agricultural societies, too. The Spanish often demanded more tribute than had indigenous overlords. For example, Andean villages had provided a labor draft called the *mita* to their Inca rulers, but after the conquest mita laborers

were forced to do something new—toil in the shafts of deep
silver mines, sometimes locked down for days. In addition, epidemic European diseases continued to decimate the indigenous
population.

By the end of the 1500s, the basic contours of Latin American ethnicities were established. American, European, and
African genes and cultures had begun to mix, creating rich
potential for human diversity, but the violent and exploitative
nature of the Encounter would sour the mix for centuries to
come. In Brazil and the Caribbean region, Europeans and Africans took the place of the indigenous populations that were
virtually wiped out. In Mexico and Peru, by contrast, Nahuatl-
and Quechua-speaking societies survived to be gradually transformed. One way or the other, the original sin of Latin American
history—the festering social injustice at the core—had done
its durable damage. How would more equitable, more inclusive
communities ever emerge from the smoking ruins of conquest?
The next step, systematic colonization, the creation of entire
social systems geared to serve the interests of distant masters in
Europe, only made matters worse.

# Friar Bartolomé de las Casas

Colonial Brazilian Church.
Statue by Aleijadinho. *Photograph by Michael Teague.
Brazil, Time World Library,
1967.*

As our story makes abundantly clear, the European drive
to extract labor and tribute explains much about the colonization of Latin America. How could it be different? At the most
basic level, conquest is always about exploitation. On the other
hand, conquerors and colonizers rarely admitted this, even to
themselves. That is how the other, more idealistic, motives
enter the picture. Most Spanish and Portuguese people who
came to the Americas in the 1500s believed that spreading the
"true religion," even by force, was a good thing. Like all people,
they tended to give their own actions the best possible interpretation. On the other hand, religious idealism truly was the
driving force for some; logically enough, these were most often
church people. The Catholic Church—Inquisition and all—
generated the most important humanitarian countercurrents
in this age of raw exploitation.

43

For example, some members of the Franciscan order who arrived in Mexico as early as 1524 showed deep respect for the indigenous people. Several Franciscans carefully gathered and preserved information about Aztec history, religion, and daily life. The most notable was Bernardino de Sahagún, who wrote that Aztec family organization and child-care practices were superior to those of Spain. Sahagún collaborated with his indigenous students to assemble a treasure trove of Aztec thought, literature, and customs in their original language, Nahuatl. Gorgeously illustrated in authentic indigenous style, his book, known today as the *Florentine Codex,* remains essential for any interpretation of Aztec civilization. Another Franciscan, Toribio de Motolinia, denounced Spanish tributes, torture, and forced labor as so many "plagues" afflicting the indigenous people. To this day, Motolinia is warmly remembered in Mexico as a defender of the conquered.

The first Jesuits in Brazil similarly worked to defend the indigenous people against the depredations of the colonists. As a first measure, the Jesuits learned a number of the variants of Tupi (which was really a family of related languages as distinct from one another as French, Spanish, and Italian). They then devised a simplified Tupi grammar and a standard vocabulary for use in the mission villages. This *Lingua Geral*, or "general tongue," was easily learned by speakers of various Tupi dialects. It facilitated religious teaching and separated the indigenous people from the settlers who wanted to enslave them.

But by far the greatest religious champion of the indigenous people was Bartolomé de las Casas, prototype for a long line of radical priests in Latin America. Las Casas was a university-educated, fortune-seeking young gentleman—no radical at all—when he came to America in 1502. He got an encomienda himself and for twelve years lived the life of an early Caribbean conqueror, watching indigenous people die by the dozen from exploitation and disease. He was about forty when, in 1514, he had a change of heart, influenced, apparently, by the fiery sermons of a member of the Dominican order who had begun to preach against Spanish exploitation of encomiendas. By 1515, Las Casas, now a Dominican himself, returned to Spain and proposed various ways to protect indigenous Americans from the encomienda system. "The reason for the death and destruction of so many souls at Christian hands," according to Las Casas, was simple greed: "gold, and the attempt to get rich quickly." One of his alternative suggestions was to rely on the labor of enslaved Africans, but then he had a better idea: the recruitment in Spain of entire farming families disposed to work for themselves. Las Casas dreamed that Spanish and indigenous societies in America might be kept separate and the use of indigenous labor might be strictly limited and supervised. But his pilot colonization project in Venezuela never got off the ground.

During the 1520s and 1530s, Las Casas wrote a stream of publications denouncing encomienda abuses, and he traveled throughout the Caribbean and Central America defending the indigenous people. In 1537, the pope issued a proclamation, partly inspired by Las Casas, saying that the indigenous people were exactly that: people, not subhuman beings, as some claimed. In 1542, largely thanks to Las Casas, the Spanish Crown issued the famous New Laws of the Indies for the Good Treatment and Preservation of the Indians, immediately limiting and eventually ending encomiendas altogether. The high-flying holders of encomiendas hated and vilified Las Casas for the New Laws that clipped their wings, but the old crusader, already in his late sixties, had no intention of stopping.

In 1550–51, Las Casas represented the cause of the indigenous people in a great debate held in the Spanish city of Valladolid to determine, once and for all, the moral status of Spanish conquest in America. At Valladolid, Las Casas passionately denied the charge that the indigenous people were naturally inferior to Europeans and therefore deserved to be enslaved. Although the official result of the Valladolid debate was inconclusive, Las Casas had made a strong impression on the imperial government. In 1552, he published the most famous of his innumerable writings, *A Brief Account of the Destruction of the Indies,* full of grisly descriptions of Spanish cruelty, rhetorically exaggerating a slaughter that was horrible enough in reality. Few pamphlets have ever found a wider European audience. Among the most avid readers of this tract were the Protestant enemies of Catholicism in a Europe wracked by religious wars. Over the next two centuries, *A Brief Account of the Destruction of the Indies* saw three editions in Latin, three in Italian, four in English, six in French, eight in German, and eighteen in Dutch, not to mention those in Spanish. The engraving on page 10 was done for a French translation of 1582.

Bartolomé de las Casas lived to be eighty-nine, a fabulously long life for the 1500s. Although his early error in calling for more African slaves remains a stain on his record, he quickly and permanently repented of the idea. Overall, the spirit and struggle of Las Casas continues to inspire idealistic churchmen and churchwomen in Latin America more than four hundred years later.

**Sor Juana Inés de la Cruz.** Women, too, chose to enter religious orders, and convents were lively centers of colonial life. Besides providing a sheltered, and therefore honorable, upbringing for young women, convents had a key role in financing agricultural production. In some situations, convents offered outlets for women's artistic and intellectual pursuits. It is no accident that Sor Juana, the most celebrated woman of colonial Latin America, was a nun. *Courtesy of Instituto Nacional de Antropología e Historia–Museo Nacional de Historia. Mexico City.*

| 1600 | 1651 | 1690s | 1776 | 1790s |
|------|------|-------|------|-------|
| Mature Colonial Period begins | Sor Juana Inés de la Cruz born | Bandeirantes discover gold | Viceroyalty of the Río de la Plata created | French Revolution triggers war in Europe |

# 2.

# COLONIAL
# CRUCIBLE

Rule by Spain and Portugal lasted three long centuries in Latin America. Despite the utopian dreams of the religiously inspired and despite continual resistance to exploitation, the bitter legacy of conquest and slavery remained strong in 1800, the eve of independence. Latin Americans had wrestled with the hierarchy of race imposed by conquest and slavery and had adapted themselves to that hierarchy. As Latin American societies grew around the hard edges of domination like the roots of a tree gradually embracing the rocks at its base, adaptation made colonization endurable but also embedded it in people's habits. Indigenous, African, and European people consorted and intermingled, fought and slept together. They misunderstood and learned about, despised, and sometimes adored each other. Over hundreds of years, most Latin Americans began to sincerely accept Catholicism and the rule of a Spanish or Portuguese king. Thus, more than merely rule by outsiders, colonization was a social and cultural, even a psychological process. The resulting patterns of domination—intricate and omnipresent—constitute the saddest product of the colonial crucible.

The contours of colonial Latin American societies revealed the priorities of the Iberian invaders. A whirlwind tour of the

colonies will explain the basic economic patterns and geographical layout. To begin, only precious metals and a few high-priced
items such as sugar (then a luxury) could repay the enormous
costs of transportation across the Atlantic Ocean. So mines
and sugar plantations loom large in the early history of Latin
America.

## COLONIAL ECONOMICS

Gold was the precious metal that first mesmerized the
Europeans—gold from Aztec and Inca treasures, gold that
could easily be panned in sandy streambeds and was quickly
exhausted. An early Caribbean gold rush had helped annihilate
the Arawaks during the first generation of Spanish colonization.
But silver, not gold, eventually structured the colonial economy
of Spanish America. The major silver mines of Zacatecas (Mexico) and Potosí (Peru) were opened in the 1540s. Zacatecas,
an area without sedentary inhabitants, attracted indigenous
migrants from central Mexico. Migrants also became miners
at Potosí, on a windswept mountain plateau at twelve thousand
feet, where Spanish smelting techniques (using a bellows) did
not work and indigenous ones (channeling the Andean wind)
had to be adopted instead. These were deep-shaft mines that
went miles under the earth, vast quasi-industrial enterprises that
attracted diverse assortments of people. Mining immediately
began to reshape Mexican and Peruvian society.

The mining zones became the great focus of Spanish activity
in America, linking the colonies economically with Europe. For
a while in the 1600s, Potosí became the most populous city in
America. And because Potosí stood more or less on the roof of
the world, too high for agriculture, almost everything except
silver had to be brought to it by mules. Sure-footed mules, bred
on the plains of Argentina, trooped up narrow Andean trails
to provide transportation. Indigenous women elsewhere in the

**Potosí.** Honeycombed with mine shafts, the "mountain of silver" looms over the city of Potosí in modern Bolivia—called Upper Peru at the time of this 1584 painting. In the foreground, silver ore is being crushed by water-powered machinery and mixed with mercury to extract the precious metal. *The Granger Collection, New York.*

Andes wove cloth to dress the miners, and farmers at lower altitudes sent food to feed them. (To apply economic concepts here, "primary" export production stimulated "secondary" supply activities.) Eventually, silver came down from the sky on mules bound for the coast. Because the high plateau of the central Andes is so remote from the coast, the Peruvian capital was established at Lima, near a good seaport. Likewise, the wealth of colonial Mexico clustered along routes connecting the northern mines with Mexico City and the port of Veracruz. The northern mining zones became a meeting place for all sorts of people, while southern Mexico, along with Guatemala, had a more strictly indigenous population. The main ethnicities in this southern region were Zapotec, Mixtec, and especially Maya—the people among whom Malinche grew up. Now all of southern Mexico, Central America, and the Caribbean became part of the supply network for the northern silver mines.

The economic priorities of the Spanish Crown determined the political organization of the colony. The "royal fifth," a 20 percent tax on mining, was the prime source of colonial revenue for the Spanish state. To keep an eye on the royal fifth, the Crown organized colonial governments in New Spain (the colonial name for Mexico, administratively embracing Central America and the Caribbean as well) and Peru (which then included much of South America), by the late 1540s. Each of these areas, called *viceroyalties* because of the *viceroys* sent from Spain to rule in the king's name, also had an archbishop and a high court. Eventually, Mexico City and Lima each developed a wholesale merchants' guild that concentrated commercial power, as well as political power, in the *viceregal* capitals. Gradually, the viceroyalties, high courts, and other administrative subdivisions multiplied in a manner guided by the principle of profitability to the Crown. Modern Colombia became the center of a third viceroyalty (called New Granada, 1717) partly because of its gold. Eventually, another jurisdiction was created to stop Potosí silver from escaping untaxed through the area of modern Argentina. This became the fourth viceroyalty (the Río de la Plata, 1776), with its capital at the Atlantic port of Buenos Aires. Despite the two new viceroyalties, however, Peru and Mexico remained the core areas of Spanish colonization.

In Brazil, sugar took the place of silver, and plantations replaced mines as the main generators of export production. Sugar plantations capitalized on rich red soils, superb for the cultivation of sugarcane, along Brazil's northeastern coast. The Northeast therefore became the core area of the Brazilian colony, with its principal centers in Pernambuco and the Bay of All Saints. For the Portuguese Crown, the taxes on exported

**A Brazilian Sugar Mill.** In this nineteenth-century engraving, sugar-cane is being unloaded from an oxcart and fed into an *engenho*'s grinding mechanism, producing gallons of sweet sap that will be boiled down into bricks of sugar for shipment. The *senhor de engenho* looks on. *The Granger Collection, New York.*

sugar—and on goods imported with profits from sugar—were the prime sources of colonial revenue in Brazil. Throughout the 1600s, sugar was "king" in Brazil, and it structured the Brazilian colony much as silver mining structured colonial Spanish America.

Sugarcane had to be milled and its juice boiled down into cakes in order to be exported. Planters rich enough to build a sugar mill (an *engenho*, or "engine" in Portuguese) became known as "mill lords," *senhores de engenho*. The senhores de engenho stood at the crux of the sugar economy, and they loom large in Brazilian social history. In each locality of the Brazilian sugar coast, a handful of mill lords, each owning hundreds of slaves, lorded over their neighbors, many of whom grew sugarcane but depended on the lords to have it milled. Like a silver mine, a big engenho was a complex and expensive economic undertaking, almost a town in itself, with a chapel, stables, storage facilities,

Guanajuato
Zacatecas
*fringe*
*fringe*
*fringe*

Orinoco R.
Amazón R.
São Francisco R.
*fringe*

Lima
Potosí
Salta
Paraná R.

*fringe*

São Paulo
and the roving
bandeirantes

Core areas
of colonization

Missions

Sugarcane

Silver

**Original Areas
of Colonization,
1500–1700**

and workshops, not to mention barracks-like slave quarters. As in the early plantation colonies of North America's Chesapeake Bay, plantations that were almost towns in themselves tended to undercut the growth of urban centers. The Brazilian colony, even its core area, was a place of few cities and towns when compared with colonial Spanish America.

Outside of its northeastern core area, most of colonial Brazil was quite sparsely settled. The Amazonian northwest, for example, remained a vast equatorial rainforest inhabited chiefly by semisedentary indigenous tribes, half a continent with a mere handful of tiny Portuguese towns and a sprinkling of Jesuit missions along the banks of its river highways. The backlands behind the sugar coast, the sertão, stayed dirt-poor cattle country. Other interior regions could be reached only by thousand-mile canoe odysseys involving arduous portages between rivers, feasible only during the rainy season. The Portuguese called these rainy-season canoe expeditions "monsoons," a word they had learned in India. South of São Paulo lay more Jesuit missions in evergreen forests outside the tropics. And beyond these forests, open grasslands stretched south to the Río de la Plata. Here, cattle and horses that had escaped from the missions ran wild, multiplied, and roamed free in numberless herds.

Overall, colonial Brazil could not compete with colonial Spanish America. Sugar was never as precious as silver. Nor could tiny Portugal equal the resources of Spain. And only slowly did Brazil become the principal focus of the Portuguese seaborne empire, with its rich African and Asian outposts. So the Brazilian colony remained in all ways less: poorer, less populous (with a tenth the people of Spanish America), and more loosely governed. Brazil's diffuse plantation economy limited urbanization and scattered administrative power. Two viceroyalties were eventually established, but only during wartime did Brazilian viceroys possess the authority of Spanish American viceroys. Portugal simply attempted less in its colonies than did Spain.

For example, there were a dozen universities in Spanish America after barely a century of colonization, but none was ever established in colonial Brazil. One might wonder how Brazil stayed a Portuguese colony for three hundred years.

## A POWER CALLED HEGEMONY

Both the Spanish and Portuguese Crowns had limited resources for colonization. Neither had large military forces in the American colonies. Iberian colonizers and their American-born descendants were a small minority even in the core areas, so how did they maintain control over so much of the hemisphere for three centuries?

To answer that question, consider the life of Sor (Sister) Juana Inés de la Cruz, a Mexican nun who died in 1695. At the age of seven, Juana had made a surprising announcement. She wanted to attend the University of Mexico (which had opened its doors in 1553, a century before Harvard). She offered to dress as a boy, but it was hopeless. A university education was supposedly over Juana's head. Never mind that she had been reading since the age of three or that she learned Latin just for fun. Forget that she stumped a jury of forty university professors at the age of seventeen, or that Juana became known throughout Mexico for her poetry. Like other women of her class, she had two alternatives: marry and devote her energies to husband and children, or become a nun. Juana chose convent life, which offered a little more independence than marriage. She became Sor Juana, as she is known to history. She collected and read books by the hundreds, studied mathematics, composed and performed music, and even invented a system of musical notation. Her poetry was published in Europe. Some of it criticized hypocritical male condemnations of women's sexual morality: "Why do you wish them to do right / If you encourage them to do wrong?" asked one poem. And, concerning the common scorn for prostitutes, she wondered who really sinned more: "She who sins for pay / Or he who pays for sin?" In the kitchen, she dabbled in experimental science. "Aristotle would have written more," she said, "if he had done any cooking." When she published a brilliant reply to one of her century's most celebrated biblical scholars, the fathers of the church became worried. Juana received instructions to act more like a woman. Her scientific interests, they said—and all her other interests, too, except for religious devotion—were unnatural in a woman. This was the wisdom of her age. She could not defy it alone, and ultimately, she consented. She sold her library, instruments, everything, and devoted herself to atonement for the sin of curiosity. Broken, she confessed to being "the worst of women." Soon after, she died while caring for her sisters during a plague.

The fathers of the church never used physical force against Sor Juana Inés de la Cruz. They did not have to. They embodied religious authority, and she was a religious woman. Revolt or disobedience was literally unthinkable for her. Similarly, the conquered indigenous people of Latin America, and the enslaved Africans, too, gradually accepted the basic premises of colonial life and principles of Iberian authority. Otherwise, Spain and Portugal could never have ruled vast expanses of America without powerful occupying armies.

Historians explain colonial control of Latin America as *hegemony,* a kind of domination that implies a measure of consent by those at the bottom. Hegemony contrasts with control by violent force. It is a steady preponderance rather than an iron rule. Though it may seem "soft," this form of political power is resilient and does devastating damage to people at the bottom. When they accept the principle of their own inferiority and, in the old-fashioned phrase, "know their place," they participate in their own subjugation.

Religion offers one of the clearest examples of cultural hegemony. When enslaved Africans and indigenous people accepted the Europeans' "true religion," they accepted, by the same token, their own status as newcomers to the truth. Catholicism, after all, had been born and developed far from indigenous America. The history of the "true church" was a European history, and its earthly capital was Rome. Most priests and nuns, not to mention bishops and the rest of the ecclesiastical hierarchy, were of European descent. The monarchs of Spain and Portugal reigned by a divine right that only heretics would question, and they enjoyed royal patronage rights, allowing them to appoint or dismiss priests and bishops as if they were Crown officials. The royal government decided where churches should be built and collected the *tithe* (an ecclesiastical tax of 10 percent, paid especially on agricultural products). To sin against Catholic teachings was, in many cases, a criminal offense.

All educational institutions were religious, so if knowledge is power (and it is), the church monopolized that power. The Inquisition kept a list of banned books that people were not allowed to read. The church even controlled time; the tolling of bells set the rhythm of the day, signaling the hours of work, rest, and prayer. Successive Sundays marked the seven-day week, which was new to indigenous people. The Catholic calendar of observances and holidays provided milestones through the year: a collective, public ebb and flow of emotions, from celebration at Epiphany and Carnival, for example, to the somber mood of Lent, Holy Week, and Easter. The milestones of individual lives, from baptism to marriage to death, were validated by church sacraments and registered in church records. Place names, too, were frequently religious. Every town and city had an official patron saint, often part of the city's full name—São Sebastião do Rio de Janeiro, San Francisco de Quito, and so on.

Another hegemonic force, omnipresent and inescapable, was *patriarchy*, the general principle that fathers rule. Fathers ruled heaven and earth, cities and families. The Spanish and Portuguese were more rigidly patriarchal than many indigenous

*What Catholicism does to a community?*

American and African societies, so the hegemony of fathers must be understood, at least in part, as a legacy of colonialism. Patriarchy structured all colonial institutions, including the exclusively male hierarchy of the church, right up to the Holy Father in Rome. Iberian law was based on patriarchal principles. Husbands had legal control over their wives as over their children. Wealthy women led shut-in, elaborately chaperoned lives, isolated from all male contact outside the family—a matter of *honor* in traditional Spanish and Portuguese sexual ethics.

Honor was a measure of how well men and women played their prescribed, and very different, social roles. Avoiding extramarital sex, in this way of thinking, became something like a woman's supreme life mission, whereas a man's sexual purity held less value. In practice, if a man could support more than one woman, that heightened his social distinction, so many men kept mistresses. On the other hand, men were supposed to defend—specifically by bloodshed—the virginity of their daughters and the sexual exclusivity of their wives. This conception of honor led to dueling and to the violent punishment of independent-minded women. This cultural pattern has pre-Christian roots in the Mediterranean world and a basic logic, worth mentioning to show the rhyme and reason in this madness, that relates to property. Women's illegitimate children, not men's, would be born into the family and inherit part of its precious patrimony: the family wealth parceled out among heirs at the death of each parent. Male "wild oats," on the other hand, would sprout on somebody else's property, so to speak. Thus, philandering implied no loss, but rather a kind of territorial gain, for the family.

Women resisted being treated like means rather than ends, of course. Fairly often, it seems, they used magic—coming from the folk traditions of Iberia, as well as Africa and indigenous America—to attract, manipulate, escape, or punish men. The Spanish Inquisition was on the alert against them. In 1592 the

Inquisition punished a poor Lima woman for reciting a prayer under her breath "so that men would desire her." That was European folk magic, meant to redirect the powers of Catholic liturgy by saying a prayer backward, for example. Inquisition files of the 1600s also reveal native Andean "witches" like Catalina Guacayllano, accused of spilling the blood of guinea pigs on sacred rocks while chewing coca and praying "Oh Lord Father who has been burned, who gives us the irrigation canals and water, give me food." Her idea of God seems to have remained strongly indigenous, giving her, and her people, a spiritual independence from Spanish religion. In explaining why he had three women whipped, a Peruvian priest reported that these witches "went neither to Mass nor to catechism class." Instead, they publicly disobeyed him and inspired their whole village to do the same.

Women doubtless got less satisfaction than men out of the colonial Latin American "honor system," which cast suspicion on any woman who did not live under male control, even a widow. Still, women's protests usually took the form of demands that men live up to their patriarchal responsibilities to be good providers and conscientious husbands and fathers. Learning to live with these values, for there was no other choice, women absorbed them. Only women of property could make the grade, though, because people without property lacked honor almost by definition. Poor women often had to work outside their homes, after all, as cooks, laundresses, or market women who moved around by themselves in the street as no honorable lady would. Not all roles were honorable, no matter how well played. Slaves, who were themselves somebody else's property, had no hope of honor. Only the most extraordinary slave, like Henrique Dias, a born fighter who led Brazilian forces against Dutch invaders in the 1600s, could achieve it. The women of indigenous communities, whose social life retained different gender patterns, lived less in the grip of this unfortunate honor system.

A **GUAMAN POMA DRAWING** denounces Spanish exploitation in the early 1600s. Here, a royal administrator, a parish priest, a notary, and other representatives of Spanish power (represented as savage beasts) menace a kneeling Indian. *Nick Saunders/Barbara Heller Photo Library, London/ Art Resource, New York.*

Viceroys who could literally "grant honors" and refined European ladies and gentlemen who provided models of "honorable" behavior—these inhabitants of colonial cities made them the heart of the honor system, as cities were the staging areas and command centers of the colonizing project generally.

## A PROCESS CALLED TRANSCULTURATION

Across the varied landscape of colonial Latin America, from Mexico to Chile, from the high Andes to the mouth of the Amazon, urban institutions created a framework of authority, hegemonic rather than absolutely dominant. In some respects, cities seemed like tiny, scattered islands of European life and architecture dotting the vastness of indigenous America. Both Spanish and Portuguese colonizers were town dwellers whenever possible. Cities were the only places in Latin America where white people could socialize mostly with each other and maintain a basically European culture. All administrative officials, bishops, judges, notaries, merchants, and moneylenders— the people whose commands, reports, and dealings with one another connected cities to Europe—were urban-based. Cities staged the great public spectacles that dramatized imperial power: solemn processions for Holy Week (preceding Easter), ceremonial welcomes for new viceroys, boisterous celebrations to commemorate royal marriages.

Especially in Spanish America, cities were laid out according to imperial directives mandating the now familiar but then innovative checkerboard of square blocks and streets that intersect at right angles. Around the central square of each city stood the governor's palace, the cathedral, and mansions for the bishop and richest families, also the seat of the city council (*cabildo* in Spanish, *câmara* in Portuguese), which was the most important governing institution outside the handful of major capitals. Urban centers were given the legal rank of village, town, or city, each under the jurisdiction of higher-ranked centers nearby, all reporting to the handful of major capitals such as Lima, Mexico City, Bogotá, and Buenos Aires. Colonial cities, like colonial people, were to be just so, according to imperial order.

But the attempt to impose uniformity was an uphill battle. The challenge lay partly in new and distinctive Latin American cultures—not Spanish or Portuguese, not indigenous or African, but fusions of two or more elements, varying from region to region in kaleidoscopic combinations. These new Latin American cultures emerged gradually from a give-and-take process called *transculturation*. Imagine transculturation as a thousand tiny confrontations and tacit negotiations taking place in people's daily lives, always within the force field of hierarchy and domination. The people on top are usually able to impose the broad outlines of things, as in the case of religion, with those below contributing subtle aspects more difficult to police from above—style, rhythm, texture, mood.

Religion, once again, provides an excellent illustration. Although church practice structured the outer contours of collective life even among indigenous people and slaves, the inner spiritual content resisted colonial standardization. Slaves, who gathered and danced on religious feast days, preserved African religion by dressing it in the clothes of Catholic saints, so to speak. A blending of indigenous, African, and European religious attitudes often occurred. The blend might be covert, as when indigenous artists integrated their own sacred plant and animal motifs (and in the Andes, symbolic rainbows) into the mural paintings of Catholic cloisters, but they could be more obvious, as in the famous case of Mexico's patron saint, the Virgin of Guadalupe. The Virgin of Guadalupe supposedly appeared on a site already sacred to the Aztecs. Her image sometimes had a dark face, and Nahuatl-speaking Mexicans continued to call her by the name of an indigenous earth goddess, Tonantzin. Thus did indigenous and African religions infiltrate Latin American Catholicism. The profusion of blood on colonial Mexican crucifixion figures, for example, was meant to evoke blood's life-giving power, a prominent element of Aztec religion. In the Caribbean and Brazil, on the other hand, Catholicism acquired a less austere, more celebratory and African tone. In Cuba, the singing of black women in church choirs created a stir—for and against—when they began to infuse Cuban music with African sensibility as early as the 1580s. In Salvador, on Brazil's Bay of All Saints, an African religious spirit, including dancing to very un-European rhythms, infused many Catholic ceremonies during the 1700s.

*City*

Transculturation happened especially in cities. Many indigenous and mestizo people, as well as blacks, both free and enslaved, were city-dwellers. From the very beginning, the impact of colonization had shaken some indigenous people loose from their native communities and forced them to migrate. Some went to the mines or Spanish estates. Some built simple housing on the outskirts of Spanish cities—Latin America's first suburban shantytowns. Torn away from their cultural roots, indigenous migrants had to regrow them in new environments, as did those other forced migrants, enslaved Africans. Urban slaves enjoyed greater freedom of association than did plantation slaves. Urban slaves could locate and socialize with people from the same part of Africa. Urban slaves could also join free black people in Catholic lay brotherhoods that provided a social support group and a sense of voluntary belonging. Slaves, and free blacks too, often worked as artisans (bakers or carpenters, for instance), and artisans came in all colors. Thus, cities were sites for the creation of distinctive new cultural forms. As mestizos, free blacks, and poor whites rubbed elbows at a shoemaker's bench or in a blacksmith's shop, they were inventing Latin American popular culture.

Transculturation had different contours in rural life. Plantation slaves worked in gangs and were often locked down at

*Rural Life*

night. Rural indigenous people had more chance to live apart, speaking Quechua or Quiché or Aymara or Nahuatl and following their own traditions. But the white people of the countryside were too few and far between to socialize, or marry, exclusively with each other. Rural people of Spanish and Portuguese descent, even when they maintained a house in town, thus acquired indigenous habits and African tastes sooner than did their urban counterparts. If transculturation happened on profitable Brazilian sugar plantations, where export earnings could pay for imported clothing, wine, and even food, it happened even more on *haciendas*, the sort of large estate more typical of Spanish America. Rather than investing huge sums in an enslaved workforce, haciendas relied on indigenous workers, who earned a small salary or shared the harvest. Instead of crops for export to Europe, haciendas produced less profitable harvests for local consumption. And as a rule, hacienda owners who had little to sell to Europe could afford few imported European goods. On rare visits to town, their speech, clothing, and behavior seemed (from the point of view of their urban cousins) rustically tinged with indigenous or African influences.

For Latin America's subjugated majorities, transculturation was both a blessing and a curse. For example, Nahuatl speakers came to worship the dark-skinned Virgin of Guadalupe because they identified her with Tonantzin, making her *their* Virgin. Thus, colonial masters and servants became a bit more like each other, seemingly a positive result. But by refashioning the colonizers' religion in their own likeness, the indigenous people more easily consented to the basic ideology of colonization and, therefore, moved more firmly under Spanish control. El Inca Garcilaso and Guaman Poma, two spokesmen for the native people of Peru, wrote books advancing an indigenous perspective on colonization, but they did so while strongly endorsing Christianity and Spanish rule. In other words, transculturation and hegemony often went together.

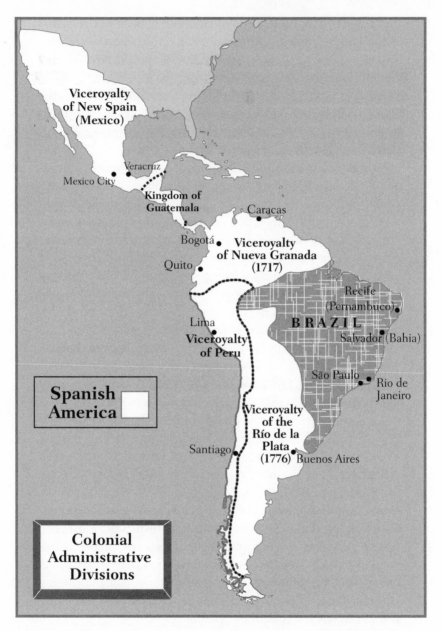

Spanish America

Colonial
Administrative
Divisions

Viceroyalty
of New Spain
(Mexico)

Veracruz

Mexico City

Kingdom of
Guatemala

Caracas

Bogotá

Viceroyalty
of Nueva Granada
(1717)

Quito

Recife
(Pernambuco)

Lima

B R A Z I L

Salvador (Bahia)

Viceroyalty
of Peru

São Paulo

Rio de
Janeiro

Viceroyalty
of the
Río de la
Plata
(1776)

Santiago

Buenos Aires

The Jesuit Antônio Vieira, who has been called the Las Casas of Brazil, exemplifies the same paradox. Vieira was one of the most famous intellectuals of the 1600s. In fact, it was a publication by Vieira that Sor Juana made the mistake of refuting too brilliantly for her own good. Vieira traveled back and forth between Brazil and Portugal, preaching fiery sermons. He studied both Tupi and the language of Angola. He tried to protect the indigenous people against the Portuguese settlers. He defended the humanity and worth of African slaves. Vieira preached that "Brazil has its body in America and its soul in Angola," but he also called on slaves to endure slavery with a good heart and await their reward in the Christian heaven. Vieira had some African heritage of his own, through his grandmother; slaves who heard him preach no doubt found him more convincing for that reason.

## THE FRINGES OF COLONIZATION

While the colonizers concentrated their efforts on silver mining and sugar cultivation, vast reaches of Spanish America and Brazil remained outside the core areas, on the "fringe" of colonization. The fringes were quite different from the core areas because they had little to export. They could not generate as much wealth for Iberian colonizers and therefore attracted fewer of them. Lack of sugar and precious metals meant less incentive to force labor from indigenous people, less capital to invest in African slaves, and, overall, fewer stark contrasts between luxury and misery. A weaker money economy meant that people's energy went into subsistence activities, especially growing their own food. Where people are few, those at the bottom of the social hierarchy become more important. Thus, people of mixed race got a little more respect in fringe areas, and even slaves received better treatment there, because their replacement price was harder to afford.

Paraguay, a large Spanish province in the heart of the South American continent, was one of the most socially peripheral areas in the empire. Like many fringe areas, Paraguay had a form of colonization characterized by missions where religious orders, Jesuits in this case, gathered indigenous people to be instructed in the Christian faith. Remote from the mining economy and almost landlocked, colonial Paraguay became thoroughly permeated with Guaraní indigenous influence. Eventually, Guaraní became the language of intimate conversation at all levels of Paraguayan society, even among nonindigenous people. Racial mixing, another characteristic of fringe societies, made Paraguay notably mestizo. Even Paraguay's chief export was native American—leaves of the evergreen *yerba mate* tree, which made a tea widely consumed in South America.

Farther south, at the mouth of the Río de la Plata, lay other Spanish American settlements, including the ports of Buenos Aires and Montevideo, much less isolated than Paraguay, but still fringes. The great rivers that feed the Río de la Plata together constitute a navigable transportation network second in Latin America only to the Amazon. Silver from Potosí flowed out of the continent here—hence Río de la Plata, or River of Silver. Herds of cattle multiplied on the grasslands around the Río de la Plata, and by late in the colonial period, the exportation of cattle hides added yet another lucrative line to this rising Spanish American fringe. Still, even after becoming the capital of a new viceroyalty in 1776, Buenos Aires could hardly compete with the splendors, refinements, and impressive buildings of Mexico City or Lima. Mobile parties of indigenous raiders still swooped down on isolated ranch houses and carried away captives to be incorporated into tribal life not so far south of the city. On the other hand, the society of the Río de la Plata could boast a kind of abundance different from that of the older colonial centers. The ratio of cattle to people was so high that virtually everyone, including slaves, ate as much beef as they wanted. Horses, too, abounded; to the astonishment of Europeans, Argentine paupers might beg from horseback.

Across the Andes from Argentina lay another Spanish fringe settlement, Chile, paradoxically isolated despite its two thousand miles of Pacific coast. To channel resources to mining, the Spanish Crown had made Chile strictly subordinate to the viceroyalty of Peru. In addition, to curb smuggling and defend the sea link between America and Europe, the Crown restricted transatlantic communications to one annual fleet that gathered at Havana bound for Spain, and another that made the return trip. As a result, Chile's only communications with Madrid involved first a voyage to Lima, then a second leg to Panama, a harrowing journey on mule over the forest-clad mountains of the isthmus, a third voyage through the pirate-infested Caribbean, a layover in Havana, and then the perilous Atlantic crossing. Nor could Chile offer settlers many tribute-paying indigenous servants. Indeed, the southern Chilean frontier had resisted colonization even before the Spanish arrived. There, Inca armies had encountered the unconquerable Araucanos, whose heads Inés Suárez famously cut off. Fighting between the Spanish and the Araucanos continued for centuries. By the 1700s, however, the Spanish controlled most of Chile, with its long central valley lying between the towering Andean ridges and the Pacific. This valley was fertile but lay outside the tropics, too far south for sugar. Instead, Chilean landowners grew wheat as part of the supply network of the Peruvian mining complex.

Spanish fringe areas were often cattle frontiers, sparsely populated lands of "cowboys and Indians," dotted with isolated mission settlements. Río de la Plata cowboys were called *gauchos*, Chilean ones *guasos*, Mexican ones *vaqueros*, and so on. In fact, the cattle lands of the southwestern United States were once a fringe of the Mexican mining zone. In later years, the Anglo settlers learned to be cowboys from the "buckaroos" (*vaqueros*, that is) who preceded them. Spanish American fringes, in other words, were a bit like the Wild West. These cattle frontiers remained poor as long as beef could be preserved only by drying it into jerky, which people in Europe refused to eat.

Much of the Caribbean region, where Columbus touched land, was a fringe area after the first decades of colonization. Cuba, the greatest of the Antilles, comprising roughly half the total land area of all the Caribbean islands, was basically cattle country until the late 1700s. The islands of Hispaniola and Jamaica remained so undeveloped that the French and English made their own territorial claims there. Likewise, on the southern shore of the Caribbean, most of Venezuela was a cattle frontier too. The Caribbean coast of Central America was another sparsely colonized fringe, which explains how the English got footholds there, especially the foothold which became Belize—an English-speaking, non–Latin American country wedged between Mexico, Guatemala, and Honduras.

New Granada (present-day Colombia) was, then as now, a place more complicated than most. It had dense populations of fully sedentary indigenous people in its Andean highlands, but lacked the great silver mines of Peru. On the other hand, it had lots of fringe area, too, including great tropical forests and extensive cattle frontiers. Ecuador, administratively part of the Viceroyalty of New Granada, also had fully sedentary people in its string of high Andean valleys. Such areas with fully sedentary indigenous inhabitants, but without silver mines, lay somewhere between core and fringe in economic terms. Guatemala and Yucatán could be described that way, as well.

Some fringe areas underwent an economic boom at the end of the colonial period. The Río de la Plata found avid European markets for cattle hides. Cuba and Venezuela found profitable plantation crops. In Cuba, those crops were coffee and, especially, sugar. *Cacao* (which English tongues turned into "cocoa") ultimately proved better suited than sugarcane to the slopes of the mountainous Venezuelan coast. Throughout the Caribbean, plantation agriculture brought high profits but, along with them, the same grim social outcome of plantation agriculture everywhere—the massive forced migration of enslaved Africans.

Brazilian fringes resembled Spanish American fringes. Missions constituted the chief expression of Iberian presence. Few representatives of royal authority, few Portuguese of any description, in fact, could be found in the Brazilian backlands. Cattle ranchers, aiming to provide beef on the hoof for coastal plantations and cities, spread inland from the sugar coast into the arid sertão, especially up the long valley of the São Francisco River. Portuguese officials rarely followed them. For the most part, Portuguese colonization hugged the coast and left the backlands to the ranchers, to the surviving indigenous people, to Jesuit missionaries, and to the remarkable frontiersmen called *bandeirantes*, whose base was the mission town of São Paulo.

Today the industrial powerhouse of Brazil, São Paulo was very much a Brazilian backwater in the 1600s. One of the few Brazilian towns not a seaport, it had been founded by Jesuit missionaries at the top of a difficult escarpment that rises steeply from the Atlantic. São Paulo's colonial society faced inland, into the forest of southern Brazil, and indigenous influence was strong there. São Paulo landowners could not compete with the plantations of the sugar coast, and, without export profits, the Portuguese settlers of São Paulo could not buy many African slaves. Therefore, they depended on the labor of indigenous people. They could not afford the luxuries that would attract Portuguese wives, either, so they tended to cohabit with Tupi women. Thus, the population of São Paulo did not follow the black-and-white pattern of the sugar coast, tending instead to be mestizo. A similar situation applied in the Amazonian region, in the arid sertão area of northeastern Brazil, and anywhere else beyond the sweet circle of the sugar economy.

In São Paulo and the other fringe regions of Brazil, the enslavement of indigenous people continued long after it had ceased on the sugar coast. To hunt slaves, São Paulo bandeirantes roamed the vast interior of the Brazilian subcontinent, traveling in canoes, not returning to São Paulo for months or years. Often, they overran missions and captured their inhabitants. Ironically, these slave hunters conversed not in Portuguese but in the generic Tupi, called Lingua Geral, that the Jesuits had used to teach Christianity. By the 1600s, Lingua Geral had become the most widely spoken language of the Brazilian interior. Gradually it disappeared, lingering only in remote Amazon regions. Some important bandeirantes, like Domingos Jorge Velho, did not speak Portuguese at all. He needed an interpreter to communicate with officials from Portugal. The bandeirantes chronically disobeyed the royal guidelines on legal enslavement, but they claimed loyalty to the Portuguese king and made themselves useful. They did not found settlements, but their explorations extended Portuguese claims deep into the continent. Velho's bandeirantes were also able to do what no other Portuguese force could—destroy Palmares, a settlement of escaped slaves, called a *quilombo* in Brazil, where there were hundreds. Palmares was one of the largest quilombos and certainly the best known, a collection of fortified villages that thrived in the hills behind the sugar coast for most of the 1600s. Zumbi, the warrior king of Palmares, led the last stand against the bandeirantes. When Zumbi died fighting in 1695, his head was stuck on a pike in a public square to quash rumors of his immortality. But the rumors were true: three centuries later, Zumbi stands incomparably as the most beloved Afro-Brazilian hero, a symbol of heroic resistance to the horrors of slavery.

Just before 1700, the bandeirantes discovered gold in the backlands. Now for the first time Portuguese settlers poured inland, and soon the precious metal upstaged sugar as the source of colonial profits in Brazil. The São Francisco River began to function as a highway for migrants from the sugar coast to the gold fields, which they named Minas Gerais, or General Mines. The bandeirantes regarded the newcomers as claim jumpers and derided their European-style clothing, calling them *emboabas*, or "fancy-pants." As the gold rush grew, however, the bandeirantes were pushed aside. Slave owners from the sugar coast brought Africans to do the real work of mining, Crown officials began to collect the royal fifth, cities were built near the largest mines, and Brazil acquired its first substantial inland settlements. Vila Rica de Ouro Preto (meaning "rich town of black gold"), the capital of Minas Gerais, became one of Brazil's most populous and prosperous cities in the 1700s, with lavish churches and close-packed two-story houses lining its winding streets. This gold financed the religious art of Aleijadinho, an affectionate nickname meaning "cripple." Aleijadinho's hands were crippled by leprosy. Sometimes unable to grip his tools, he had to tie his chisel to a ruined hand in order to work. But work he did, adorning church after church with his vigorous, expressive statues of biblical figures. Today, Aleijadinho, a mulatto, is recognized as the greatest Latin American sculptor. (The statues on page 43 are his work.)

The discovery of more gold, and even diamonds, in remote locations of the Brazilian interior—thanks, once again to the wandering bandeirantes—began the settlement of Goiás and Mato Grosso, even further inland. São Paulo frontiersmen began to breed mules on the southern plains and drive them north to serve the mines. Brazil became more economically integrated. But the great Brazilian gold boom soon went bust. As generally occurs with gold rushes, the best deposits were easily panned out. Although many newcomers stayed to raise cattle, many others drifted away from Minas Gerais. Still, the Brazilian colony had changed shape as gold pulled its demographic and economic center southward. In 1763, the capital of Brazil was transferred from Salvador to Rio de Janeiro, a port city closer to Minas Gerais. Former fringe areas, Minas Gerais and Rio de Janeiro now counted as part of central Brazil.

Of course, the distinction between core and fringe is only a rough guide, a conceptual model, not a neat physical reality. In fact, in the late 1700s the variety and distribution of Latin America's local cultures was already infinitely more complex than can be explained in a few paragraphs. Still, basic principles such as the core/fringe distinction help us understand many permutations.

## Late Colonial Transformations

A final colonial pattern remains to be delineated: change over time. After the 1500s, the century of the Encounter, indigenous populations gradually recovered, and African slaves arrived in ever-larger numbers. During the 1600s, the basic social outlines of Spanish America and Brazil became well established as the descendents of conquerors and conquered found a *modus vivendi*. Contact with Europe was fairly limited, New World societies were fairly autonomous, and local political control was fairly stable. In the 1700s, economic forces, such as the Brazilian gold rush, gradually expanded the areas of Iberian settlement, and new viceroyalties were added, as has already been described. Around 1750, a further sort of transformation occurred, one that, in the long run, would spell trouble for Spanish and Portuguese dominance.

The transformation began when royal administrators in both Spain and Portugal planned to tighten their control over their New World possessions and extract more revenues from them. This new attitude was associated with the Bourbon dynasty that now ruled Spain and with a particularly powerful royal minster in Portugal, the Marquis de Pombal, and so the transformations are called Bourbon or Pombaline reforms, respectively. These reforms intended to rationalize and modernize the governance of overseas dominions by making them act more like colonies. The descendants of the conquerors liked to think that their heroic forefathers had carved out rich New World kingdoms for their monarchs, kingdoms equal in importance and dignity to Old World kingdoms. But the Bourbon and Pombaline reformers regarded that as an old-fashioned idea. Modern European nations, they believed, should have *colonies* that served the economic interests of the mother countries. Among themselves, the reformers spoke of New World "colonies," rather than "kingdoms," but even if they avoided using the offensive term *colonial* in public discourse, their actual reforms were offensive enough.

The reformers' chief concern was increasing the profitability of the colonies for Spain and Portugal. Therefore, they raised taxes across the board and introduced all sorts of provisions to insure better collection of existing taxes, especially by revamping the framework of colonial administration. A frequent technique was the creation of state-controlled monopoly enterprises to oversee trade or production and sale of basic commodities, such as tobacco or alcohol, in order to maximize the revenue that they produced for the state. Mining, the single most lucrative sector of the colonial economy, received special attention in both Spanish America and Brazil, both to promote technical improvement and to stifle smuggling of untaxed gold and silver. To insure that colonial economies would serve Spain and Portugal better, the reformers also tightened limitations on production of certain goods, such as cloth or wine, in the Americas. They wanted colonials to buy cloth and wine from Spanish and Portuguese producers, not compete with them. To facilitate transatlantic economic integration beneficial to the mother countries, the reformers loosened restrictions on shipping, as long as the colonies traded exclusively with Spain and Portugal.

By tightening colonial control to serve European interests, the Bourbon and Pombaline reforms naturally injured the interests of people living in Spanish America and Brazil. Tax increases fell directly on some, such as indigenous people, who were little able to pay. The limitations on various sorts of trade and production put people out of work, and the new monopoly enterprises resulted in rising prices. No wonder the period after 1750 saw widespread revolts and protests with economic motivations, a relatively new form of unrest. The people with the most at stake in this situation were the native-born Spanish American and Brazilian ruling classes, who lost influence in all sorts of ways. The Bourbon and Pombaline reformers reasoned, logically enough, that colonial officials would have European interests most at heart when they were themselves Europeans, while the native-born elite was much more likely to defend its own local interests. Because European-born Spaniards and Portuguese were regarded as superior agents of imperial control, they received systematic preferment throughout the civil and ecclesiastical power structures. The proud heirs of the conquerors began to lose the judgeships and administrative positions that they had previously enjoyed, a tremendous blow to their pride and to their opportunities for social advancement. And native-born elites suffered in other ways from the reformers' tightening of colonial control, too, particularly when the reformers expelled the Jesuit order from both Brazil (1759) and Spanish America (1767). The Jesuits had offered a prestigious career path to capable young men of the New World, and they had provided rare educational opportunities to the ruling class. But the Jesuits had a habit of resisting royal authority, something that the reformers would not tolerate.

Young men of haughty elite families were bumping up against a glass ceiling just as socially climbing young men of more humble families crowded them from below. The late colonial period saw a marked rise in the portion of the population that was not white, not indigenous, and not African, but culturally and racially mixed. Mixed people were people-in-between. They occupied the middle rungs on the social ladder, with whites above them and Africans and indigenous people further down. They were products of centuries of transculturation, speaking a variety of languages, well able to negotiate the various social worlds of the colonial environment, superbly adapted to succeed in their diverse social milieu. Not by accident were they culturally *and* racially mixed.

Transculturation usually occurred along with some sort of race mixing. Obviously, transculturation can happen without any mixing of genes, and vice versa. Nevertheless, in Latin American history, transcultural mixing and race mixing go together.

Race mixing could mean several things here. It could mean social interaction and shared experience—rarely on a basis of equality, of course, but still meaningful in human terms—as when apprentice artisans of various colors labored and caroused together, or when white rural families spent their whole lives— their childhood, their workaday routine, their moments of deep personal significance—surrounded by slaves, indigenous people, or free people of mixed race. On the other hand, race mixing often meant sex as well. Intermarriage among poor whites, blacks, and indigenous people was common, as were consensual partnerships. Often *not* consensual, or only superficially so, were the sexual encounters between social unequals of different race, as when "gentlemen" hired prostitutes or forced themselves on enslaved women.

The story of Xica da Silva is extreme rather than typical, memorable rather than anonymous. Xica became celebrated, and also notorious, in the diamond fields of Brazil. Her mother was African and her father was Portuguese. The riches of the diamond fields flowed into the pocket of the king's royal diamond contractor. He could buy whatever he wanted. What he wanted was Xica da Silva for his mistress, but she did not come cheap. For her he had to provide rich clothing, a place of honor at church, a dozen maids-in-waiting, a park with artificial waterfalls, even an artificial lake with a miniature sailing ship. (Xica had always wanted to see the ocean.) Now she wore a powdered wig, and people came to her seeking access to her lover, the diamond contractor. One of her sons—not the diamond contractor's—studied at European universities. Her disdainful reference to certain Portuguese visitors rang in people's memories. "Butler," she famously said, "take care of the *sailor boys*," using the scornful Brazilian slang for Portuguese immigrants just off the boat. When she called the Portuguese "sailor boys," Xica da Silva, a Brazilian woman of mixed race, was daring to look down on European men—flying in the face of the *caste system.*

To exercise control over colonial Latin American societies, the Iberian Crowns sorted people into fixed categories called *castes*, as in India. The caste system was all about pedigree, so it more or less corresponded to what people today call "race." In practice, the caste system also factored in other characteristics, such as education, clothing, and especially wealth. "Money whitens," according to a famous phrase expressing the importance of wealth in the Latin American caste system. A person's caste classification was noted in the baptismal register at the time of baptism, and people of low caste were legally prevented from becoming priests, attending the university, wearing silk, owning weapons, and many other things. A person wholly of European descent occupied one category in the system, and a person entirely of African descent occupied another. That much is quite familiar from US race relations. But the child of a European and an African belonged to a third category—half European, half African, logically enough. There was a fourth category for a child with a European father and an indigenous mother, and a fifth for a child whose parents were indigenous and African. And indigenous people had a category to themselves, making six. And this was just the beginning.

Members of these six categories continued to produce babies with each other, despite official rules against this, creating new "people-in-between" who confounded the categories and strained the system. At least in theory, caste categories prolif-erated geometrically—to sixteen or more, including some with animal names, *Lobo* and *Coyote*—during the last century of colonial rule. These names are from the 1700s in Mexico, where many series of paintings were commissioned to illustrate the caste system. Such caste paintings were entitled, for example, "An Español and a Mulata make a *Morisco*," with father, mother, and child shown in a domestic setting, each with the appropri-ate clothing, demeanor, and skin color. Caste paintings were sent to Spain, where imperial officials viewed them much as species classifications in natural history. Above all, these strange works were intended to help impose order on the unruly reality of race mixing. The dozen or so new caste names never really gained everyday currency, and they should be viewed mostly as a symptom of the strain that progressive race mixing was put-ting on the caste system by the late 1700s.

Also in these years, successful people of low caste (prosper-ous mule drivers or artisans, for example) presented a different challenge to the caste system. Perpetually in need of money, the Spanish Crown sometimes allowed such people to buy an official exemption that made them legally white and eligible to occupy positions of distinction and authority. This exemption was called *gracias al sacar*. Whites with little else going for them except for caste privilege complained bitterly about the sale of legal whiteness, saying it undermined the whole caste system. The sale of gracias al sacar also exemplified the Latin American tendency to think of race as a negotiable spectrum, a ladder that families might ascend. Families could climb the ladder, even without legal exemptions, when daughters and sons were able to marry "up"—which is to say, find partners lighter than themselves. Note, however, that moving "up" by marrying for skin color also meant buying into the logic of the caste system, with its premise of white superiority. Therefore, race mixing provides a tracer of transculturation (and cultural hegemony) in action.

Whether valued, abhorred, or merely tolerated, race mixing was a fact of colonial life in Latin America. By 1800, near the end of the colonial period, people of mixed blood already made up roughly a quarter of the Latin American population, and these "people-in-between" were also the fastest-growing group. The African and indigenous majority had adopted much from the Spanish and Portuguese. They had made a cultural impact of their own. In living together, with all the conflicts that entailed, people of diverse origin had created shared identities and unifying webs of loyalty. By the year 1800, even white Spanish Americans and Brazilians, roughly another quarter of the population, were noticing that many of their habits and preferences, such as their taste in music, now made them different from their European cousins and in some ways a bit like the people below them in the colonial hierarchy. Still, few colonials assigned much importance to a distinctive American identity in 1800.

The wars of independence would change that.

# COUNTERCURRENTS:
## Colonial Rebellions

Durability and stability were the most surprising traits of colonial rule in Latin America, but there were many small rebellions—and a few notably large ones—especially toward the end. Some of these uprisings were aftershocks of the Iberian takeover. Others, the later ones, can be taken as signs of rising tensions and, thus, precursors of independence.

THE REBELLION OF GONZALO PIZARRO, 1544–49. The most important early rebellion was carried out by the conquistadors of Peru. It occurred when the New Laws limiting encomiendas (in 1542) arrived in Peru along with the first viceroy to be sent by the Spanish king. The leader of the revolt was Gonzalo Pizarro, brother of the Peruvian conqueror, Francisco Pizarro. Pizarro's followers feared losing their encomiendas altogether as a result of the New Laws, and they reacted violently, capturing and killing the viceroy in 1546. Within three years, the rebellion had run its course. Gonzalo Pizarro was beheaded for treason, and a new viceroy resumed royal control of Peru.

INDIGENOUS REVOLTS, 1500–1800. Indigenous people often revolted once the first shock of conquest had worn off. The 1560s Andean movement called Taki Onqoy was a particularly interesting example. In it, indigenous people heard their old gods calling them and, as in Europe's Saint Vitus's Dance of the 1300s, they suffered uncontrollable fits of shaking and dancing. However, most indigenous revolts, of which there were hundreds, were small and isolated, seldom threatening to overall Spanish or Portuguese rule. The 1680 Pueblo rebellion of New Mexico was an exception. In that year, the Pueblo people rose up and, for more than a decade, expelled all things Spanish from their land. Yucatán, at the other end of Mexico, was the site of repeated uprisings. In 1761, a Yucatec Maya took the name Canek (a legendary indigenous leader) and led a brief but serious revolt. He was captured within the year and executed by being torn limb from limb. Punishments for indigenous revolts were, as a rule, truly savage.

REBELLIONS AGAINST BOURBON REFORM MEASURES, 1740S–80s. The Bourbon attempt to tighten royal control and extract greater profits from the American colonies sparked resistance in several places. In 1749, Venezuelan cacao growers revolted against the government's monopoly control of their product. In 1765–66, urban crowds staged an uprising to protest tax hikes in Quito (Ecuador). In the *Comunero* uprising of 1781, inhabitants of a town in present-day Colombia revolted because of tax increases and new monopoly restrictions on the cultivation of tobacco. Often, such rebellions united people across caste lines for a short time, but their alliances usually broke apart, precisely along those lines, within a few weeks. In addition, these rebellions targeted specific Bourbon reform measures and not Spanish rule per se. In fact, the rebels often proclaimed their loyalty to the Crown at the very moment of revolt, shouting "Long Live the King! Death to Bad Government!"

QUILOMBOS AND PALENQUES, 1500–1888. We have already encountered the great Brazilian quilombo (refuge of escaped slaves) called Palmares. Refuges also existed in the Spanish Caribbean, where they were termed *palenques*. (The Spanish word describes the palisade of tree trunks that often fortified a camp of escaped slaves.) Uprisings in which slaves took revenge on masters were much less common, but never out of the question.

**"FRENCH-STYLE" CONSPIRACIES IN BRAZIL, 1789 AND 1798.**
An early tremor or two showed those ideas at work in Brazil
as well. In a few cities, circles of daring men began to discuss new political philosophies—namely, the overthrow of
monarchies to form republics—then emanating from France
and the United States. The city of Ouro Preto, in Brazil's
mining region, was one such place. Informers revealed the
conspiracy almost immediately, however, and the partici-
pants were swiftly arrested. Most, being white and well-off,
were merely exiled. But one, a mulatto army officer (nick-
named Tiradentes, "Tooth-puller," because he practiced
dentistry on the side), was publicly executed. Today Tiradentes is Brazil's greatest patriot martyr. A similar "French-
style" conspiracy, called the Tailor's Rebellion because
several of the conspirators practiced that trade, was exposed
in Bahia nine years later. There, most of the conspirators
were blacks or mulattos, a circumstance particularly frightening to the white elite.

**THE REBELLION OF TUPAC AMARU II, 1780–83.** This most
important of colonial rebellions shook the high Andes and
sent shock waves throughout Spanish America. The mestizo who called himself Tupac Amaru II claimed royal Inca
descent, but whether or not he had it, the Inca name itself
was the main point. He took it in memory of Tupac Amaru
I, an Inca resistance leader and folk hero who fought a rear-
guard action against the conquest in the 1500s. The initial
proclamation of the new rebellion was anti-"Peninsular" (a
name given to Iberian-born Spaniards) and called for an
alliance among American-born whites, mestizos, and indigenous people. Once begun, however, the rebellion became
primarily indigenous and raged out of control, leaping south
through the high plateaus of dense indigenous population

like a grass fire, into Upper Peru (modern Bolivia), where it set off another, more stubborn revolt, involving a leader who called himself Tupac Catari. The rebellion, which consumed perhaps a hundred thousand lives before it finally burned out, thoroughly terrified the Peruvian elite and profoundly affected their behavior in the coming wars of independence.

**THE LIBERATOR SIMÓN BOLÍVAR.** Bolívar, who helped create five nations, was the single greatest general of independence. Bolívar was from Caracas, the son of a plantation-owning family who gave him a privileged education—including a European walking tour with his brilliant tutor, Simón Rodríguez, a man afire with new ideas. But white, upper-class generals like Bolívar could not win independence without the support of Latin America's nonwhite majority. Indigenous patriots figure prominently in this Bolivian painting. *Courtesy of Hulton Getty Picture Collection.*

| 1807–8 | 1810–14 | 1815 | 1820 | 1824 |
|--------|---------|------|------|------|
| Napoleon invades Iberia | Spanish American revolts begin | Brazil raised to status of kingdom | Liberal revolutions in Spain and Portugal | Battle of Ayacucho |

# 3.

# INDEPENDENCE

Latin American struggles for independence erupted suddenly and unexpectedly. There had been a few ominous tremors before 1800, but the most remarkable thing about colonial rule continued to be its overall stability. Therefore, nobody saw an imperial collapse coming, and when it came, everybody improvised. One might expect those at the bottom to rise up when European control slipped; that did happen in some places, notably Haiti, where slaves literally took over. But the outcome in Spanish America and Brazil was more conservative. In general, the white people at the top of the social hierarchy stayed there, while blacks and indigenous people stayed at the bottom. On the other hand, Latin American independence created a dozen of the world's first constitutional republics. The fighting dealt the caste system a deathblow and brought new honor to many people of mixed race.

The fighting itself changed much in Latin America. Many men of color became honored war heroes because of their bravery in combat. But winning the wars of independence required more than blood; it also required a sense of belonging and shared purpose. The modern nations of Latin America did not yet exist, even as a pipe dream, when the wars began. What did an African slave, a Quechua-speaking villager, a landowner of

**THE HAITIAN REVOLUTION.** The great slave uprising that began in the French colony of Haiti in 1791 crushed the master class, defeated several French armies sent to repress it, and created a vivid worst-case scenario for a generation of Latin American slave owners. *Schomburg Center/Art Resource, New York.*

pure Spanish blood, and a mestizo artisan have in common just because all had been born (for example) in the viceroyalty of Peru? Not much, obviously, aside from being subjects of the Spanish Crown, which treated them almost as different sub-species of human being. So patriot leaders faced a great chal-lenge. They had to imagine new nations and get other people with little in common to imagine those nations, too. The image had to be so vivid that people would betray their king, kill, and risk death for it. The patriotic vision of the wars of indepen-dence introduced elements of the two big ideas, liberalism and nationalism, that have animated Latin American political life ever since.

To understand people's actions during the crisis years of 1808–25, to see how independence came so unexpectedly, then so quickly, how it changed so much and yet so little, we must observe how violent events in Europe suddenly destabilized colonial rule. Then we will see how Latin Americans reacted—a story with several different threads. Core areas like Mexico and Peru followed one pattern, fringe areas like Venezuela and Argentina another. Brazil followed its own quite distinctive path to independence. These winding roads can get a bit compli-cated, but understanding them is worthwhile, because the wars of independence cast a long shadow on the history of Latin America.

## REVOLUTION AND WAR IN EUROPE

Spanish Americans experienced a grueling couple of decades after 1788 under the calamitous rule of an incompetent king, Carlos IV, who shirked his royal responsibilities and left govern-ing to a hated minister widely known to be the queen's lover. Misrule had combined with a series of costly wars to bankrupt the Spanish state during the 1700s. The bankruptcy of the Crown led to higher taxes, as well as to other irritating practices like the sale of high office, which put incompetent people in

positions of command, and highly unpopular government
foreclosure of long-term loans. Worse, war with England, beginning in 1796 and lasting off and on for the next decade, meant
confronting the world's most powerful navy, for these were
the years when "Britannia ruled the waves." The Spanish
navy was overwhelmed, and the number of Atlantic sailings
dropped drastically, strangling colonial trade. Spanish Americans watched all this with dismay but without seeing it as a
cue to rebel. After all, foreign wars often evoke feelings of loyalty to king and country, and the English were hereditary enemies who frequently attacked Spanish American ships and
ports. Neither Spain nor Portugal could escape the widening
repercussions of the French Revolution (1789–99) and the sub-
sequent Napoleonic Wars (1799–1815) that eventually engulfed
all of Europe. In practical terms, Spanish American independence began to exist de facto in 1808, when the Spanish king
was imprisoned by Napoleon.

In Brazil, things worked out differently. Portugal had maintained a friendly relationship with England since the 1300s,
a relationship described in the 1386 Treaty of Windsor as "an in-
violable, eternal, solid, perpetual, and true league of friendship"—
a relationship that England dominated. England would prove a
valuable but demanding ally. But, English ally or no, the French
Revolution and Napoleonic Wars started the process of independence in Brazil as well.

French revolutionaries of the 1790s had challenged the idea
of monarchy based on divine right, even executing the French
king and queen, Louis XVI and Marie Antoinette. These revolutionaries took inspiration from the intellectual awakening
called the Enlightenment. They proclaimed "Liberty, Equality,
and Fraternity," questioned traditional authority, and remade
the political order. They sneered at idiot kings who, thanks to
their royal bloodlines, possessed power they did not deserve.
Instead, the revolutionaries argued for *popular sovereignty*,

meaning that the people of each nation (not yet including women, however) had the right to determine who would rule them according to a written constitution. French revolutionaries set out to overthrow other European kings and establish republics. Somewhat perversely, the revolutionary creed became an ideology to justify military aggression, as French armies led by General, then First Consul, and finally Emperor Napoleon Bonaparte began "liberating" other countries into French control. Spain and Portugal were two of these.

The new political ideology of liberty and liberation—liberalism, in a word—was almost as much English as French in origin. England's own Civil War and revolution in the 1600s had enshrined the principle of popular sovereignty in the unwritten English constitution. England preserved its monarchy, as it does to this day, but it is a limited monarchy, subordinate to an elected legislature, the House of Commons, which liberals regarded as the voice of "the people." England opposed the radicalism of the French Revolution and led the fight against Napoleonic expansionism. That aligned England with anti-Napoleonic Spanish and Portuguese patriots during Latin America's independence period, as we will see. In sum, liberalism, whether coming from France or England, inspired all sides in the Napoleonic Wars. It was the impact of those wars, and their aftermath, in turn, that triggered Latin American independence—all under the ideological banner of popular sovereignty.

In late 1807, when the Portuguese refused to close their ports and declare war on their old ally, England, Napoleon invaded Portugal. The Portuguese royal family fled, accompanied by a glittering entourage of nobles and government officials, swarms of servants and courtiers—over ten thousand people, as well as the royal treasury—sailing from Lisbon only days before Napoleon's troops arrived in the Portuguese capital. British warships were on hand to escort the royal flotilla and, most especially,

Prince João (who exercised power in the name of the queen, his demented mother) to Brazil. For more than a decade, João made his court in Rio de Janeiro, safely outside the reach of Napoleon. Meanwhile, both the Spanish king, Carlos IV, and his heir, Prince Fernando, had fallen into Napoleon's hands and, under pressure, both abdicated their claims to the Spanish throne. Napoleon then had his own brother Joseph crowned king of Spain, a move that most Spaniards and Spanish Americans refused to accept.

One aspect of colonial hegemony had been the gradual acceptance of the Spanish and Portuguese monarchs as rightful rulers by almost everyone in the colonies. The Crown had strong *legitimacy*: authority that inspires obedience. By 1810, a startling contrast existed. The Portuguese Crown was closer than ever to Brazil. The Spanish Crown, usurped by a foreigner, was further than ever from Spanish America. Brazilian history shows how much difference the king's presence could make.

João's royal court in Rio de Janeiro had become the political center of the Portuguese-speaking world, and the people of Rio, always fond of glamour, were delighted to have it there. Thousands of rich European courtiers flooded the city, sparking a boom in building and profitable services, from livery stables to hairdressing. The presence of the royal court also favored the Brazilian elite, for the opportunity to speak a few words directly into the king's ear is valuable indeed. The end of colonial trade monopolies favored Brazil as a whole. Before, Brazilian trade had all been channeled to Portugal, but now João allowed Brazilians to trade with everybody (chiefly the British, who had pressed strongly for this trade opening), and imported goods became less expensive. João liked Rio and enjoy placid naps in his botanical garden as ships from Europe and Spanish America brought news of one distant upheaval after another.

Back in Portugal, an anti-Napoleonic patriot uprising began in 1808 soon after João's departure, and fighting in the Iberian peninsula dragged on for years as Portuguese and Spanish guerrillas, supported by British troops, fought hit-and-run actions against the French. In Spanish America, chronic fighting broke out as well. Independence was declared here and there. Meanwhile, Rio bustled and Brazil remained peaceful. Whatever social and economic pressures had built up during the colonial period, whatever rivalries existed between Portuguese and Brazilians, they did not explode now. So content was João in Rio that even after Napoleon met ultimate defeat in the battle of Waterloo (1815), the Portuguese king conspicuously failed to hurry back to Lisbon.

Events in Spanish America between 1808 and 1815 contrasted totally with the picture in Brazil. Spanish Americans were shocked at the eclipse of the legitimate monarchy. The Spanish government had not vanished entirely, because provincial resistance movements in Spain sent representatives to a national resistance committee, called the Central *Junta*. The Central Junta expected Spanish American support, but Spanish Americans had other ideas. The Central Junta had been chosen entirely in Spain. It therefore represented the Spanish people, but not the Spanish *American* people, and they rejected its dictates. In the wake of the Napoleonic takeover of Spain, most Spanish Americans professed fervent loyalty to their legitimate king, Fernando VII, but in so doing, they also rejected the idea that Mexico or Peru or New Granada were colonies. Instead, they reaffirmed the old idea that the Spanish king's throne had two pillars of support: his European kingdoms in Iberia, and his American kingdoms in the New World. They argued that, although loyal to Fernando, the American kingdoms were equal to the European ones and not subservient to them. In other words, paradoxically, the Napoleonic crisis led Spanish American patriots to invoke the principle of popular sovereignty against Spain itself. Soon, they began to form their own juntas to rule locally in Fernando's name. These "caretaker" juntas were often created at an open meeting of the town council, a *cabildo abierto*.

By 1810, the Spanish resistance to the French occupation
had been pushed to the southern port city of Cádiz, where it
continued to function under British naval protecton. The Spanish liberals who led the resistance now called for a constitution
to be written by elected representatives from both Spain and
Spanish America. The Constitution of Cádiz was a truly liberal
document and, if implemented, would have profoundly altered
the Spanish empire. But it was never fully implemented. By
the time it was completed, patriot rebels had already raised the
cry of anti-Spanish rebellion in Mexico, Venezuela, Argentina,
and elsewhere.

## The Spanish American Rebellions Begin, 1810–15

But who were these patriot rebels? In most cases, the initiatives for independence came from native-born whites, called
Creoles to distinguish them from Spaniards born on the Iberian
Peninsula. Iberian-born Spaniards were now called Peninsulars
or, often, nastier things that do not translate well. We should
backtrack a bit to explain what the Creoles were after.

By the late 1700s, Spanish American Creoles had grown quite
resentful of the Peninsulars, with whom they competed socially.
Spanish birth made Peninsulars the preferred agents of imperial rule. Peninsular Spaniards normally got the best ecclesiastical and government offices, the key positions on boards of
trade, and so on, gaining privileged access to wealth and power
over their American-born Creole cousins. But this rivalry existed
only at the top of Spanish American society. The other three-
quarters or four-fifths of the population—people of indigenous,
African, or mixed descent—had little at stake in the Creole-
versus-Peninsular contest, because the caste system put them
out of the competition altogether. Sometimes they disliked the
Creoles more than they disliked the Peninsulars, because the
Creoles were the masters and overlords who annoyed them in

daily life. Creoles generally owned the land, and much of the Spanish American population lived under the thumb of landowners. In the towns, it was Creoles, not Peninsulars, who feared the social climbing of prosperous people of mixed race and fought to keep them "in their place." In other words, the majority of Spanish Americans had plenty of reason to revolt—but not particularly against the Peninsulars.

Mexican independence shows these dynamics at work. Mexico was by far the Spanish Crown's brightest imperial jewel by the early 1800s, vastly the most profitable colony, and home to four out of ten Spanish Americans. Peninsulars numbered only a fraction of 1 percent, but Creole resentment against them ran high, so the Creole-dominated cabildo of Mexico City seized the 1808 crisis in Spain as a chance to gain ground against their privileged European cousins. Affirming their continued loyalty to the imprisoned Fernando VII, the Creoles convinced the viceroy to call a representative assembly to provide legitimacy while the king was out of the picture. The colony's powerful Peninsulars would have none of it, however. They actually unseated the viceroy to forestall such an assembly. Creole anger smoldered.

Then, in 1810, Spanish America's political upheavals began in earnest. A Creole conspiracy in Mexico's northern mining region sparked a massive rebellion of indigenous and mestizo peasants. The man who let the genie out of the bottle was a Creole priest, Father Miguel Hidalgo. A reader of banned French books who also studied indigenous languages and defied the Catholic rule of sexual abstinence for clergy, Hidalgo was an impulsive nonconformist, and the Inquisition already had a file on him. Informed that the Spanish authorities would soon arrest him for his part in the conspiracy, Hidalgo hurried to his parish church and rang the bell. He then spoke to the gathering crowd using religious language that his audience well understood— not about independence, but about the need to defend Mexico against the Peninsular usurpers of legitimate authority and the enemies of Fernando VII. Hidalgo presented the rivalry between Creoles and Peninsulars as a unanimous Spanish American revolt against Spain. He spoke of how Spanish conquerors had stolen Indian lands. In point of fact, it was the Creoles, and not the Peninsulars of 1810, who descended from those conquerors. In truth, Hidalgo had more in common with most Peninsulars, his social peers, than with his indigenous parishioners. But his rhetoric constructed a simple dichotomy: Americans versus Europeans. His battle cry was "Long live the Virgin of Guadalupe, and death to the Spaniards!" The appeal worked.

Poor rural people flocked by the thousands to the banner of the Virgin of Guadalupe, now a potent symbol of Mexican identity. The throngs included men, women, and children, whole families, burros, and cattle. Their weapons were mostly farming tools rather than firearms. A recent famine in the mining zone had left many humble Mexicans with little to lose. When terrified Peninsulars in the important mining center of Guanajuato saw twenty thousand angry indigenous peasants coming at them, they hurriedly barricaded themselves in the largest, strongest building in town, the massive granary—but to no avail. Peninsulars died by the hundreds in Guanajuato and then all along the route of this rampaging ragtag army. And not only Peninsulars: Creoles died, too. Hidalgo's patriotic rhetoric had theoretically drawn the line between the Peninsulars and everyone else, but Creoles and Peninsulars resembled one another. Many Peninsulars had Creole wives and children. Furthermore, Peninsulars cornered by the rebels commonly claimed to be Creoles. The downtrodden indigenous and mestizo peasants who followed Hidalgo lacked military discipline, and to them, Creoles and Peninsulars seemed equally arrogant. As Hidalgo's multitude reached sixty, seventy, eighty thousand, it began to look to many Creoles like their own worst nightmare.

Few Mexican Creoles, or town dwellers of any description, joined Hidalgo, and his unruly followers dispersed after only a few months. Hidalgo himself was captured, forced to repent publicly, and then executed. As an exemplary lesson, Hidalgo's head was dangled in a metal cage on a corner of the Guanajuato granary where so many Spaniards had died. But the revolutionary genie would not go back into the bottle. In southern Mexico, where indigenous communities retained village identities and lands from before the conquest, one of Hidalgo's officers still raised the torch of rebellion. He, too, was a priest, but a modest and practical one, very unlike the grandiose visionary Hidalgo. Father José María Morelos was not a Creole at all, but a mestizo, and a more able leader in every way. His army was well organized and his main goals were clear: an end to slavery, to the caste system, and to the tribute paid by indigenous people. Morelos prohibited the use of caste classifications. All born in Mexico were simply "Americanos." In 1813, he declared outright independence. His movement still did not attract many Creoles, but it had staying power—at least until Father Morelos was caught and executed in 1815. By then, small bands of patriot guerrillas had been fighting for years in several regions of Mexico, and with Morelos gone, they continued to defy the government, causing heavy military expenses, living off the land like bandits, and gradually gnawing away at the fabric of colonial rule.

In Peru, independence got a slower start. Peruvian Creoles had already glimpsed their nightmare scenario a few decades earlier, in the 1780s, when the great indigenous rebellion of Tupac Amaru II rocked the Andes. Although a generation in the past by 1808, Tupac Amaru's rebellion was far from forgotten, and it had given Peruvian Creoles a vivid appreciation of the dangers inherent in mobilizing the indigenous people against the Peninsulars. So they avoided revolt, aside from a few early protests, even at the cost of putting up with arrogant Europeans who got all the best government jobs. Overall, Peru, along with other Andean areas such as Bolivia and Ecuador, remained comparatively quiet during the crisis years of the early 1810s as major revolts erupted elsewhere.

Leading Creoles in "fringe" colonies such as Venezuela and Argentina were less cautious. They chafed under imperial trade restrictions that favored silver production in the core areas of Peru and Mexico. And the grassy plains of both Venezuela and Argentina abounded in horses and horsemen, very useful in premechanized warfare. Unlike the movements of Hidalgo and Morelos, which were uprisings from below, the patriot juntas of Caracas and Buenos Aires began as *cabildos abiertos*, gatherings of the most influential men in the two cities. This was revolution from above, led by confident, well-traveled Creoles, some of whom had witnessed European events firsthand. When the crisis of legitimacy began in Spain, Creoles in Caracas and Buenos Aires reacted like those elsewhere. Gradually, however, they shelved their protestations of loyalty to the king, embraced the liberal revolution, and moved toward full independence. Their critics called this "taking off the mask of Fernando."

In Venezuela, all this had already happened by early 1811. The problem was making it stick. The first Venezuelan republic crumbled when an earthquake, convincing evidence of divine disapproval, struck Caracas a year later. Nor was the earthquake the patriots' only problem. In the heart of Venezuela, beyond the mountainous Caribbean coast with its plantations of cacao, lay the flood-prone tropical plains of the Orinoco River basin, a land of cattle and dark-skinned cowboys called *llaneros*, who ate mostly beef, carried lances, and rode as if born on horseback. To put it mildly, the llaneros had no sympathy for the elite, plantation-owning revolutionaries of Caracas, who regarded them more or less as scum. When the Caracas junta went so far as to deny the authority of Fernando VII, the llaneros opted to defend their king, and their horses' hooves kept the ground trembling long after the earthquake had subsided. As long as the llaneros opposed them, the patriots would never win in Venezuela.

In Argentina, the revolutionary junta had an easier time gaining military dominance. The patriot advantage began back in 1806 and 1807, when the Spanish and the British were enemies. During those years, two British expeditions landed in the viceroyalty of the Río de la Plata. They were both defeated, not by Peninsular forces, but by local militias. So Creole patriots there had the upper hand militarily when Spain's Napoleonic crisis began. By May 1810, Peninsular control had ended once and for all in Buenos Aires. Other regions of the Río de la Plata viceroyalty, however, showed little inclination to follow the lead of Buenos Aires. Whether patriots or royalists, people in the interior resented the airs of overweening Creole aristocrats from the capital. The wars of independence in the Río de la Plata therefore consisted mostly of fighting between armies from Buenos Aires on the one hand, and provincial armies, whether royalist or patriot, on the other.

By 1815, with the execution of Morelos in Mexico, royalist victories in Venezuela (and elsewhere, such as Colombia and Chile), Peru still firmly in Spanish hands, and patriots fighting among themselves in the Río de la Plata, the wars for Spanish American independence stood at a low ebb. The patriots had not yet succeeded in getting enough people on their side. What did they really have to offer, anyway?

## The Patriots' Winning Strategy: Nativism

After all, it was *not* the exploited majority, as one might have expected, who initiated independence movements. Radical doctrines such as republicanism did not hold much appeal for conservative country people who had received little exposure to such ideas. Moreover, most of the movements' Creole leaders had little interest in helping the masses or making colonial society more egalitarian. Instead, they simply wanted to rule it themselves. Mexican and Peruvian Creoles, particularly, worried about losing control of large populations of indigenous peasants who had shown a fearsome penchant for rebellion. Consequently, Mexican Creoles backed away wide-eyed after a look at Hidalgo's ragged multitude of 1810, and Peruvian Creoles, mindful of Tupac Amaru II, preferred not to risk declaring independence at all. Venezuelan and Argentine Creoles, on the other hand, showed more confidence in their ability to hold the tiger by the tail. To do so, they somehow had to reach out to "the people." The Creoles were just too few to win independence without help from below.

The winning strategy for independence-minded Creoles was *nativism*. Nativism glorified an American identity defined by birthplace, something Creoles shared with the indigenous people, with those of mixed blood, even with the children of African slaves. *Americanos* was the nativist keyword. From Mexico to Brazil to Argentina, patriots defined theirs as the *American* cause, and their enemies as everyone born in Spain or Portugal. Nativism had many advantages. The name *Americanos* fit easily and comfortably over multihued Spanish American and Brazilian populations, contrasting them with Europeans. And nativism drew on powerful emotions. Resentment is always at the heart of nativist attitudes, resentment of foreigners and foreign influence. Resentment against the idea of colonial inferiority and, more particularly, against resident Spanish and Portuguese, now foreigners in nativist eyes, was widespread in America at all social levels. Finally, nativism linked arms with liberal ideology in an obvious way. "Who should govern? The People! And who are the People? *Americanos!*" No patriot fighters could ignore the rhetorical appeal of nativism, and all used it sooner or later.

For maximum wartime appeal, the definition of *Americanos* had to be as broad as possible. Few revolutionary leaders really wanted to see social equality, however. Most simply wanted popular support to win independence, leaving the social hierarchy more or less intact. As long as that hierarchy remained in place, the Creoles expected to be the leaders of the emerging sovereign nations.

Brazilian independence provides a good illustration of the way this worked. As Spanish America underwent military upheaval and political mass mobilization during the 1810s, Brazil remained relatively undisturbed under the rule of João VI. Of course there was some discontent. To have the royal court in Rio de Janeiro was expensive, as people noticed after the novelty wore off. A ruinous and unpopular war with Spanish-speaking neighbors began on Brazil's southern border. And João caved in to British pressure and legally restricted the slave trade, which irritated slave owners, even though the restrictions were ineffective. British ships had once participated aggressively in the slave trade, but the British government later renounced the practice and pressured other nations to do the same. The policy responded both to humanitarian antislavery sentiments and to the hope of expanding the market for British goods by turning slaves into consumers.

Foreigners, especially the British and French, had flocked to Brazilian ports since 1808. They took advantage of free trade, brought liberalizing changes of attitude, and stimulated political ferment. The year 1817 saw a localized but notable political explosion in the major northeastern province of Pernambuco, an attempted liberal revolution more significant than any preceding it in Brazil. During a few heady weeks, the Pernambucan rebels declared a republic, discussed a constitution, and called each other "patriot," clearly showing the influence of up-to-date political ideas. This liberal republicanism theoretically favored the great majority of Brazilians, but liberalism was still too unfamiliar to inspire mass support in Brazil. Therefore, the revolt of 1817 was easily crushed after a few weeks, when João's forces arrived in Pernambuco to put it down.

Portuguese actions nudged Brazil closer to independence in 1820. Since Napoleon's defeat, Portugal had wanted its king back

*King João*
*Brazil ← Colony to Kingdom*
*= Portugal*

in Lisbon, and the Portuguese assembly had begun to insist that João return. The assembly was very unhappy with João's 1815 declaration raising Brazil from the legal status of colony to that of kingdom, like Portugal itself. That declaration made Brazil and Portugal juridically equal, with João king of both. The old aspiration not to be a colony had finally been granted, but the Portuguese assembly wanted Brazil reduced once more to colonial status. João returned to Lisbon in 1821, leaving his son, Prince Pedro, behind in Rio to watch the Brazilian situation. The moment was fraught with uncertainties. Various Brazilian provinces established liberal juntas and sent their own representatives to Lisbon, bypassing Rio. Faced simultaneously with the threat of recolonization *and* a loss of control over the provinces, the Brazilian elite of Rio de Janeiro discovered the patriotic pride of native birth and popular sovereignty.

By 1822, Rio's native-born elite had formed a Brazilian Party that claimed to represent the Brazilian people against Portuguese recolonization. While defining "the Brazilian people" to include everyone (except slaves) born in Brazil, the Brazilian Party also accepted Portuguese-born converts to the cause of Brazilian patriotism, and they found a crucial convert in the Portuguese-born Prince Pedro himself. Pedro had been prepared for this eventuality by his father, who foresaw that Brazilian independence might become inevitable. If Pedro himself declared Brazil independent, the monarchy might be preserved, and Brazil could at least be kept in the Braganza royal family. When the Portuguese assembly demanded that Pedro, too, return to Portugal, the prince publicly announced his refusal from a palace balcony, and the people of Rio celebrated deliriously in the public squares. By year's end, Pedro had officially declared Brazil an independent constitutional monarchy with himself as monarch, and he called for representatives of the sovereign people to write a constitution. A handful of Portuguese army garrisons in the north and south refused to recognize Brazilian independence, but all were defeated or withdrew

**CORONATION OF PEDRO I.** The 1822 crowning ceremony of Emperor Pedro I of Brazil deployed the traditional pageantry of monarchy, a tried-and-true formula that contrasted with the innovative but difficult and risky republican experiments then beginning in Spanish America. *Wikimedia Commons.*

within a few months, without any need for the mass military mobilization that had proved so risky for Spanish American elites. A mass mobilization would certainly have threatened the institution of slavery in Brazil, where half the potential fighters were slaves.

By the end of 1823, the Brazilian Party had achieved its goal. It had made Brazil independent while maintaining the social hierarchy that kept the slave-owning elite in charge. Even the provinces that had lately formed their own liberal juntas accepted the proposition that Prince Pedro—now Pedro I, Emperor of Brazil—embodied the cause of Brazilian patriotism. Had the emperor not promised a constitution? There was disappointment ahead, but for now, the cloning of a legitimate monarchy had provided Brazil a political unity that contrasted starkly with Spanish America.

## Patriot Victories in Spanish America, 1815–25

Meanwhile, Spanish American nativists regained momentum after 1815. By that time, Napoleon had met defeat at the battle of Waterloo. Fernando VII had recovered his throne, renounced the liberal constitution of Cádiz, and set out to crush patriot rebels in America. Spanish recalcitrance left the rebels nowhere to go but forward. In South America, Spanish royalist forces held the Peruvian Andes until ultimately defeated—in a great, continental "pincer" maneuver—by patriot armies that had originated on the distant plains frontiers of Venezuela and Argentina. In Mexico, Creoles entered an alliance with the heirs of the Morelos movement and backed reluctantly into independence.

The guerrilla followers of Father Morelos had remained strong in the rugged country south of Mexico City after their leader's death in 1815, continuing their stubborn fight but unable to defeat the royalists. Then European events intruded once again when Spain had its own liberal revolution in 1820. Spanish liberals forced the tyrannical Fernando VII to restore the constitution. The mystique of the monarchy suffered, and many formerly royalist Mexican Creoles felt betrayed. Within months, a Creole army commander named Agustín de Iturbide began to parlay with the guerrillas. His contact on the patriot side was Vicente Guerrero, a mestizo and man of the people. When Iturbide and Guerrero joined forces, the independence of Mexico was at hand.

Iturbide and Guerrero rallied a winning coalition with guarantees of an independent, constitutional Mexican monarchy that preserved traditional religious and military privileges and offered social "union" (vaguely implying the equality of all Americanos with Peninsular Spaniards). According to the traditional social hierarchy, Iturbide and not Guerrero was the natural candidate for monarch. In 1821, a triumphant Iturbide entered

Mexico City, where enthusiastic crowds called for his coronation the next year as Agustín I. But the monarchical solution
did not work in Mexico. Crowned or not, Iturbide was a Creole
like the rest, without a drop of royal blood, and years of patriot
struggle had generated political convictions and animosities not
easily soothed by a make-believe monarch. When, after a short
year in power, Iturbide closed the newly formed congress, composed of representatives of the sovereign people, military leaders ejected him and ushered in a republic.

Meanwhile, patriot armies from Venezuela and Argentina,
former fringe areas of Spanish America, were converging on the
second great core area of the Spanish colonization, Peru.

Despite many previous failures, the tenacious man who
became the single most important leader of Spanish American
independence, Simón Bolívar, "the Liberator," began his string
of triumphs in 1817. Bolívar had participated in the Venezuelan
independence struggle from the start. The early defeat of patriot
forces by the royalist llaneros had been Bolívar's personal defeat.
He learned from it and planned to get the llaneros on the patriot
side. Setting up his base in the Orinoco plains, far from Caracas, Bolívar used feats of physical prowess and Americano nativism to attract llaneros. Here was one Caracas aristocrat whom
the tough tropical cowboys could respect. When the llaneros
switched sides, the momentum moved to the patriot cause. In
August 1819, Bolívar's army of llaneros crossed the Orinoco
plains during the floods of the rainy season, then climbed the
Andes and took surprised Spanish forces from behind. The
viceregal capital of Bogotá fell to Bolívar in a sudden, shattering
triumph. By late 1822, Bolívar's forces also captured both Caracas and Quito, now controlling all of northern South America.

Far to the south, during those years, the brilliant general José
de San Martín had trained a combined Argentine-Chilean
patriot army in western Argentina, then crossed the Andes unexpectedly, in a surprise attack similar to Bolívar's, and decisively

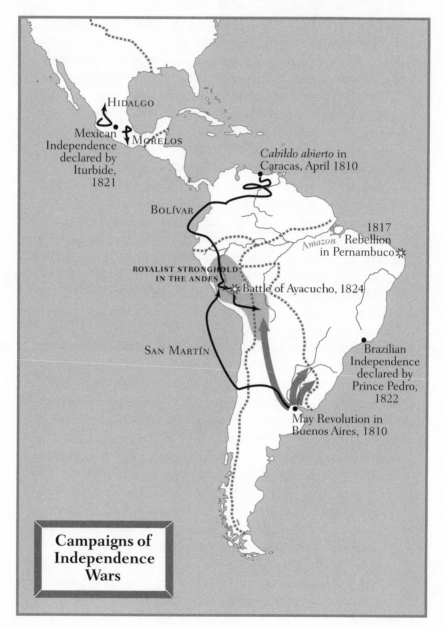

HIDALGO

Mexican
Independence
declared by
Iturbide,
1821

MORELOS

*Cabildo abierto* in
Caracas, April 1810

BOLÍVAR

*Amazon*

1817
Rebellion
in Pernambuco

ROYALIST STRONGHOLD
IN THE ANDES

Battle of Ayacucho, 1824

SAN MARTÍN

Brazilian
Independence
declared by
Prince Pedro,
1822

May Revolution in
Buenos Aires, 1810

**Campaigns of
Independence
Wars**

defeated Chilean royalists. San Martín met a hero's welcome in the Chilean capital, where his movement gathered strength for three years before launching an expedition northward against Lima. The viceroy of Peru withdrew from Lima into the Peruvian highlands. Then San Martín's frustrations began. A year after capturing Lima and declaring Peruvian independence, his army had bogged down, unable to finish the job. At this point, Bolívar invited San Martín to a personal meeting in the port city of Guayaquil. What passed between the two patriot generals at their Guayaquil meeting was confidential, but whatever was said, San Martín immediately returned to Chile, then to Argentina, and eventually to Europe, leaving Bolívar to lead the final assault on Spanish power in South America.

It took Bolívar two years to equip an army equal to the task, but resounding victories in 1824 made Bolívar the liberator of two more countries, one of which, Bolivia, even took his name. In the second of these battles, Ayacucho, fought at an exhausting altitude of over ten thousand feet, the patriots captured the last Spanish viceroy in America. Everything after the battle of Ayacucho was essentially a mop-up operation. The long and bloody Spanish American wars for independence were finally over. Only Cuba and Puerto Rico remained under Spanish control, where they would stay for the rest of the 1800s.

## Unfinished Revolutions

Flags waved, cheering crowds lined the streets, and victorious patriot armies paraded throughout Latin America, but independence meant less than met the eye. The broad contours of colonial Latin American culture and society underwent no profound, sudden change. After all, liberal ideas had never been the popular driving force of independence movements that derived more energy from what we might call identity politics. And for all the talk of "America for the Americans," the old hierarchy of status and race created by colonization, with native Americans and Africans at the bottom, remained substantially unaltered. The language and laws of the Iberian colonizers became those of the new nations, and the Creole descendants of the conquerors continued to profit from the ill-paid labor of the conquered and the enslaved. In that sense, <u>independence did not undo colonialism in Latin American nations. Rather, it made them postcolonial</u>—now self-governing, but still <u>shaped by a colonial heritage.</u>

Many things changed hardly at all. Latin American women, for example, would find the new republics nearly as patriarchal as the old colonies, even though women had fought hard for independence and often died for it. Patriot women became powerful symbols. Andean women had led the way back in the 1780s. Imagine Manuela Beltrán, a poor woman, stepping up to a royal edict announcing new taxes, pulling it down, and trampling it as an angry crowd roared its approval. That was in Colombia's Comunero rebellion. Imagine Micaela Bastidas and Bartolina Sisa, tormented and executed in front of another crowd, this time a jeering group of enemies, alongside their husbands, Tupac Amaru and Tupac Catari. That was in Peru and Bolivia.

Juana Azurduy, another Bolivian, was remembered for wearing a man's uniform and leading a cavalry charge in which she personally captured the enemy flag, a feat that normally defined the superior male. Because of her exploits, we know more about Azurduy than some of the others. She was a mestiza whose Quechua-speaking mother apparently "married up" into a family of property. Born in 1780, Juana grew up in Chuquisaca, a city of courts, churches, convents, a university, and many Peninsular Spaniards, one of whom apparently killed her father but went unpunished—because he was a Peninsular. Now an orphan, Juana entered a convent but rebelled and was expelled at the age of seventeen. She married a man who shared her affinity for indigenous culture. In addition to Quechua, Azurduy learned the other major indigenous language of Bolivia, Aymara. The official commendation after the cavalry charge congratulated her for "heroic actions not common at all in women." Interestingly, though, during those same years, the name of the martyred patriot women of Cochabamba, a Bolivian city where many had heroically died rather than surrender to the Spanish, became synonymous with a fighting spirit. Whenever special courage was needed in battle, patriot officers taunted their men with a famous challenge: "Are the women of Cochabamba present?"

In 1816, the same year as Juana Azurduy's glorious charge, Policarpa Salavarrieta was hanged in Bogotá. She had been caught carrying messages, a more usual activity for patriot women, like providing supplies—not to mention keeping households running, crops planted, and animals tended in the men's absence. Both Salavarrieta and the Mexican woman María Gertrudis Bocanegra de Lazo de la Vega became patriot martyrs despite their Spanish heritage—both women had Peninsular parents. Gertrudis Bocanegra saw her son and her husband executed as patriots. Then, like Policarpa, she too was caught with a message and executed. Like Policarpa, she spoke for the patriot cause in the moments before her death.

The wars of independence provided stories of patriotic heroism to inspire future generations. But in the aftermath of war, many patriot leaders became disillusioned. Bolívar himself came to think that Spanish Americans "did not understand their own best interests," and his mood turned authoritarian. Before his death in 1830, he complained that he had "plowed the sea," accomplishing nothing.

Immediate change was not the measure of independence, however. The long-term impact was more important. Wherever the patriot cause had resorted to mass mobilization, fighters of indigenous, African, or mixed blood gained political prominence. The old social hierarchies, no matter how stubborn, lost their explicit, public justification in new republics with liberal constitutions. To gain independence, white elites from Mexico to Argentina had vigorously waved the banner of popular sovereignty. Now they would have to govern through new institutions, such as elected assemblies, always in the name of "the people": the Brazilian people, the Chilean people, the Colombian people.

The old rallying cry "Americanos!" was no longer sufficient, as Spanish America shattered into a dozen national pieces. The viceroyalty of the Río de la Plata alone broke into four independent countries: Bolivia, Uruguay, Paraguay, and Argentina. It would take years for these new nations to acquire much legitimacy in people's minds. After the Spanish and Portuguese outsiders were defeated, it became much harder to sell the idea of a common political purpose uniting all Brazilians or Chileans or Colombians, whether they be mighty plantation owners or hardscrabble peasants. Despite the achievement of independence, the struggle to decolonize Latin America in a deeper sense was only just beginning.

# COUNTERCURRENTS:
## The Gaze of Outsiders

Traveler and indigenous porter
in the Colombian Andes. *In
Edwuoard André, Voyage dans
l'Amerique Equinoxiale, Paris,
1879.*

After independence, outside travelers, especially North
Americans, English, and French, poured into Latin America.
Great curiosity surrounded the mysterious empires that Spain
and Portugal had for centuries kept off-limits to most outsiders. Many travelers went for business—mining, trade, finance.
A few were Protestant missionaries or naturalists collecting
new specimens to classify and name. In hopes of expanded
trade, England and the United States quickly recognized the
new nations of Latin America and sent diplomatic personnel.
Other travelers went for the thrill, or mainly to write a book
about the area. Among the first European travel writers to
explore Latin America was Alexander von Humboldt, who visited Cuba, Venezuela, Colombia, Ecuador, Peru, and Mexico.

A scientist, Humboldt carefully collected information and wrote many influential books about his travels. Travel books like his became an important branch of popular literature in the 1800s. These books reflected—and also shaped—attitudes toward Latin America in the English-speaking world.

Latin America loomed in the US and British imagination as a lush, exotic land of opportunity, especially commercial opportunity. In the very first years of independence, travelers reported sixty British firms in Rio, twenty in Lima, thirty-four in Mexico City and Veracruz, and so on. In 1833, Brazil was Great Britain's third largest overseas market. Meanwhile, in Rio, English residents were outnumbered by French merchants, teachers, and professionals, who set the tone in the city's fashionable districts. A similar invasion occurred in major ports throughout the region. Traveler Maria Graham reported in her *Journal of a Residence in Chile during the Year* 1822:

> English tailors, shoemakers, saddlers, and innkeepers hang out their signs on every street; and the preponderance of the English language over any other spoken in the chief streets would make one fancy Valparaíso a coastal town in Britain.

Yankee traders from the United States often visited Latin American ports, too. Overall, though, early business ventures were disappointing, as we shall see.

Lost investments, defaulted loans, and dashed hopes— not to mention the chronic banditry of the countryside— compounded the scornful, superior attitude that many travelers brought with them to Latin America. In his *Journal of an Expedition 1400 Miles up the Orinoco, 300 up the Arauca* (1822), a British traveler mentions "a corrupt, stupid, beggarly and dishonest set of beings, chained in ignorance and swayed by superstition and the most gloomy bigotry." Sadly, such attitudes were typical. "It's the vilest place I ever saw," wrote an important British diplomat about the plains of the Río de la Plata, "and I certainly should hang myself if I could find a tree tall enough to swing on." The place had "no theater that can be endured," he moaned, "nothing good but the beef." The bias of such writers is hard to miss. "Superstition" and "gloomy bigotry" were Protestant code words for Catholicism, and denunciations of Latin American "vileness" were plainly racist. Latin Americans as a whole did not rate very high in English-language travel books. Henry Hill, a US consul in Rio, considered the Brazilian people "wholly incapable of self-government." Sometimes, travelers suggested that Latin Americans did not deserve the natural wealth of their own countries. According to scientist John Mawe's *Travels in the Interior of Brazil* (1823): "No territory perhaps in the world is so rich in natural products and at the same time so neglected for want of an enlightened and industrious population."

Women travelers, on the other hand, often wrote of Latin Americans more sympathetically. One was Frances Calderón de la Barca, a Scottish woman married to a Spanish diplomat in Mexico City. She called Mexico City "one of the noblest-looking cities in the world." In contrast to many travelers, she found Mexican religious fervor overpoweringly sincere and often praised the personal habits of humble people. "The common Indians, whom we see every day bringing their fruit and vegetables to market, are, generally speaking, very plain, with a humble, mild expression of countenance, very gentle and wonderfully polite in their manners to each other," she wrote. "Occasionally, in the lower classes, one sees a face and form so beautiful, that we might suppose such another was the Indian [she means Malinche] who enchanted Cortés." On the other hand, like many others, she faulted the traditional limits to women's education in Latin America. Even jewel-encrusted elite women received little education: "When I say they read, I mean they know how to read; when I say they write, I do not mean they can always spell." In many ways, she was as biased as any male traveler.

For all their negative attitudes, travelers' views are useful, in part precisely because they were those of outsiders who noticed and commented on things that local writers took for granted. Take slavery. Only travelers from the southern United States knew slavery at home. Most travelers were mesmerized and horrified by the spectacle of human bondage, which also provided sensational descriptions to sell their books. On the other hand, travelers' testimony is impressionistic. Often they did not fully comprehend what they were seeing; their vision was partial, too, for no individual traveler sees things from all angles. Therefore, travel accounts provide an excellent example of the subtle problems that arise in interpreting historical evidence.

Consider the following views of wet nurses, women who breast-feed the babies of rich families. In Brazil, many wet nurses were slaves. An enslaved wet nurse was a status symbol, as this 1862 traveler's description from Rio de Janeiro makes clear: "The black girl, richly and splendidly dressed, approaching with her head held high, a superb smile on her lips, as majestic as an ancient goddess, will obviously establish with her fine attire and the embroidered garment of the child she carries, the immense wealth of her masters." But a much starker view emerges in this 1845 newspaper ad, also from Rio:

> FOR RENT: An eighteen-year-old girl, wet nurse, healthy and with much good milk for the last two months. She is for rent because her child has died. Inquire at 18A Candelaria Street.

**ENSLAVED WOMEN.** In this photo, taken by a French traveler to Brazil, enslaved women are preparing food for the midday meal of field workers. In spite of independence, Latin American societies remained models of social inequality, in which hierarchies of race and class defined people's lives. The persistence of slavery is among the most extreme examples. But only in Brazil and Cuba did outright slavery continue long after independence. Elsewhere in Latin America, social inequalities took a more subtle and more enduring form. *In Charles Ribeyrolles,* Brazil pittoresco, *Paris, 1861.*

| 1828 | 1829 | 1830s | 1840s | 1848 |
|---|---|---|---|---|
| Remaining Spaniards expelled from Mexico | Rosas takes power in Argentina | Conservative trend throughout region | Guano boom in Peru | US troops occupy Mexico City |

# 4.

# POSTCOLONIAL
# BLUES

Liberty. Equality. Popular sovereignty. America for Americans. These ideas, loosely grouped under the banner of liberalism, had made Latin American independence possible. They had inspired patriot dreams and justified revolt by explaining why Americans should rule themselves. They had solidified the patriot alliance with vague promises of future equality, and they became basic premises for the constitutions of a dozen new republics. In 1825, only Brazil remained a monarchy. Even the Brazilian emperor, Pedro I, considered himself a liberal.

All across Latin America, liberals came forward to put their ideas into practice—with disastrous results. Many liberal governments were overturned by force within only a few years, and then presidents and constitutions followed one another at dizzying speed. It is during these years that Spanish America (Brazil had better luck, as we shall see) gained a reputation for political instability, a bitter disappointment of patriot dreams. What happened?

In a nutshell, the first governments of independent Spanish America possessed few resources and faced tremendous obstacles. Liberal dreams of prosperous, progressive new countries soon dissolved in disappointment and economic failure. Hopes for true democracy were crushed by old habits of conservative hierarchy. Recurring patterns of political violence and corruption alienated most people from the governments that supposedly represented them. Politics became, above all, a quest for the personal benefits of office. In sum, the first postcolonial generation (1825–50) saw Latin America going nowhere fast.

## Liberal Disappointment

From the outset, Latin American liberals suffered collectively from a split personality. The Creole leadership of the patriot armies had waved the banner of liberalism, but governing by liberal principles was not so easy. The liberal emphasis on legal equality for all citizens had radical, disruptive implications in societies that were still fundamentally hierarchical. It is important to observe that liberalism grew out of social and economic transformations (such as the rise of capitalist trade, manufacturing, and a middle class) that had occurred more in England and France than in Spain and Portugal. The new Spanish American republics and Brazilian monarchy inherited strongly traditionalist societies. For generations, Spanish and Portuguese thinkers had emphasized collective responsibility over individual liberties and religious orthodoxy over religious freedom. Spanish American and Brazilian societies were much further from the liberal model than was US society at independence. The exception was the US South, which, with its plantation economy and slave system, looked rather like Latin America. At any rate, the liberal vision was more difficult to implement in strongly hierarchical societies with exploitative labor systems.

A formal public commitment to legal racial equality, for example, had been the price of mass support for Latin America's independence movements. In the generation following independence, the various mixed-race classifications typical of the caste system were optimistically banished from census forms and parish record keeping. In republics, all but slaves were supposed to be citizens, equal to all other citizens. Slavery receded everywhere in Latin America, except in nonrepublican Brazil, Cuba, and Puerto Rico. In practice, however, very few elite Latin Americans, who remained in leadership everywhere, could accept the idea of broad social equality. The basic contradiction between political theory and social reality fatally undermined the stability of the new republics.

Theoretically, liberals sought "government of the people," but in Latin America, liberal leaders, who were typically white and upper class, had mixed feelings about "the people." They considered indigenous people and their lands a national problem, never a national asset. Admiration of Europe made liberals Eurocentric, and their interest in new political ideas made them ideological. Despite the importance of liberal thought in the recent struggles for independence, liberalism remained an exotic plant on Latin American soil. Conservative leaders soon rose to challenge the liberal agenda. In contrast to liberals, conservatives openly proclaimed that the common people should "know their place" and leave governing to their "betters." Even so, conservative defense of traditional values appealed to many common people.

Church-state conflicts offer an excellent example. The church represented reverence for colonial traditions in general. So liberals called for freedom of worship and the separation of church and state. Conservatives, on the other hand, wanted Catholicism to remain the official religion of the new republics. Liberals believed in public schools, whereas conservatives were satisfied to let the church retain its dominant role in education. And so on. The liberals had Protestant merchants and educational reformers on their side on this issue. But the defense of the Catholic Church was highly popular with pious, tradition-minded peasants and landowners alike. The church issue became the chief litmus test distinguishing liberal from conservative cultural outlooks, and it was a winning issue for conservatives.

Gradually, all Latin America divided along liberal versus conservative lines: the liberals, oriented toward progressive—especially US, English, or French—models; the conservatives, harkening back toward colonial or Spanish models. Popular sovereignty, enshrined by the wars of independence, was the one political principle espoused, at least publicly, by everyone. But how would "the people" become engaged in the political process? Formal party organizations—often, but not always, called the Liberal Party and the Conservative Party—formed slowly. After all, partisan politics—with electoral campaigns, newspapers, and speeches—was new in Latin America (and in the rest of the world, too, for that matter). Under colonial rule, there had been few forums for public debate. Meanwhile, there was much to be debated. These new nations faced enormous difficulties, both economic and institutional.

Horrendous economic devastation had occurred during the wars of independence. Hardest hit were the Mexican and Peruvian silver mines. Their shafts flooded, their costly machinery wrecked, the mines needed major injections of capital. Yet there were only a handful of banks in Latin America before 1850. Local moneylenders charged astronomical interest rates, and, after some initial failures, London bankers showed little interest. They had safer investment opportunities in industrializing, railroad-building, commercially booming England and the United States. Colonial Latin America had produced much of the silver in world circulation, but the region ran very short of capital after independence. As for trade, colonial restrictions had ended, and nobody regretted that except the Spanish merchants who lost their former monopoly. But control of import/export trade passed from the hands of Peninsulars directly into the hands of British, French, and US traders. Creoles had little experience in commercial business and preferred to invest in land.

Another major economic problem was the lack of transportation infrastructure. With few navigable rivers—Mexico, for example, had none to speak of—and lots of steep mountains and tropical forests, transportation was costly indeed. Colonial merchants had responded by keeping quantities small and profit margins high. A few mules loaded with silver or with the luxury goods that mine owners imported did not need much of a road. Transporting bulky agricultural products for the new high-volume trade of the mid-1800s was a different matter. British traders offered consumer goods, such as cotton cloth and steel tools, at low prices. This trade could not prosper until crates of sugar, stacks of hides, bolts of cloth, and bags of coffee could be transported more cheaply. Adequate port facilities, roads, and bridges—not to mention railroads, which belong to a later period of Latin American development—did not yet exist. Without capital to build them, Latin America had to wait half a century to realize its trade potential. Meanwhile, Latin American economies grew slowly or, as in Mexico and Peru, even experienced decline.

So much to be done, and fledgling liberal governments had few practical assets. Everywhere but in Brazil, the governing institutions had to be rebuilt from scratch, an expensive undertaking. Meanwhile, another institution, the army, was already overdeveloped—another negative impact of the protracted independence wars. These armies were frequently top-heavy with salaried officers who got testy when their pay was late. And wobbly new states possessed little political legitimacy to inspire obedience in societies made turbulent by war. The vogue of republican institutions such as constitutions was recent, their efficacy untested. Most ordinary people had heard of constitutions, presidents, and legislatures but regarded them as new-fangled importations. When push came to shove, nobody was sure whether constitutions would be binding. Loyalty to the king had taken generations to develop, and so would loyalty to republican institutions.

In the meantime, the new republics were fragile. And fragile, understaffed governments found it hard to administer (that is,

make people pay) taxes. Latin American states relied on import/
export tariffs, high-yield taxes that could be charged at the
docks by a few inspectors and a handful of soldiers. But tariffs
were only as lucrative as the meager import/export trade they
taxed. To meet basic needs, revenue-starved liberal governments borrowed what money they could. Often, they defaulted.

Overall, the deck was stacked against the liberals who held
the reins of government in Spanish America after independence.
Their vision implied sweeping change, but they had neither the
resources nor the allies they needed to achieve it. They presided
over countries wracked by war—militarized societies where
many had new guns and old grudges—and their innovative
plans often offended powerful vested interests and provoked
violent confrontations. The postindependence period of liberal
ascendancy ended in most countries after only a few years. Conservatives cried "Anarchy!" and called on generals to impose
order and protect property. The rapid fall of Latin America's first
republican governments further undermined their legitimacy
and set a tragic precedent, as one constitutional president after
another was overthrown militarily.

Between independence and the 1850s, strings of presidents
held office for only months, or even days. Few governments
were able to implement their programs. Conservatives—in the
ascendancy by the 1830s—basically wanted things *not* to change.
And many, conservatives and liberals, saw politics mostly as a
path to office and personal enrichment—the traditional colonial
approach. Their objective was to take over the government and
distribute the so-called spoils of office, a pattern that also characterized US politics of the day. People in power could distribute
spoils to their friends and followers to reward their loyalty. These
spoils, also called *patronage*—government jobs, pensions, and
public works—loomed large in societies with sluggish economies. Spoils fueled the "patronage politics" and caudillo leadership that characterized postcolonial Latin America.

## PATRONAGE POLITICS AND CAUDILLO LEADERSHIP

Patronage politics made corruption (channeling government benefits to one's cronies and clients) a necessary part of the system. Patronage flowed through personal relationships, sometimes replacing party platforms altogether. A local justice of the peace—whom we can call Don Miguel, as a hypothetical example—would use his office to secure benefits not only for his extended family, but also for his political allies (in return for past and future favors), for his informal "clients" (for example, his godchildren and their families), and for his faithful servants and employees. These people's support of Don Miguel and his party had little to do with abstract principles of liberalism and conservatism. Loyalty was what counted. At election time, clients held up their end of the patronage bargain by voting the way their "patron" wished. If the patron joined a revolution, his clients would be expected to pick up weapons and follow him. Don Miguel, in turn, received favors and honors from a patron wealthier and more powerful than himself—a cabinet minister, say, or the state governor—and so on, up to the highest patron of all, the party's national leader, or *caudillo*.

A caudillo in office would be president; in opposition, he was the second most powerful man in the country. Caudillos were typically large landowners who could use their personal resources for patronage or for maintaining private armies. The first caudillos rose to prominence during the wars of independence and then carried their wartime fame as leaders of men into peacetime politics, which were not especially peaceful, as we will see. Caudillos were often war heroes who embodied ideal masculine qualities—bravery, loyalty, generosity, and sexual glamour—in their followers' eyes. A string of romantic conquests and mistresses only enhanced a caudillo's reputation. Most caudillos were from well-off families, though some rose from the ranks. Either way, they generally cultivated a "common touch," the special ability to communicate with, and manipulate, humble followers, including mestizos, free blacks, and indigenous people—a rapport often called *charisma*. Caudillos could be liberals or conservatives, but their folksy style fit more naturally with conservative traditionalism. Caudillos were defined by their army of followers, not by formal ranks, offices, and institutions. Sometimes they were generals in the regular army, sometimes not. The focus on personal leadership expressed itself in language. The supporters of Don Miguel would be known simply as Miguelistas.

Or Rosistas, in the case of the caudillo Rosas. Juan Manuel de Rosas, who dominated Argentina from 1829 to 1852, exemplifies caudillo rule. Rosas was a rancher of the great cattle frontier called the *pampa*, and frontier militias stiffened his grip on the city of Buenos Aires. He made routine use of violence against his political opponents, but also shrewd use of political imagery and mass propaganda. Rosas had his picture placed on church altars and ordered the people of Buenos Aires to wear red ribbons signifying their support. Anyone caught not wearing the red ribbon might be beaten in the street. Rosas represented himself as a man of the people, able to identify with hard-riding gauchos of the pampa and poor black workers in the city, while depicting his liberal opponents as effeminate Eurocentric aristocrats, out of touch with the real Argentina. The powerful ranchers of the pampa saw Rosas as one of them, and he protected their interests. For example, the nonsedentary indigenous people of the pampa remained unconquered in the mid-1800s. They had been pushed back by a line of forts, but they often raided herds and ranch houses. Rosas made war on the indigenous people to expand the territory open to ranching, but he also negotiated with them skillfully, sometimes in their own language. Finally, Rosas won patriotic glory by defeating British and French interventions in the 1830s and 1840s.

**ANTONIO LÓPEZ DE SANTA ANNA.** Mexico's Santa Anna was among the most notable of the "men on horseback," or caudillos, who held sway in Spanish American countries during the mid-1800s. *Texas State Library and Archives Commission.*

Antonio López de Santa Anna of Mexico was another famous Latin American caudillo and, by all accounts, a great rascal and political opportunist. Here was a Creole who fought against the patriot cause of Hidalgo and Morelos, finally accepted independence with Iturbide, and then helped overthrow Iturbide, making him, oddly enough, a founding father of the Mexican republic. During the 1830s and 1840s, thanks to his influence over the army and his status as a war hero, Santa Anna seemed to install and remove presidents at will. He made himself president, too, over and over, first as a liberal, then as a conservative. Santa Anna's opportunism was displayed by many caudillos. They moved in a world of friends, enemies, followers, and factions where abstract principles faded into the background. One source of Santa Anna's otherwise perplexing public popularity seems to have been his military victories against a last-gasp Spanish invasion of Mexico in 1829 and against a small-scale French intervention of 1838. Like Rosas, Santa Anna had a keen sense of political theater. When he lost a leg fighting the French invasion of 1838, he famously had it buried with full military honors.

The history of Spanish America during the mid-1800s can be told as a succession of caudillos. Interestingly, this is true even in Central America, which had never revolted against Spain, becoming independent on Mexico's coattails, so to speak. The liberal first generation was defined in Central America by Honduran-born caudillo Francisco Morazán, whose French connections and federalist convictions were typical of liberals. But, also typically, Morazán's liberal reforms, such as anti-church measures and a legal code imported directly from the United States, proved unpopular. In the late 1830s, Rafael Carrera, a conservative caudillo, overthrew Morazán and dominated Central America for the next quarter century. Carrera was Morazán's social and ideological opposite. A rural mestizo with close ties to Guatemala's indigenous peoples, Carrera protected their welfare—their village lands, above all—as few other national leaders in Latin American history. Like Rosas, Carrera shielded the Catholic Church from liberal assaults, and he honored the local folk culture that made Eurocentric liberals shudder. Absorbed in governing Guatemala, Carrera allowed the United Provinces of Central America to fall apart, becoming today's cluster of independent minirepublics.

Minirepublics were especially susceptible to one-man rule. In South America, Paraguay was governed from 1814 to 1840 by a most unusual caudillo. Dr. José Gaspar Rodríguez de Francia was a scholar, a doctor of theology, rather than a war hero. An austere conservative dictator who permitted no dissent, El Supremo, as Francia styled himself, tried to seal off Paraguay totally from European cultural influences. He allowed only a few European merchants to visit Paraguay, and generally they returned wide-eyed with tales of El Supremo's omnipresent spies. Some foreign visitors became Francia's permanent guests, such as the French naturalist Aimé de Bonpland, who spent ten years under house arrest and never returned to Europe. Francia's strategy of isolation seems paranoid, but it more or less worked. Paraguay became independent, self-sufficient, and relatively prosperous, with no thanks at all to Europe. The Paraguayan caudillos who followed Francia lessened the country's isolation but continued the emphasis on national autonomy.

Francia and a few other dictators did away with the trappings of liberal constitutionalism, such as elections, but most caudillos did not. During the first generation of independence, politics became a double game in Latin America, differing markedly in theory and practice. Constitutions mattered enough for people to keep writing them, over and over. Colombia seemed to have a new one every ten years. Everyone knew, as a matter of experience, that each new constitution might soon be canceled, that each new president might soon be replaced by revolution. In political practice, individual people remained more important than laws, and toppling governments by revolution became not an exception to the system, but the system itself. Although the efficacy of republican institutions in Latin America stood at a low ebb by the 1840s, few saw an alternative. Constitutions and elections remained essential symbols of popular sovereignty and were rarely eliminated altogether. Rather than measures of majority opinion, elections became contests of force that showed who controlled each locality; the party that got the most ballots into the ballot box—by whatever means—was, by definition, the strongest. Governments frequently manipulated vote counts and used the police to determine the outcomes of elections. Stolen elections often provoked revolutions led by the caudillo of the opposition party. Gradually, most Spanish Americans lost faith in the promise of democracy during these years. Often prevented from voting, the common people rarely spoke for themselves in politics. Most often, "the people" exercised their sovereignty through action in the street.

By the middle of the 1800s, most Latin American countries were ruled by conservative caudillos whose sole public service was to maintain order and protect property. Political conflict had completely shaken apart several of the new Spanish American republics. When state or provincial governments gained the upper hand over central governments, federalism often became a first step toward dismemberment. Greater Colombia, as the former viceroyalty of New Granada was called after independence, started as a single republic but split into the present three countries of Colombia, Ecuador, and Venezuela. As mentioned, the original Central American Republic splintered into five parts—Guatemala, El Salvador, Honduras, Nicaragua, and Costa Rica—dividing Spanish America into a total of sixteen sovereign political fragments, not counting Spanish-controlled Cuba and Puerto Rico. Colombia, Venezuela, Peru, Argentina, and Mexico all seemed headed for further fragmentation in contests between centralists and federalists.

## BRAZIL'S DIFFERENT PATH

Was this the necessary price of decolonization? The contrasting example of mid-century Brazil suggests that retention of colonial institutions such as the monarchy lent stability, although at a heavy price. Brazil had retained a European dynasty; a nobility of dukes, counts, and barons sporting coats of arms; a tight relationship between church and state; and a full commitment to the institution of chattel slavery, in which some people worked others to death. On the other hand, despite a few attempts to form breakaway republics, Portuguese America remained united, and the Brazilian government had never been violently overthrown. The Brazilian elite was extremely proud of this achievement and fond of contrasting Brazil to revolution-wracked Spanish America.

The independent Brazilian Empire sprawled grandly over half the South American continent. It had a specialized cadre of circulating provincial governors, not elected but rather designated by Rio. Brazilian society had not been militarized at independence. Unlike the situation in Spanish America, where regional caudillos ran rampant, the Brazilian imperial army was unrivaled in power, its generals unswervingly loyal to the emperor. Brazilian plantations also escaped the sort of destruction that hampered early republican Spanish America. The original heartland of Portuguese colonization along the northeastern coast still boiled down tons upon tons of sugar for European desserts, but a newer plantation crop, coffee (an excellent accompaniment to dessert), now competed with sugar as the prime product of slave labor. By the 1840s, coffee emerged victorious. Brazilian coffee cultivation boomed as the dark brew replaced tea on breakfast tables in the United States and many parts of Europe. Coffee would be to independent Brazil what sugar had been to colonial Brazil. It also contributed directly to the economic and political strength of the imperial capital,

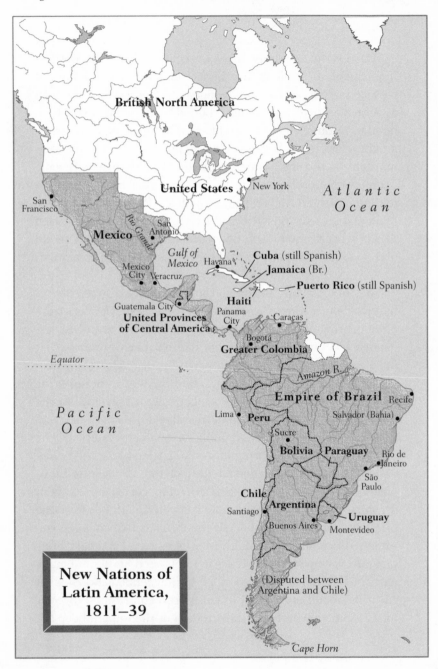

British North America

United States    New York

Atlantic
Ocean

San
Francisco

Río Grande

Mexico    San
Antonio

Mexico
City    Veracruz

Gulf of
Mexico    Havana    **Cuba** (still Spanish)
**Jamaica** (Br.)
**Puerto Rico** (still Spanish)

Guatemala City    Panama    **Haiti**
City    Caracas
**United Provinces
of Central America**

Equator    Bogotá
**Greater Colombia**

Amazon R.

Pacific
Ocean    **Empire of Brazil**    Recife

Lima    **Peru**    Salvador (Bahia)

Sucre

**Bolivia    Paraguay**    Río de
Janeiro

São
Paulo

**Chile    Argentina**

Santiago    **Uruguay**
Buenos Aires    Montevideo

(Disputed between
Argentina and Chile)

Cape Horn

**New Nations of
Latin America,
1811–39**

because the coffee boom began in the province of Rio de Janeiro itself.

This Brazilian success story obscures the saga of Brazil's own liberal hopes and disappointments. In fact, liberalism had created a miniature version of the tempestuous Spanish American experience during the first decades of independence. Pedro I fancied himself a liberal, but he had an authoritarian temperament. After consenting to the creation of a constituent assembly in 1822, he impatiently closed it when liberal representatives took the notion of popular sovereignty too seriously for his taste. In practice, Pedro aimed to rule "by the grace of God," *not* by the permission of the Brazilian people. He convened a few advisors to write a constitution that, he taunted the assembly, would be more liberal than any they could devise. But his 1824 constitution called for a senate appointed for life, and it placed the emperor's so-called moderating power above the other branches of government. True liberals were not fooled, and Pedro's blundering impetuosity—his inflationary policies, his unpopular wars in the south, his scandalous adultery, and, worst of all, his continued involvement in Portuguese politics—gave the advantage to his enemies.

Liberals found their most popular issue in the irritating presence of many Portuguese-born merchants, bureaucrats, and army officers, who still occupied positions of power in independent Brazil. Ordinary Brazilians who cared nothing for political theory identified with cries of "Brazil for the Brazilians." Anti-Portuguese rioting became frequent. Pedro tended to surround himself with Portuguese-born advisors, and he was, after all, Portuguese by birth himself. In addition, his father's death in 1826 made him legal heir to the throne of Portugal. Pedro renounced the Portuguese throne in favor of his daughter but remained deeply engrossed in Portuguese affairs. What if the Crowns of Portugal and Brazil were reunited? Liberals warned of possible recolonization. By early 1831, anti-Portuguese resentment in Rio had reached fever pitch, and Pedro, feeling royally unappreciated, decided to abdicate the Brazilian Crown and return to Portugal. But, like his father, João VI, Pedro I left his son to take his place in Brazil. Although he was only five years old, the prince, named Pedro after his departing sire, had been born in Brazil. No one questioned his authority. Nevertheless, until he came of age, the child emperor would need adult guardians, called *regents*, to rule in his name.

The *regency* years, 1831–40, were the stormiest in Brazilian history. The regents represented the liberal forces that had unseated the despotic Pedro I. Since they wanted to limit the power of the central government, they reduced the size of the army and gave more authority to local and provincial officials. Very quickly, however, they began to want their power back. The liberal notion that "all men are created equal" (even leaving women and slaves out, as most liberals then did) contradicted the powerfully hierarchical social organization of Brazil. Most of the time, equality remained an abstract concept, a pretty lie, a rhetorical gambit. Like Spanish American liberals during the wars of independence, Brazilian liberals now needed allies among the common folk, and they took a similar tack. Exalting the importance of native Brazilian birth and invoking the menace of Portuguese recolonization, liberals in a number of provinces rebelled against the central government, which they thought too timid by half. By the late 1830s, liberal rebellions raged simultaneously in four provinces, from far north to far south, and these were not the last. Ephemeral republics were declared. Slaves were getting involved here and there. The regents panicked.

Liberals among the imperial elite now did an abrupt about-face. Maybe the conservatives had been right, they admitted. Maybe Brazil needed strong royal authority more than democracy. Decolonization was put on hold. In 1840, even though Prince Pedro was still only fourteen, the national assembly voted to put him on the throne anyway. It canceled earlier liberal reforms, built up the imperial army, and instituted a centralized national police force. Liberalism had failed, and the conservative Brazilian success story of the mid-1800s—slaves, coffee, and monarchical stability—could now be told.

## CONTINUITIES IN DAILY LIFE

Whatever the political alterations after independence, the texture of people's daily lives—their work, their families and other social relationships, their amusements and beliefs—changed less than one might think. The great economic engine of transformation that would eventually touch everyone, capitalism, was still idling spasmodically in most countries (for reasons already explained) and would not roar to life until after 1850. In the meantime, however, things were not so bad for most Latin Americans.

Indigenous people farmed communal lands belonging to their villages, relatively unmolested by outsiders. During the period 1825–50, the economic slowdown took pressure off indigenous land and labor. Colonial labor drafts such as the mita had ended—except in extraordinarily backward cases—and indigenous people preferred, whenever possible, to avoid wage labor and grow their own food. Especially in Mexico, where indigenous villages had governed themselves through Spanish institutions since the 1500s, village elders administered their own communities, giving them an independent voice in political matters. But most indigenous people cared little for republican politics. They wanted to live apart, observing their own customs, speaking their own language, and generally minding their own business.

In some cases—Colombia, for example—free peasants of mixed blood far outnumbered the inhabitants of indigenous communities. Sometimes, rural people lived as "attached workers," called *peons*, on the property of a large landowner and became, in effect, his economic and political clients. For attached workers and their families, the standard name for the landowner was, in fact, *patrón*. Having a patrón provided security but also carried obligations. Typically, hacienda peons worked part time for the patrón and part time growing food for themselves. On the other hand, much virgin forest still existed here and there, where peasants might clear a field and farm their own crops without having to work as peons or fight battles for any landlord. In sum, during the period 1825–50, most rural Latin Americans depended, one way or another, on subsistence agriculture rather than the market for their food.

At the other end of the rural spectrum, African people and their children still slaved in the fields of plantations, especially in Brazil and Cuba. They, too, raised food in their own provision fields, but spent most of their time, when not household servants, cultivating and processing the export crop. In fact, Brazilian coffee planters had imported record numbers of Africans in the period 1825–50, despite the English-inspired legal prohibition of the trade. Some laws were on the books, according to the old Brazilian expression, merely "For the English to see." Cuban plantation owners, benefiting particularly from the abolition of slavery in Jamaica, Barbados, and the other sugar-growing islands colonized by England, also imported vast numbers of enslaved workers. Cuba was becoming one big sugar factory, highly capitalized and relentlessly productive, an indicator of things to come elsewhere.

Rich or not, landowners held the balance of power in postcolonial Latin America. They complained about bandits and impassable roads but enjoyed greater social prestige and political influence than in their parents' generation. In the wake of independence, liberals had eliminated powerful urban merchant guilds and instituted free trade. The massive importation of foreign machine-made fabrics had then bankrupted urban weavers. Now most of Latin America's export opportunities were agricultural, putting new *economic* clout in the hands of landowners. Landowners' *political* clout got heavier, too. Urban merchants and bureaucrats had fewer followers than the owners of plantations and haciendas, and numerous clients counted in elections and revolutions.

Transculturation, the give-and-take creation of new Latin American cultures, was encouraged by the postcolonial prestige of national identity and the rise of the landowning class. By the mid-1800s, landowners were less likely to maintain a house in town and more comfortable seeing themselves as country people. Years of nativist rhetoric had proclaimed the essential patriotic dignity of "Americanos," and the countryside, rather than the cities, was thought to define the native identity. The folk dances of poor mestizos, long condemned by the colonial authorities as inappropriate for anybody, now enjoyed a broad vogue as representations of a national spirit. Mexican *jarabes* and Colombian *bambucos*, two such dances, were cheered on stage by patriotic audiences that might hiss at actors with Portuguese or Spanish accents. Even in Spanish-controlled Cuba, people danced—at rustic wedding parties, seedy dance halls, or elite social clubs—to music with an Afro-Cuban lilt. Place of birth had been enough to define native identity during the wars of independence, and it remained a crucial reference point. Defining the national "us" partly happened through opposition to a foreign "them." But national identities needed more than boundaries. They needed substance, and transculturation provided it.

Latin American literature of the mid-1800s played a key role in elaborating and promoting these new national identities. Most writers of the period believed that the landscape and distinctive customs of the new nations were the proper subject matter for new national literatures. A particular literary form called *costumbrismo* (from *costumbres*, the Spanish word for "customs") became popular throughout the region. Costumbrista writers created national self-portraits by describing not only the dances, but also the dress, speech, and lives of ordinary folk, particularly those of the countryside, who were believed to embody the national essence. Costumbrista sketches were often published in the newspapers and scripted for presentation on stage during intermissions between the "serious" European dramas that constituted the normal fare.

The nativist spirit, a key to independence, remained strong for several decades afterward, before gradually fading. Peninsulars who had remained in republican Mexico, for example, were expelled following widespread nativist agitation in 1828. Conservatives, along with and eventually more than liberals, also used nativist imagery. Rosista publicists created folksy newspaper characters like Pancho Lugares, *The Gaucho*, who dispensed homespun advice and made fun of Eurocentric liberals in 1830s Argentina. Nativism remained antiforeign, but it lost its liberal emphasis on social equality.

By 1850, the oppressed majority of Latin America, the descendants of the conquered and the enslaved, were clearly not going to overthrow the descendants of the conquerors. Overall, the upper classes of the new nations still looked like the upper classes of the colonies—with a few darker faces, now, in the elite group portrait. There were only a few isolated cases in which mass rebellions threatened to sweep aside the existing social hierarchy. The most famous was the mid-century Caste War of Yucatán, in which Mayan people rose up, inspired by prophetic religious messages from a talking cross, to cleanse their land of white and mestizo intruders. They called themselves Cruzob, a mixed Mayan/Spanish word meaning "people of the cross," but their worldview was more Mayan than Spanish. In general, truly radical rebellions occurred only where the rebels, like these Mayas, kept a cultural distance from the larger society. The Bahian slave conspiracy of 1835, perhaps the most famous of independent Brazil, occurred among slaves, many of

**COSTUMBRISMO**, the depiction of customs and lifeways, was important in Latin American graphic arts, as well as literature, during the mid-1800s. This illustration shows the folk costume distinctive to one of Colombia's many regions. *La Comisión Corográfica/Biblioteca Nacional de Colombia.*

whom were Arabic-speaking Muslims, the Malês, impervious to the Christian ideology of Brazilian society. Their Muslim identity helped the Malês organize, but it also limited them by alienating Christian slaves, some of whom revealed the conspiracy.

White minority rule in Latin America still exercised the subtle, resilient power of cultural hegemony. Whereas whites had once ruled because they represented the colonizing power and the true religion, now they represented "civilization." What was civilization? A silly question! Civilization was Paris, London! It was free trade and steam power and romantic poetry. It was everything money could buy from Europe. Whoever accepted this outrageously Eurocentric definition of civilization more or less had to accept the "more civilized" white ruling class with it. The black Muslim rebels of Bahia and the Cruzob Mayas of the speaking cross did not need the white man's definition of civilization, nor his values, because they had their own and could envision a radically different world. But these were the exceptions. In most of Latin America, transculturation had, over the course of centuries, created societies that shared basic values and attitudes despite huge differences in wealth. The result was continued hegemonic control for the elite minority. An example is the awe attached to writing.

Spanish and Portuguese had been the languages of empire, and writing in those languages remained the vehicle of law, administration, and all long-distance communication. Although educational opportunities expanded slightly after 1825, most Latin Americans could neither read nor write. Meanwhile, new nations, as well as states and provinces within them, now had legislatures to draft laws and newspapers to air political debate. Political hopefuls of all kinds orated endlessly in electoral campaigns and then, if fortunate, on the floor of the senate or the balcony of the presidential palace. So important was rhetoric and oratory to public life that many a semiliterate caudillo captured a capital city only to slink back to his hacienda in tongue-tied embarrassment, amid snickers from the educated elite. Politics constituted the principal venue for this kind of language, but special glamour went also to the young man who could write poetry in proper meter and rhyme, recite classical wisdom in Latin, or show easy familiarity with untranslated English or French authors. Only men could have this glamour, for the most part, because university education was still closed to women.

Indeed, the tumultuous public life of the new nations—the biggest transformation of independence—largely excluded women altogether. Women's names became well-known either because of their connections to powerful men or because they broke the gender rules—or both. Domitila de Castro, for example, known to history by her title Marqueza de Santos, became the best-known woman in Brazil after the Empress Leopoldina, because she was the emperor's mistress. She had a reputation for giving excellent parties at the lavish villa that Pedro built for her near the beach in Rio. Pedro gave titles of nobility to several members of Domitila's family, too, and officially recognized his paternity of their daughter, whom he made Duchess of Goiás. By most accounts, his behavior virtually killed the Empress Leopoldina with humiliation. Pedro had introduced Domitila among Leopoldina's ladies-in-waiting and for a time had her and the infant duchess living in the imperial palace. Leopoldina was a vigorous, intelligent, and loyal woman who had borne six children and died from complications of her seventh pregnancy. Born in Austria, she was much loved in Rio despite her foreign manner. She had helped persuade Pedro to make Brazil independent in 1822. Her death in 1826 discredited Pedro in the hearts of many Brazilians, preparing the way for his downfall.

Encarnación Ezcurra, the wife of Argentine caudillo Juan Manuel de Rosas, played an important political role, but mainly behind the scenes. When Rosas was away from Buenos Aires, ranching or leading military expeditions, Ezcurra took over his political affairs. She greeted and offered hospitality to poor as well as rich Rosistas. She dealt with other caudillos and wrote her husband frequent, detailed political reports. Her correspondence shows a proud, strong, tough-talking Rosista. She dismissed slanders directed at her by her husband's enemies: "But none of this intimidates me. I will put myself above it. And they will pay *dearly*." Still, she did not assume any public office, although Rosas proclaimed her "Heroine of the Federation." When she died in 1838, the banner on her casket put her life achievements in the order believed proper for a woman: "Good mother, faithful wife, ardent patriot."

Her daughter, Manuela de Rosas, soon stepped into her shoes. Manuela (more commonly, Manuelita) now managed the public relations of her father's rule. When still a girl, she had famously joined in the dancing when the black people of Buenos Aires paid their respects to Rosas. Later, she entertained visiting diplomats, playing the piano and conversing with them in French. More than one wanted to marry her, but her father opposed her marriage: he needed her. So she remained "la Niña" to all Buenos Aires, one of the most popular people in public life. She finally did marry, against her father's wishes, after he was overthrown.

Camila O'Gorman, a friend of Manuelita's, was famous for an awful scandal. This young woman of "decent family" fell in love with a young priest. When they ran away together in 1847, a tremendous outcry arose, not only from the church and from Camila's father, but also from Rosas's enemies, who loudly bewailed the moral corruption of Argentina under Rosas, and from Rosas, who loudly vowed to find and punish the lovers "even if they hid underground." The lovers had changed their names and gone to live in a distant village, but they were quickly found. Manuelita Rosas tried, but failed, to save her friend. Camila now symbolized danger to the social order. Even though she was pregnant, she and her lover faced a Rosista firing squad, side by side.

Obviously, Iberian patriarchy remained virulent in postcolonial Latin America. The political activities of an Encarnación Ezcurra were, though not unique, infrequent. Women's exclusion from the new political arena of public life merely continued a colonial practice, but it found new justification in republican theories assigning women specifically to the domestic sphere. Women bore the total burden of arduous but indispensable tasks—cooking, cleaning, sewing, and child rearing—that took place in the home. Poor women often had to work outside their own home and inside someone else's, still cooking, cleaning, and rearing children, even breast-feeding someone else's children. Women also took in laundry to wash, starch, and iron for their social "betters," and crowds of washerwomen could be seen scrubbing on the rocks and extending clothes to dry on the grass at choice riverbank locations. Prostitution, too, remained a standard feature of urban life.

Eugenia Castro, a poor woman thirty years younger than Rosas, never got much from him, nor did he ever publicly recognize his six children with her. Unlike the Marqueza de Santos, Eugenia Castro led a shut-in life, hidden from public view. Rosas had been her legal guardian, and she had been raised as a sort of respectable servant in his house. Eugenia had nursed the dying Encarnación Ezcurra and then took her nightly place in the bedroom of the "the Illustrious American," as Rosas allowed admirers to call him. In private, she sat with him at the same table (reported a surprised visitor), and Manuelita was affectionate with her and her children. But when Rosas later invited her to share his exile in England, she stayed in Argentina.

Women of higher status continued to suffer the tyranny of the honor system that so limited their experiences and movements, but honor itself was evolving. Honor had always been partly assigned by hierarchy and partly earned through behavior. Scoundrels with the right pedigree could claim honor, and so could more humble people who showed themselves to be personally virtuous. After independence, the second, more modern definition of honor increased in importance, as befitted societies of supposedly equal citizens. Women who had achieved ideals of chastity or motherhood could demand social recognition as honorable people, despite having been born in poverty or with the "wrong" skin color. Military service could compensate for a similarly dishonorable background in men, at least hypothetically. As the caste system declined after independence, honor served as an auxiliary sorting principle for the new class system.

Caste, usually determined by skin color or some other physical characteristic, had been a fixed aspect of people's social being, but class was a bit easier to change. Class depended especially on wealth, and poor people sometimes struck it rich. Exceptionally prosperous black, indigenous, or mixed-race people had been held down in the colonial period by laws that kept them out of silk clothes and high-status jobs, unless they bought an exemption to make them "legally white." These caste laws disappeared after independence. In addition, the political turmoil of the early 1800s resulted, as we have seen, in increased social mobility for successful military and political leaders. White upper-class families worried about the social climbing of mestizo competitors. They had reason to worry. People of mixed race made up an ever-larger portion of the population. Indigenous people who knew Spanish and lived outside traditional communities increasingly abandoned an indigenous identity and became competitors, too.

The multiple categories of the caste system were collapsing, gradually, into two basic class categories: the self-described, mostly white, "decent people" at the top, and the common people, *el pueblo* in Spanish, *o povo* in Portuguese, below. The so-called decent people zealously patrolled the perimeters of their privileged social space. Diamond jewelry or an ostentatious coach with matched horses driven by a uniformed servant could help the daughters of a mestizo general get a foot in the door of "decency," so to speak, but those already inside held new arrivals to strict standards of behavior and fashion. The daughters of the mestizo general might buy the most costly materials for their dresses, but did they have the most up-to-date Parisian pattern? Did they know proper ballroom etiquette? Could they play the piano? If so, how well?

No less than in the colonial period, European norms defined what was "civilized," "stylish," and, ultimately, "decent" in the eyes of postcolonial Latin Americans. Those at the top of the social hierarchy and most in touch with Europe obviously held the winning cards in this parlor game. Was Latin America merely passing from formal, overt colonialism to a more subtle kind? In some ways, that is exactly what was happening.

Overall, Latin American states had gotten off to a rocky start between 1825 and 1850. Economically, these were stagnant years; politically, unstable years. Liberals had failed to create inclusive political communities, law-abiding commonwealths of equal citizens. At mid-century, old habits of hierarchy appeared to have triumphed in most of Latin America over liberal dreams of transformation. In the long run, however, the tide of history favored change. When the liberals got their second wind after 1850, they had much better luck.

Mexico and the US Border before 1848

Only Cuba and Puerto Rico remained outright colonies, but all Latin America remained culturally and economically oriented toward the outside world, highly receptive to European influence, especially from France and England. Spain and Portugal retained little influence and instead attracted angry disdain from Latin American liberals, who faulted Iberian colonization for what they found wrong with their societies. Conservatives were a bit more sympathetic to the "mother countries," but not much.

Both liberals and conservatives regarded the United States, on the other hand, as worthy of imitation. But their admiration was mistrustful, and with reason, as we will see. US traders had begun to operate in Latin America soon after independence. Their presence was welcome indeed. Since 1823, the US government had also promoted a mostly self-serving diplomatic vision of hemispheric solidarity, the Monroe Doctrine, which called for "European hands off" the Americas. England and France paid little attention. Since US influence paled beside the awesome commercial and naval power of Great Britain in the 1800s, the Monroe Doctrine remained mostly theoretical for decades. Nor could the cultural achievements of the United States rival those of England or, especially, France in Latin American eyes. But US trade grew stronger as years went by, and so did the aura of US technology and prosperity.

Together, the United States, England, and France began to define Latin America's new relationship to the outside world. As embodiments of Civilization and Progress, they became models of everything that, according to liberals at least, Latin America should aspire to be. Furthermore, traders from these countries would gladly provide the look and feel of progress, ready-made, if only Latin Americans had francs or dollars or pounds sterling enough to buy it. Generally, however, Latin American economies were weak in the first decades after independence, exporting little and importing little.

A famous exception is Peru's *guano* boom. Formerly the mighty center of Spanish-speaking South America, its very name synonymous with silver, Peru had suffered a series of turbulent military caudillos in the wake of independence. But already in the 1840s, a new export product rescued Peruvian fortunes or, more precisely, the fortunes of the "decent people" of Lima. This product was guano, the old fertilizer from Inca days, seabird manure, that had accumulated for thousands of

years on offshore islands where the birds nested. Easy—if
not exactly pleasant—to mine, guano deposits stood in great
mounds, waiting to be shoveled aboard ship, and European
farmers could not get enough of the nitrogen-rich fertilizer.
Guano export required substantial capital for ships, crews,
installations, and shovel men, but British capitalists saw it as
a safe investment. British guano exporters operated offshore,
even bringing workers from China to keep the process totally
under outside control. The Peruvian government, for its part,
got a direct cut of the profits, usually more than half, because
the guano islands were government property. As Peruvian
export earnings doubled and doubled again, the formerly
poverty-stricken national government had a bonanza on its
hands.

Guano money immediately began to build one of Latin
America's first railroads. Lima got public gas lighting and
other urban improvements, not to mention public jobs for the
"decent people," a kind of export-driven growth that became
common in Latin America as a whole only half a century
later. But now (or later), little of this prosperity reached the
other Peru—the *sierra*, the Andean highlands that rise sharply
behind Lima and the narrow coastal plain. Since the Peruvian
government no longer depended on Andean silver or on the
head tax paid by indigenous people of the sierra, it could afford
to neglect that region. This, too, was a portent of the future.
Progress, when it finally arrived, would be very unevenly distributed in Latin America.

During the 1830s and 1840s, England, France, and the
United States occasionally sent gunboats and landed soldiers
on Latin American shores, sometimes to protect their citizens (the merchant community), sometimes to "punish" Latin
American governments for some reason (such as lack of coop-
eration collecting debts owed to foreign citizens). Incidents
of this "gunboat diplomacy" became common, especially in

defenseless Caribbean and Central American countries. A few larger invasions also occurred. Both Rosas and Santa Anna earned patriotic glory by defeating European expeditionary forces, as we saw. By far the largest outside intervention before 1850, however, was the US war on Mexico, sparked by a rebellious Mexican territory called Texas.

The Mexican government had made a major mistake when, soon after independence, it allowed slave-holding US southerners to settle in Texas. When Mexican centralists tried to limit Texas autonomy, these settlers, eventually outnumbering Mexicans, rebelled and, in 1836, declared Texas an independent republic. They were determined to preserve slavery, which Mexico had formally abolished in 1829. Although defeated at the famous battle of the Alamo, the Anglo-Texans won the war and remained independent for almost a decade. Mexico did not recognize Texas independence, however, and so when Texas became a US state in 1845, fighting soon erupted again. Mexicans feared US desires to acquire more Mexican land, especially California, but Mexico was too weak to defend itself against the United States. In 1848, US troops occupied Mexico City and took huge spoils of war: control over all or part of the future states of New Mexico, Arizona, Nevada, Colorado, and Utah, along with California and, of course, Texas. Although sparsely settled, these lands constituted about half the territorial claims of Mexico. The heroic (and suicidal) last stand of Mexican military cadets against US soldiers became a potent patriotic symbol in Mexico, and Mexicans' early admiration of the United States took on the darker tones of a love-hate relationship.

**BENITO JUÁREZ.** Mexico's great liberal president, a contemporary and friend of Abraham Lincoln, was an indigenous Zapotec villager who learned Spanish as a teenager. Juárez represents the hard-fought triumph of Mexican liberalism at mid-century. Liberalism had encouraged the rise of a few talented mestizo and even indigenous men like Juárez, though the upper classes remained white overall and the prestige of racist ideas was on the rise internationally when this photograph was taken in the 1860s. *Courtesy of Bancroft Library, University of California at Berkeley.*

| 1855 | 1861 | 1868 | 1874 | 1888 |
|---|---|---|---|---|
| Juárez Law in Mexico | Liberal gains in Colombia and Chile | Sarmiento becomes president of Argentina | Transatlantic cable connects region to Europe | Slavery abolished in Brazil |

# 5.

# PROGRESS

In 1850, Latin American conservatism stood at high tide. Then, over the next quarter century, the liberals made a stunning comeback and oversaw a long period of export-driven economic expansion. At last, Latin American countries were fully integrated into the free flow of international trade. The social and economic transformations liberals had so desired in 1825 now finally gathered momentum.

The liberal comeback was, in part, a simple return swing of the pendulum. Any official ideology, any ruling cadre, tends to discredit itself after decades in power. Conservative rejection of liberal pipe dreams had promised "a return to sanity" in the 1830s, a soothing reestablishment of order, a rosy appeal to traditional values. But the virtues of security faded as the years passed and the benefits of peace seemed ever more narrowly distributed. Gradually, all those outside the charmed circle of official patronage began to pine for a change. Maybe, thought more and more Latin Americans, the liberal dreams of a transformed society were not so crazy after all. Landowners wanted a chance to sell coffee or hides or tobacco on the international market. The urban middle classes wanted paved streets and libraries, sewers and parks. Many pinned their hopes on new energies surging through the international economy after 1850.

The Industrial Revolution was accelerating in Europe and the United States during the period 1850–75. Industrialists regarded Latin America as a potential market for their manufactured goods. European and US industrial workers constituted a market for sugar and coffee grown in Latin America. Especially in England, which, unlike the United States, had no civil war to divert it in these years, industrial profits produced more capital than could be reinvested at home. Latin America's previous investment drought now ended in a rain of international capital. Governments borrowed and so did private businessmen who wanted to build railroads or port facilities. The Industrial Revolution, the mechanization of manufacturing, had not yet begun in Latin America. Factories were rare. But nineteenth-century steam technology did revolutionize Latin America's connection to the outside world.

**Progress Comes to Peru.** Railroads were a prime symbol of what nineteenth-century people called "progress." The Verrugas Bridge in the high Andes was constructed by Henry Meiggs, a New York entrepreneur who built railroads in several Latin American countries. Hence, both the Peruvian and US flags fly on the bridge. *Courtesy of Elio Galessio.*

The transportation revolution in Latin America meant, above all, steamships and railroads. Wooden sailing ships were at the mercy of fickle winds, and they carried less cargo than the iron-hulled steamships that gradually replaced them. Steamers plowed the waves faster and more reliably than did sailing ships. Steam-powered trains would eventually transform overland transportation, which had relied principally on pack mules or oxcarts. In general, mules and carts limited profitable export agriculture to the coastal plains. Railroads cost a lot to build, but once built, opened access to enormous areas, creating agricultural boomlets in practically every locality along the length of their tracks. As if steam were not enough, telegraph lines,

**THE TRANSATLANTIC TELEGRAPH CABLE.** Along with the advent of steamships, the laying of telegraph cables across the ocean floor constituted another communications innovation linking Latin America to Europe and the United States in the mid- to late 1800s. *Terra Media.*

able to transmit written messages instantaneously, introduced another nineteenth-century technological wonder—electricity. Stringing wires was easier than laying rails, blasting tunnels, and erecting bridges, so telegraph lines often outran train tracks. By 1874 a transatlantic telegraph cable had already been laid across the bottom of the Atlantic Ocean connecting Brazil to Europe.

New technology transformed Latin America's hazardous, unpredictable, and expensive communications with the rest of the world. That world would soon come to call, and elite Latin Americans, for whom Europe remained a cultural beacon, began to feel nervous at the prospect. After all, the "decent people" claimed social priority because of their European race and culture. But how would they measure up in the presence of the real thing? Would Europeans smirk at the "decent people's" attempts to imitate them? Would they find Latin American countries devoid of *Progress*?

Progress (with a capital P) was the great theme of the West in the nineteenth century. The industrial and transportation revolutions had massively reordered societies and touched everyone's lives in one way or another. Even when people suffered as a result, they stood in awe of the change. Somehow, the idea of inevitable, all-conquering technological advancement—a notion still with us today—had already taken hold of people's imaginations. Here was a new hegemonic idea to replace the old colonial version. In a world where Progress seemed unstoppable, well-informed elite Latin Americans wanted to be part of it. Like other ruling classes in the West, they worried about modern materialism eroding traditional values, but they embraced materialism anyway. Exporting something for pounds sterling or dollars or francs was the obvious way to satisfy their desire to be up-to-date in European terms. Export earnings, after all, could buy fence wire and sewing machines and steam engines. In other words, export earnings could literally import Progress, or so the elite believed.

In the mid-1800s, Progress was becoming a sort of secular religion, and liberals were its prophets. Back in 1810, their vision of progress had a political emphasis: republics, constitutions, elections. As it turned out, that kind of progress bogged down in a morass of conflicting interests. Technological progress, on the other hand, still had an invincible reputation, and Latin American liberals reaped the benefits of the idea's awesome persuasiveness. The years 1850–75 saw a political sea change all across Latin America as the inevitability of Progress became simple common sense for the educated elite. People continued to follow caudillos and patrons. Economic interests still collided. But everywhere in Latin America, the liberals gained advantage by riding the wave of the future.

Upwardly mobile families tended to join the Liberal Party, whereas long-established status made other families Conservatives. Opposition to the Catholic Church—its wealth, its power, and its abuses—remained the litmus test for liberals. In essence, liberals always represented change, and the church symbolized the colonial past. To conservatives, who remembered colonial days as a peaceful age when uppity mestizos knew their place, the past was attractive. But the past was the opposite of Progress. And after mid-century, Progress seemed unbeatable. The ever-dramatic history of Mexico provides an excellent example.

## Mexico's Liberal Reform

Nowhere had the colonial church been more sumptuous, more omnipresent in people's lives than in Mexico. The Mexican church owned vast properties, real estate bequeathed in wills or taken in mortgage for loans over the centuries when the church was Mexico's chief moneylending institution. This property had accumulated steadily, because the church was a landowner who never died and whose property was therefore never subdivided among heirs. By the mid-1800s, the church

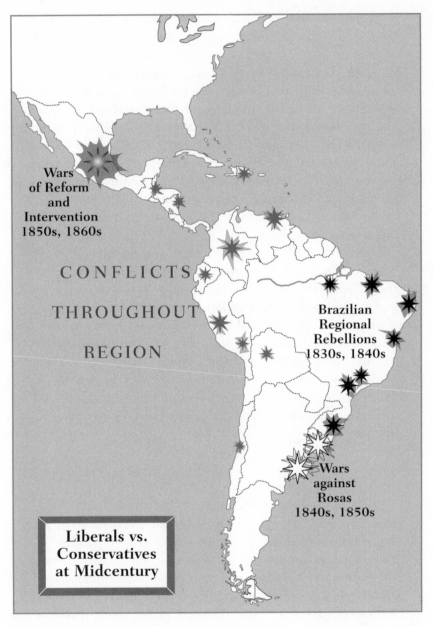

Wars
of Reform
and
Intervention
1850s, 1860s

CONFLICTS

THROUGHOUT

REGION

Brazilian
Regional
Rebellions
1830s, 1840s

Wars
against
Rosas
1840s, 1850s

Liberals vs.
Conservatives
at Midcentury

owned about half the best farmland in Mexico, as well as mon-
asteries, convents, and other urban real estate, not to mention
the church buildings themselves. Especially in central and
southern Mexico, rural society was organized around agricultural villages, and each of these around a church. Generally,
the priest was a local leader and, sometimes, a petty tyrant.
According to traditional Spanish law, still in force, the clergy
enjoyed a broad legal exemption called a *fuero*, and parish
priests often supported themselves by charging fees for their
religious services. In addition, Mexicans were legally obligated
to pay a tenth of their income to the church as a tithe.

The independence era had been a time of progressive priests
like Hidalgo and Morelos, but these seemed to vanish by mid-
century, when the pope himself led a spiritual counterattack
against the gospel of Progress. Europeans called this ecclesiastical conservatism *ultramontane* because it emanated from
beyond the Alps, that is, from Rome. Ultramontane conservatism now became official Catholic policy, and assertive churchmen, especially a wave of militant priests who arrived from
Spain in these years, refused to accept government control
over ecclesiastical affairs. All of Spanish America and Brazil
too felt the impact of ultramontane conservatism, but again,
nowhere felt it as much as Mexico.

Religion and politics had always gone together in Mexico.
The language of Mexican independence struggles, years before,
had been infused with religion, and even most liberals of the
1830s and 1840s had viewed the church as a necessary part
of the country's social order. Then, as the mid-century church
became explicitly antiliberal, liberals became more antichurch.
This did not make them necessarily irreligious—although some
were. Leading Mexican liberal Melchor Ocampo, for example, caused great scandal by announcing the nonexistence of
God. For the most part, Mexican liberals directed their anger
against the Catholic Church as an institution; they were more

anticlerical than antireligious. The church's unproductive wealth and the fuero exemptions enjoyed by the clergy were affronts to Progress, reasoned the liberals. The anger of liberal anticlericalism comes out in a story (true or not) that Ocampo liked to tell about a priest who refused church burial to a dead boy until the boy's family paid his fee. Asked by the boy's father what he should do, the priest in the story replies: "Why don't you salt him and eat him?" For Mexican conservatives, on the other hand, religion, church, and clergy were one and the same. "Religion and Fueros!" became their battle cry.

When Mexican liberals began their great mid-century uprising—the beginning of an entire period called the Reform—the president was once again the old caudillo Antonio López de Santa Anna, who had worked overall to keep things from changing for a generation. Santa Anna finally left for exile in 1855. If Santa Anna represents Mexican politics as usual in the early postindependence era, the liberals who gathered against him represent an alternative Mexico. At their head was Juan Alvarez, a tough mestizo caudillo from the tangled mountains of indigenous southern Mexico. Alvarez had been a patriot since the 1810s, when Santa Anna was still a royalist. Now an old man, and not much of a politician, Alvarez became the figurehead president after the departure of Santa Anna. But the real liberal crusaders of mid-century were younger men, educated men of words and laws. One was Melchor Ocampo, already mentioned. Like Alvarez, Ocampo was a mestizo, a man of humble background but extraordinary talent—an amateur scientist, economist, linguist, dramatist, and professional lawyer. Ocampo exemplifies a particular kind of liberal leadership—young, urban, mestizo, upwardly mobile men for whom progress offered personal advancement. Benito Juárez, the first person of fully indigenous ancestry to become governor of a Mexican state, likewise provides an atypical, but highly symbolic, example.

Juárez, like Ocampo, was an orphan with nowhere to go in life but up. At the age of twelve, he tired of watching over his uncle's sheep in the mountains, left his Zapotec village, and traveled to the provincial city of Oaxaca, where his sister worked as a cook. There he put on European clothes (becoming famous, in fact, for the relentless formality of his black frock coat), perfected his Spanish, and eventually studied law at Oaxaca's new public Institute of Arts and Sciences, which existed thanks to Mexico's postindependence liberal government. Juárez then practiced law in Oaxaca, at one point representing poor villagers against a supposedly abusive priest, a case that landed Juárez in jail for a few days. Eventually, he was elected to the state legislature and national congress and served five years as governor of Oaxaca. But Juárez left his Zapotec identity behind when he donned his black frock coat. He did not represent the interests of the Zapotecs in particular, or of indigenous people as a group. To call him an *indio* was to insult him, and he sometimes used rice powder to lighten his dark complexion. Yet everyone in Oaxaca—and, one day, all Mexicans—knew where Benito Juárez came from. His enemies might call him "a monkey dressed up as Napoleon," but to many Mexicans, the personal rise of Benito Juárez confirmed the promise of liberalism.

Among the first decrees of the liberal Reform was the Juárez Law (1855), which attacked military and ecclesiastical fueros and thrust its author into the national limelight. A couple of months later, the liberals decreed the Lerdo Law (1856), abolishing collective landholding. The Lerdo Law struck primarily at the church, which would now have to sell off its vast properties, but its secondary effect was to jeopardize the communal lands of indigenous villages. The Reform credo enshrined individual effort, property, and responsibility. According to the liberals, distributing village lands to individual families as private property would motivate each family to work harder because of the selfishness inherent in human nature. But indigenous villagers had their own vision, and they believed that communal lands benefited them. For that reason some indigenous villagers joined the "decent people" and other conservatives under the banner of "Religion and Fueros" and opposed the liberal Reform of the 1850s.

The Reform lasted for only a few years before a conservative general seized the presidency and dissolved Congress in 1858. A full-scale civil war then erupted. Fleeing toward the liberal strongholds in the mestizo mining towns of the Mexican north, the reformers chose Benito Juárez to command their forces. They chose well, because even those who disliked Juárez respected his determination. The conservatives controlled most of the army, but the liberals now enjoyed widespread popular support. The Juárez government soon retook Mexico City, but the liberals' troubles were not over. The civil war had bankrupted the Mexican state, and Juárez suspended payment on foreign debt. France, Spain, and Britain retaliated by collectively occupying Veracruz. At first, this occupation seemed simply another episode of gunboat diplomacy. The French, however, had an ulterior motive.

In desperation, defeated Mexican conservatives reached for their secret weapon: a monarch. Napoleon III of France wanted to expand French influence in Latin America. In fact, the French invented the name "Latin America" during these years as a way of making their influence seem natural. Before the mid-1800s, people had talked of Mexico or Brazil or Argentina, and also of "America," but never of "Latin America." Because French, like Spanish and Portuguese, is directly descended from Latin, the term "Latin America" implied a cultural kinship with France. Napoleon III obligingly supplied Mexican conservatives with a potential monarch obedient to French interests. The would-be emperor of Mexico, Maximilian, was a truly well-intentioned man from one of Europe's greatest royal dynasties, the Hapsburgs. Before accepting the plan, Maximilian asked earnestly whether the Mexican people really wanted an emperor. Mexican conservatives falsely assured him that they did.

So French troops invaded Mexico in 1862 and installed Maximilian as emperor two years later. Benito Juárez retreated northward to lead the resistance. The French invasion had fueled a nationalist reaction that aided Juárez. In an attempt to satisfy the patriotic feelings of Mexicans, on his first independence day in Mexico Maximilian made a public pilgrimage to the church where Father Miguel Hidalgo had begun the fight for independence in 1810. The emperor engaged in a bit of political theater by ringing the bell of Hidalgo's church and on other occasions wearing a serape and exhibiting his taste for Mexican food. But nationalism was a losing issue for the conservatives in this case. Juárez, Zapotec in spite of the rice powder, was simply a more convincing nationalist symbol than Maximilian dressed as a mariachi.

In addition, Juárez found a powerful ally in the United States. The French invasion had presented an obvious challenge to the Monroe Doctrine. Napoleon III had attacked during the US Civil War, when there was little danger of interference from the United States. In 1865, however, that war ended, US aid to Júarez increased, and Napoleon III decided to withdraw French forces from what had become an expensive mess. Maximilian stayed in Mexico, where he was captured and executed. When he faced the firing squad, among his last words were "Viva Mexico!" His wife, the glamorous Empress Carlota, escaped. She managed to return to Europe but was insane for the rest of her life.

Benito Juárez returned to Mexico City as president. Mexican conservatives had utterly disgraced themselves by inviting the French invasion. They would never again rule Mexico. Nor would Catholicism ever regain its former prominence in Mexican society.

## OTHER COUNTRIES JOIN THE LIBERAL TREND

Colombia, Chile, and Central America further illustrate the rising fortunes of liberalism throughout the hemisphere. The church issue was especially crucial in Colombia and Chile.

Colombian liberals had attacked the church ever since Bolívar's day. Then came the conservative reaction of the post-independence generation. The 1840s governments restored the ecclesiastical fuero, which liberals had eliminated, and even invited the Jesuit order to return to Colombia. The Jesuits, known for their loyalty to the Vatican, had been too Catholic even for the Spanish Empire. They were expelled from Spanish America in 1767. When Colombian liberals began their comeback in the 1850s, they threw the Jesuits out again and went through the usual anticlerical drill, removing the fuero, making tithes voluntary, insisting on government control over Catholic clergy, even legalizing divorce.

In 1861, Colombian caudillo Tomás Cipriano de Mosquera rode into Bogotá at the head of an army and inaugurated two solid decades of liberal rule. Mosquera was a classic Spanish American caudillo: an independence hero, a general by the age of thirty, no political idealist. Like Mexico's Santa Anna, Mosquera had the distinction of being president, eventually, for both liberals and conservatives.

At the other end of South America, Chile had a stately and exceptional air in the 1800s. In an era when presidential palaces seemed to have revolving doors and their residents rarely served a full term of office, Chile was governed by only three presidents, all of them conservatives, each of whom served two consecutive terms—a full ten years—and none of whom was overthrown by a revolution: Joaquín Prieto in the 1830s, Manuel Bulnes in the 1840s, and Manuel Montt in the 1850s. The Chilean state owed its remarkable stability mostly to its excellent system of rigged elections. Still, the conservative governments permitted unusual freedom of thought and expression, and they oversaw a period of export expansion. This formerly remote corner of Spanish America now fairly buzzed with European traders. And what flourished under these conditions? Liberalism, of course.

Chile had an early dose of revolutionary liberalism during the struggles of independence and in the 1820s, before the conservatives took over, but nothing so traumatic as in Mexico. Chile was a different sort of place from Mexico. Its small indigenous population, now called Mapuches, descendants of the semisedentary Araucanos, inhabited the far south, beyond a line of forts. The Mapuches were not part of the national society at all. The principal landowning class of Chile lived in a compact central valley paralleling the coast. Wheat from Chile's central valley had found an advantageous export outlet, along with copper and silver, soon after independence, while Mexico's economy continued to sputter.

As in Mexico, Chilean liberals made an issue of church-state connections during the mid-1800s. Because the Chilean church had never been as rich and powerful as the Mexican church, the issue in Chile was not so bitter. Still, freedom of worship constituted a core liberal value. An official state religion, according to Chilean liberals, was a vestige of Spanish colonialism. Severeal Chilean liberals wrote fiery denunciations of all things Spanish, which were contrary, in their eyes, to Progress and Civilization.

Progress was already making its debut in Chile by the 1850s. Montt, the president in those years, had once been minister of education, and he led many progressive projects, including railroads, telegraphs, waterworks, and schools. Gradually, the conservative agenda had fallen out of step with Chilean life. So, when the Chilean church felt the militant influence of ultramontane conservatism, trouble ensued. President Montt himself got embroiled in a conflict with the archbishop, and, at the end of his second term in 1861, Montt favored a liberal candidate for president. The switch was peaceful but decisive. Chilean liberals remained in control for thirty years of orderly administration and progress, during which they curtailed the influence of the church, modernized Santiago, the capital city, and rigged elections with the same skill as the conservatives who had preceded them.

As should be plain by now, the post-1850 liberal comeback in Latin America has a repetitive quality. It might be turbulent, as in Mexico and Colombia, or peaceful, as in Chile. But sooner or later the liberals took over everywhere. Each nation's particular history imparted a special character and timing to the liberal takeover. Nicaraguan history, for example, slowed liberalism down temporarily by giving Progress a bad name.

Overall, Central America repeated the basic pattern of liberal triumph. In 1850, all the Central American republics had conservative rulers, the most powerful of whom was the great Guatemalan caudillo Rafael Carrera, mentioned in the previous chapter. Then liberals triumphed in one Central American country after another. El Salvador, the traditional liberal stronghold of the isthmus since independence, led the way in the 1850s. Costa Rica, Guatemala, and Honduras followed, after a delay, in the 1870s. Only Nicaragua resisted the liberal tide; Nicaraguan liberals had disgraced themselves, much as Mexican conservatives did at about the same time, by inviting foreign intervention.

Reaching out for a monarch like Maximilian was not liberal style, however. In their search for outside allies, Nicaraguan liberals instead imported a few dozen mercenary adventurers from that stronghold of world liberalism, the United States. These adventurers were led by one William Walker, a name people in the United States can never seem to remember but Central Americans can never forget. Walker was a visionary fundamentalist Christian from Tennessee, and, in his own eyes, a missionary of Progress. The liberal plan backfired when Walker attempted, on his own initiative, to colonize Nicaragua for the United States. With liberal support and force of arms, Walker briefly made himself president of Nicaragua. He proclaimed Progress, including freedom of worship, adoption of English, and land grants for US immigrants. Walker also legalized slavery, which had been abolished in Nicaragua years before. The freebooting Walker was captured and executed in 1860 by a joint Central American army, but the bad smell he left in Nicaragua kept the Liberal Party out of power there for decades. Nicaragua did not join the hemisphere's liberal trend until the 1890s.

## THE LIMITS OF PROGRESS FOR WOMEN

Progress can be interpreted many ways, obviously. What did it mean for women? In the long run, liberalism led in positive directions for women, expanding their education and life opportunities. During the mid-1800s, however, few Latin American women benefited from these changes. Education for girls expanded with excruciating slowness, and domestic walls still hemmed in the lives of "decent" married women. Few, very few, were the women able to play leading roles in public life during the 1800s. Those who did, however, could thank liberal Progress. Today, we look back on them as pioneers. In their own time, most people thought them strange.

The few women who became famous in their own right did so in the world of letters. Gertrudis Gómez de Avellaneda, for example, left her native Cuba at the age of twenty-two and wrote her celebrated poetry, plays, and novels in Spain, where she lived for the rest of her life; Latin American literature claimed her early, nevertheless. In 1841, she published a novel that was banned in Cuba. The chief protagonist of the novel *Sab* is a Cuban slave in love with the white woman who owns him. Sab has to watch her marry a blue-eyed Englishman, who is cruel to him, but the slave still sacrifices his life for her. At the end of the novel, the woman realizes Sab's moral superiority despite his slave status. Like the novel *Uncle Tom's Cabin* in the United States, *Sab* was a literary argument for the abolition of slavery.

At mid-century, plantation slaves in western Cuba grew nearly a third of all the sugar sold on the world market. And Cuba was still a land of opportunity for ambitious Peninsular Spaniards, from opulent dukes and duchesses to officious royal bureaucrats and ill-paid soldiers and store clerks. The royal Spanish governor of Cuba ruled with an iron hand, and when a Cuban patriotic spirit arose in the 1860s, he suppressed it savagely. Now Cuba's own grueling wars of independence began. The first installment was the Ten Years' War, 1868–78, which Spanish forces were able to contain in eastern Cuba, away from the big plantations, partly by building a fortified line all the way across the island. During the war, a Cuban revolutionary newspaper in New York reprinted *Sab* for patriotic readers.

These days, the *Sab* story may seem a melodramatic "sob story," but people of the mid-1800s found sentimental romanticism powerfully moving. The theme of *Sab* allowed Cuban readers to explore the meaning of their society's racial divisions and the possibility of somehow overcoming them through love. The theme of interracial love was considered scandalous, especially the love of a black man for a white woman. Avellaneda broke social rules in her writing, as she did also in her own notorious affairs with various men. Women who became public figures were already breaking the normal gender rules, so they often flouted sexual conventions, too. Avellaneda's spirit was said to be "too masculine" for a woman.

The Argentine Juana Manuela Gorriti was another of the few Latin American women whose talent won them fame in the 1800s. Gorriti's writings were "feminine" and instructive, rather than scandalous. More than Avellaneda, Gorriti concerned herself with women's issues. It is her life, rather than her writings, that inspires us today.

Gorriti was a little girl of eight when she entered a convent school. Argentine politics interrupted her education in 1831, when the caudillo Facundo Quiroga forced her liberal family to emigrate to Bolivia. She was fifteen when she met and married a dark young man, Manuel Isidro Belzú, who would one day become president of Bolivia. Belzú was an obscure captain at the time, and the tall, talented, blonde Gorriti was considered quite a catch. She bore three daughters and also taught school as Belzú's career advanced, but he abandoned her after nine years of marriage.

Gorriti moved to Peru, where she again taught and also began to publish. Her star rose in Lima, where she became an influential journalist. She also regularly hosted events called *tertulias* or "salons." These were evening gatherings where fashionable men and women of Lima discussed literature and Progress. They also enjoyed music and amateur drama, but not dancing, the main event in other salons. Gorriti thought women danced enough already—Progress called for more serious pursuits. Gorriti's literary salon made her a celebrated figure of Lima's public life. Unlike her tertulias, Gorriti's journalistic writings were mostly for women. They were didactic, instructing her readers on the proper behavior and ideas of a modern woman, often taking inspiration from US or European examples.

Gorriti's life was less conventional than her writings. In 1866, when a Spanish naval expedition was carrying out gunboat diplomacy on the coasts of Chile and Peru, it shelled Lima's port, and Gorriti served as a pioneer battlefield nurse in the style of Florence Nightingale. By this time she had gotten a divorce from Belzú (a scandal, even though he had abandoned her) and then had a child without remarrying. Somehow, her status as an exceptional woman allowed her to be accepted by polite society anyway. In 1878, Juana Maria Gorriti returned to Argentina—not to the remote region of her birth, but to Buenos Aires, the capital of Latin American Progress. Buenos Aires greeted her with public pomp as one of the most notable Latin American women of her century.

Before leaving Lima, Gorriti had helped launch the career of a younger and even more important writer. Clorinda Matto de Turner had already made a stir at the National Women's Secondary School of Peru, where she sought extracurricular instruction in "unfeminine" subjects like physics and biology. She was not quite fifteen when she married in 1871. Turner was her husband's name; in traditional usage, the husband's surname was added to his wife's using the preposition *de*. Thus, Clorinda Matto became Clorinda Matto de Turner.

Matto de Turner wrote *Birds without a Nest* (1889), one of the most important early Latin American novels about indigenous people. Earlier literary views of Latin America's indigenous people had presented them as romantic "savages" of some quasi-mythical past, but Matto de Turner's book depicted them as poor Peruvians inhabiting the present. Like Avellaneda's *Sab*, the novel told the story of an interracial love affair—in this case, between a white man and an indigenous woman. The woman is an orphan whose parents died trying to defend themselves from abusive whites. Once again, a Latin American novelist was exploring—and seeking to overcome—her country's deep racial divide. Although white and "decent," Matto de Turner was from the sierra, from the old Inca capital of Cuzco. She regarded the indigenous people as the most authentic Peruvians and crusaded journalistically on their behalf. Like a good liberal of her day, she also crusaded against what she saw as the corrupting influence of immoral priests. Evil priests appear in several of her novels. In fact, the star-crossed white youth and Indian maid cannot marry in *Birds without a Nest* because the father of both, as they eventually learn to their tearful horror, is the same philandering priest.

Like her mentor Gorriti, Matto de Turner organized a literary salon and founded a periodical for women. She also published articles controversial enough to get her newspaper burned and herself formally expelled from the Catholic Church. In 1895, the government of Peru deported her. Like Gorriti, she then traveled to Argentina, where she lived the rest of her life as a respected educator.

The lives of these exceptional women focus our attention on education and literacy, on race, and on the importance of US and European models in liberal visions of Progress. We will see these same forces driving the liberal comeback in Argentina and Brazil.

## MODELS OF PROGRESS

Argentine liberal leaders were among the most European-oriented and literarily inclined of all. Three in particular represent Argentine liberalism: Alberdi, Mitre, and Sarmiento. All had spent long years in exile during the conservative reaction of the 1830s and 1840s, a reaction personified in Argentina by the great caudillo Juan Manuel de Rosas. During the Rosas years, Argentina's liberal intellectuals gathered nearby in Uruguay and Chile, fuming at Rosas and writing passionate political literature. These were men of words, above all. Their lives exemplify both the liberal infatuation with all things European and liberalism's close link with written culture—education, books, newspapers. Well beyond the customary liberal faith in Progress, Argentine liberals dedicated themselves to transforming the Argentine people—culturally, through education, and physically, through massive European immigration.

Juan Bautista Alberdi, a man who spent most of his adult life in exile, influenced Argentine liberalism through his words alone. Born in the provinces, Alberdi had studied law in Buenos Aires and become a sort of literary salon radical in the 1830s. But even literary liberals risked bodily injury under Rosas. So

Alberdi fled across the Río de la Plata to Montevideo, where he spent his time lobbing literary bombshells back at Buenos Aires. Montevideo was full of liberal exiles. It was, in fact, an international liberal stronghold protected by the British and French navies, defended by international crusaders like the Italian hero Giuseppe Garibaldi. Alberdi spent almost ten years of his long, partly self-imposed exile in Chile.

When Rosas was overthrown in 1852, Alberdi published a treatise titled "Bases and Points of Departure for the Political Organization of the Argentine Republic" and sent copies to the delegates who were gathering to write a new constitution. But as liberal enemies of Rosas streamed back into Argentina, Alberdi stayed in Chile, eventually serving as an Argentine diplomat in Europe, where he died more than twenty years later. Given his obvious personal preferences for everything European, his prescriptions for Argentina should not surprise anyone. Alberdi urged the government to encourage European immigration, not only because the Argentine population was small (less than two million) but also because European immigrants were supposedly superior people, full of moral virtues and marketable skills. *Gobernar es poblar*, "To govern is to populate," became the liberal slogan. Alberdi also recommended modern education to transform Argentine culture and open it to European influences. Rather than studying Latin to read the wisdom of the ancients, argued Alberdi, Argentines should learn English, the language of technology and commerce.

Bartolomé Mitre was more a man of action. He was also a "liberal" writer in all senses. He wrote history, biography, poetry, a novel, Spanish translations of European classics—that sort of thing, as well as political editorials by the fistful. Unlike the shy Alberdi, Mitre also excelled at formal public speaking. He was a military leader and a statesman, and both talents were needed in the Argentine politics of the 1850s.

Mitre and Alberdi ended up on opposite sides during the stormy decade after the fall of Rosas. They agreed on European immigration and public education; separating them were regional rivalries within Argentina. At issue, above all, was the relationship between Buenos Aires (city and province) and the other Argentine provinces.

The city of Buenos Aires—rich, haughty, domineering—was the former viceregal court and Argentina's gateway to the world. It dwarfed all other Argentine cities in political, demographic, and economic importance. Yet it lacked a good harbor. The waters off Buenos Aires were so shallow, in fact, that ships had to stop six or seven miles offshore and unload their passengers and goods into smaller boats. The boats had to stop forty or fifty yards out and unload into carts half submerged in the shallow water. A lot of merchandise and many passengers got soaked in the process. The pastures surrounding Buenos Aires were the country's most productive, but they were not the only rich lands in Argentina.

In the 1850s, steam power made it practical for seagoing vessels to churn directly upriver, bypassing inconvenient Buenos Aires. Those upriver applauded, but Buenos Aires was determined not to be bypassed. Tensions with the rest of the country kept Buenos Aires out of the new Argentine Confederation, established in 1853. Instead, the Confederation made its capital three hundred miles upriver. While Alberdi represented the Argentine Confederation in Europe, Mitre served Buenos Aires. The great city and its surrounding province remained separate from the rest of Argentina until 1860. When the forces of Buenos Aires, led by Mitre, finally defeated the Confederation, Mitre became president of a united Argentina.

Another anti-Rosista who had returned from exile to serve independent Buenos Aires (as director of schools) was Domingo Faustino Sarmiento, the most influential Latin American liberal of all. His anti-Rosas tract, *Civilization and Barbarism: The Life of Facundo Quiroga and the Geography and Customs of the Argentine Republic* (1845), written in Chile, became the classic denunciation of caudillo rule in Spanish America. Sarmiento embraced the international culture available through writing and education. His favorite book, which he studied as fervently as any Philadelphian or Bostonian, was the *Autobiography* of Benjamin Franklin. In Chile, where he lived for much of the 1830s and 1840s, Sarmiento worked as a teacher, a clerk, a mine foreman, and a newspaper editor before becoming engaged in the organization of Chilean public schools. He studied English at night and practiced it by translating the novels of Sir Walter Scott. Sarmiento personally created the first spelling book and the first teacher-training institute in Chile, and he traveled to the United States and Europe to study education techniques. When Mitre became president, Sarmiento returned to the United States as his diplomatic representative. In 1868, he succeeded Mitre as president—elected, in fact, while in the United States—and stepped off the ship in Buenos Aires with ten Bostonian women whom he put in charge of teacher training in each of Argentina's ten provinces.

Argentina's liberal rulers uniformly promoted public education, but Sarmiento most of all. School enrollment almost doubled during his presidential term. Nearly a hundred public libraries were created. And Sarmiento, in turn, chose his minister of education to be the next president. In addition, liberal efforts to promote immigration had succeeded. Immigrants were arriving from Europe by the hundreds of thousands. European culture and European people would transform Buenos Aires into a city more reminiscent of Milan or Paris than of Caracas or Lima.

Turning toward European models, especially English and French ones, the liberals rejected traditional Argentine culture, particularly rural culture, as unbearably "barbaric." They rejected non-European racial heritage, too. Country people like the gauchos often had indigenous and African, as well as European, ancestry. Liberals considered race mixture a disgrace. Leading scientific theories of the 1800s advanced racist premises. Like it or not, that was Progress, according to the best experts of the day. And, like it or not, most Latin American countries had a lot of race mixing, as we have seen. Here was the "national tragedy" faced by so many Eurocentric liberals. How would they handle it?

Disappointingly, Sarmiento, the great educator, also embodies the darker side of Latin American liberalism in his thinking on race. Sarmiento was the first of many Argentines to make a literary reputation writing about gauchos. In his famous descriptions, gauchos are dangerous characters, capable of incredible exploits but, like awe-inspiring dinosaurs, clearly doomed to extinction. In 1861, Sarmiento wrote chilling words in a letter to Mitre, words justifying harsh measures against the followers of a rebellious backland caudillo: "Do not try to economize the blood of gauchos. It is fertilizer [like the blood of animals from the slaughterhouse] that must be made useful to the country. Their blood is the only part of them that is human." In truth, Sarmiento had little faith in the mass of the Argentine people. His government maintained rigged elections as a standard feature of politics in liberal Argentina.

Brazil had its own, typically Brazilian, problems with liberalism. It was still a monarchy and still a slave-owning society, two obvious contradictions to liberal thinking. Brazil also had a large free population of African and mixed descent that made up-to-date liberals, influenced by European "scientific racism," shake their heads sadly, as if announcing a terminal illness for the entire country. If Brazil could go liberal, anywhere could.

As often happens, war became a catalyst for change. The Triple Alliance War of 1865–70 was the most terrible ever fought in South America. It was a fiasco even for the winners— Argentina, Brazil, and Uruguay—and wreaked utter devastation on the loser, Paraguay. Ruled by Francisco Solano López, a dictator whom many believed insane, Paraguay had acquired a powerful army and maintained its standoffish attitude toward the outside world. Convinced that Argentina, Uruguay, and Brazil menaced his outlet to the sea through the Río de la Plata, López attacked first. The allies fought ostensibly in self-defense, supposedly to topple the dictator, but they also sought commercial, strategic, and territorial advantage. The armies of this war wore uniforms and used weapons like those of the contemporaneous US Civil War. Death tolls were similarly high. In a series of bloody battles, the allies ground the Paraguayans to a pulp. Paraguay's adult male population practically vanished in the war. Brazil and Argentina both gained land at Paraguayan expense. But the war also generated a national mood of disillusionment in Brazil.

The Brazilian Empire had called up hundreds of thousands of volunteers to fight Paraguayan "tyranny" in the name of Civilization. The whole Brazilian nation, more or less, had been enlisted rhetorically in a liberal cause—a cause heartily approved in Europe, particularly by the British, who hoped to gain better trade access to Paraguay. But victory over that small Spanish American republic had come so slowly, and at such a cost, as to call Brazil's supposedly superior Civilization into question. And for many Brazilians, a crusade against Paraguayan "tyranny" rang hollow in the presence of Brazilian slavery. When the war began, slavery had recently been abolished in the United States, making Brazil and Spanish-held Cuba the last slave-holding societies in the Americas. Free blacks, and even some slaves in search of their freedom, joined the ranks of Brazil's Patriotic Volunteers, who marched off, brass bands playing, to fight in Paraguay. The contradiction was too obvious.

After a generation of lethargy, Brazilian liberalism began to recover its voice during the war. Brazilian conservatives had gained decisive dominance back in the 1840s, as the reader may recall. Liberal ideas, ran the comfortable mid-century consensus among Brazil's ruling class, were simply too advanced for

Brazilian society, a society founded on slavery and hierarchy. Reluctantly—and their disappointment was real or not, depending on the person—elite Brazilians had resigned themselves to a life of privilege in an admittedly "backward" country, one not yet ready for democracy. Emperor Pedro II, now grown into a tall, thick-bearded man, said such things for the record.

Pedro II seems genuinely to have believed—*and* genuinely to have regretted—Brazil's supposed unreadiness to do without him. An emperor more unlike his impetuous father is hard to imagine. Pedro II was a soft-spoken, studious man who dressed in somber suits like an English banker. As monarch, he took his responsibilities seriously and worked hard at them, exercising considerable, but not absolute, power. He could name provincial governors, cabinet ministers, senators-for-life, and members of the imperial nobility. He could dissolve the national assembly and call new elections at will.

Although his personal style was conservative, Pedro II was a philosophical liberal who endorsed neither of Brazil's two parties, Conservative or Liberal, but held an unshakable faith in science, innovation, and Progress. If he were not an emperor, it was said, he would have been a schoolteacher. He traveled extensively in Europe and the United States, where he talked to scientists such as Louis Pasteur, philosophers such as Ralph Waldo Emerson, novelists such as Victor Hugo, and inventors such as Alexander Graham Bell. Pedro II hoped aloud that Brazil would one day need neither a monarchy nor a slave-labor system, and he freed his own slaves in 1840. When republicans, explicitly proposing to end the monarchy, reappeared on the Brazilian political scene years later, Pedro went so far as to make a leading republican intellectual his grandson's personal tutor.

Like their emperor, the Brazilian elite endorsed liberalism in principle while embracing conservatism in practice. Then, in the 1860s, times began to change in Brazil as elsewhere. A number of conservative leaders, convinced of the need for reform—and thinking especially of slavery—broke ranks and joined the liberals. Then a liberal prime minister clashed with Brazil's conservative military commander during the Triple Alliance War, and Pedro sided with the commander, infuriating the liberals. A liberal manifesto of 1869 called for reform of the imperial system, to make it more democratic, and for the gradual emancipation of the slaves. The document ended with the threat: "Reform or Revolution!" An even more radical liberal group issued a second manifesto the same year, demanding limitations on the emperor's power and immediate abolition of slavery. In 1870, a third manifesto also called for the end of slavery and, further, for the emperor's ouster and the creation of a Brazilian republic. Something had to give.

In 1871, the conservative government caved in to liberal pressure and enacted a "free birth" law: Slaves would remain slaves, but their children would be born free. Because the slave trade had stopped around 1850, the "free birth" law signaled a public commitment to end slavery sooner or later. Pedro II was pleased. But the last years of the trade in the 1830s and 1840s had brought hundreds of thousands of young Africans to Brazil, ensuring that slavery would last for decades. In the meantime, children born officially "free" were still required to work until adulthood for their mother's owner.

Although Brazilian conservatives ruled through most of the 1870s and 1880s, Progress gradually conquered hearts and minds. The more progressive coffee growers (those of São Paulo) began to attract and employ Italian immigrant agricultural workers. Bit by bit, the coffee-export economy fueled the growth of cities. And urban Brazilians—better educated, more cosmopolitan, and not directly connected to plantation life—were more likely to be persuaded by the liberal vision of Progress. The signers of the above-mentioned republican manifesto of 1870, for example, included ten journalists, thirteen engineers and merchants, and twenty-three doctors of law or medicine, but only one self-described planter.

In the 1880s, slavery again became a contentious political issue. The leading abolitionist spokesman was now a liberal named Joaquim Nabuco. Nabuco became a popular celebrity whose image appeared on cigar and beer labels. Even Rio de Janeiro's carnival paraders took up abolitionist themes. Nabuco and the other abolitionists of the 1880s spoke moral truths about slavery but condemned it, most of all, as an obstacle to Progress. Unquestionably, slavery *was* a thing of the past. After 1886, when the Spanish abolished slavery in Cuba, progressive Brazilians bore the international shame alone. By this time, some provinces without coffee had already freed the slaves, and on profitable coffee plantations, slaves had begun to run away in the thousands. Finally, overwhelming public pressure forced total abolition without financial compensation to the former slave owners. Pedro was in Europe, so his daughter Princess Isabel, herself an abolitionist, signed the "Golden Law" of freedom in 1888. Four centuries of American slavery were over at long last.

The next year, another outmoded institution, the Brazilian monarchy itself, collapsed, its day over too. Abolition had offended formerly stalwart monarchists, and change was in the air. Ranking army officers had grievances against the imperial government, and republican militants saw their chance. Always weak electorally, the republicans had strong influence in the army. Benjamin Constant Botelho de Magalhães, the emperor's grandson's republican tutor, mentioned earlier, became a celebrated professor at Brazil's military academy, where he channeled the military discontent and linked it to republicanism. In November 1889, the military proclaimed a republic. Pedro and his family quietly left for Europe while telegraph wires carried the news across the country, provoking astonishment but also immediate acceptance. Brazilians unanimously bowed to "the inevitable march of Progress," as if they had understood long ago that the emperor had to go but had been too polite to say so.

By century's end, liberalism served, in one form or another, as the official ideology of every Latin American country. A powerful consensus reigned among the region's ruling classes, seconded by its urban middle classes. A long period of stable liberal hegemony at last emerged. Progress, after the model of England or France or the US, was the order of the day.

Area of fighting in Chaco War

Area of fighting in Triple Alliance War

Bolivia

Won by Paraguay in the Chaco War

Lost to Brazil in Triple Alliance War

Brazil

Lost to Argentina in Triple Alliance War

Argentina

Lost to Argentina in Triple Alliance War

**Paraguay in Two Wars**

Only a handful of large wars have been fought between Latin American nations. Yet wars have had a powerful effect on the combatant countries. Mexico lost vast territory in its war with the United States (1846–48). The Triple Alliance War (1865–70) gave Brazil a national shock treatment, consolidated the Argentine national state, and virtually liquidated poor

Paraguay. Both Argentina and Brazil carved off Paraguayan territory to compensate themselves for that war.

The Paraguayans fought again, and triumphed, in a war against Bolivia, the Chaco War (1932–35). The Chaco is a desolate region of suffocating heat, alternating flood with drought, west of the Paraguay River. Competing claims to the region had long put Paraguayans and Bolivians at odds, but the claims suddenly flared with the discovery of oil there in the 1920s. Soldiers from the Bolivian highlands suffered particularly in the difficult and unfamiliar Chaco environment. Paraguayan victory in the Chaco War doubled the national territory and worked wonders for national pride. The Chaco War turned out to be the only major war fought among American countries in the 1900s.

Bolivia's defeat in the Chaco War was another bitter blow for a country on the losing side of two earlier wars fought on the Pacific Coast. The War of the Peruvian-Bolivian Confederation (1836–39) had resulted from the unification of Peru and Bolivia under the mestizo caudillo Andrés de Santa Cruz. The Chilean government minister, Diego Portales, more powerful than the president of Chile at the time, refused to tolerate the unification and launched his country into a full-scale attack, ultimately defeating Santa Cruz and ending the Peruvian-Bolivian Confederation.

Chile repeated its victory a half century later in the War of the Pacific (1879–84). This war, somewhat like the Chaco War, concerned a desolate zone where the discovery of mineral resources precipitated conflicting territorial claims. The desolate zone in this case was the Atacama Desert, a six-hundred-mile stretch of Pacific Coast where scarcely a drop of rain has ever fallen. Spanish colonial boundaries were never clear in this region. At independence, Bolivia claimed a portion of this coast, along with Peru and Chile. By the 1870s, all three countries were selling concessions to mine sodium nitrate deposits

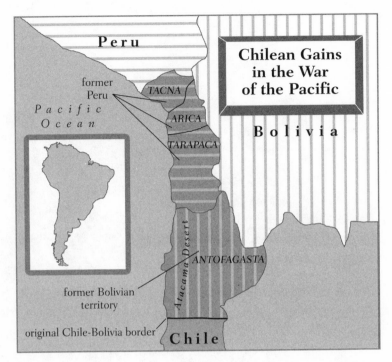

Peru

former
Peru

*Pacific
Ocean*

TACNA

ARICA

**Chilean Gains
in the War
of the Pacific**

Bolivia

TARAPACA

*Atacama Desert*

ANTOFAGASTA

former Bolivian
territory

original Chile-Bolivia border

Chile

in the Atacama. In 1879, conflicts over these mining concessions led to a Chilean offensive against Peru and Bolivia. Both
Peru and Bolivia lost territory, including Bolivia's only outlet
to the sea. Chile, on the other hand, gained territory rich in
mining resources. Nitrates of the Atacama region would provide the backbone of Chilean government revenues for the
next forty years.

**"UNCLE SAM'S NEW CLASS IN THE ART OF SELF-GOVERNANCE."** This cartoon exemplifies the neocolonial notion that only people of European heritage could govern themselves well. Two black Cuban independence fighters are shown squabbling like boys, while the great Philippine independence fighter Emilio Aguinaldo is shown wearing a dunce cap. Uncle Sam, who has just "liberated" these ill-behaved children from Spain in 1898, seems justified (according to the cartoonist) in whipping them. *From Harper's Weekly Magazine, 1898.*

| 1880 | 1898 | 1900 | 1912 | 1922 |
|------|------|------|------|------|
| Great export boom underway | US intervenes in Cuba | Rodó publishes *Ariel* | Nicaraguan intervention begins | Pan-American Conference of Women |

# 6.

# NEOCOLONIALISM

The liberal plan to make Latin America resemble Europe or the United States partly succeeded. But Progress turned out differently in Latin America. True, massive changes occurred, changes that affected the lives of everyone, rich and poor, urban and rural. Major Latin American cities lost their colonial cobblestones, white plastered walls, and red-tiled roofs. They became modern metropolises, comparable to urban giants anywhere. Streetcars swayed, telephones jangled, and silent movies flickered from Montevideo and Santiago to Mexico City and Havana. Railroads multiplied miraculously, as did exported tons of sugar, coffee, copper, grain, nitrate, tin, cacao, rubber, bananas, beef, wool, and tobacco. Modern port facilities replaced the spectacularly inadequate ones of Buenos Aires and elsewhere.

Landowners and urban middle-class people prospered, but the life of Latin America's rural majority improved little, if at all. To the contrary, agrarian capitalism laid waste to the countryside and destroyed traditional lifeways, impoverishing the rural people spiritually and materially. And Progress brought a new brand of imperialism from Great Britain and the United States. The same countries that modeled Progress for Latin America helped install it there, so to speak—and sometimes owned it

**LA AVENIDA DE MAYO.** Completed in the 1890s, the spacious main avenue of downtown Buenos Aires was flanked by impressive buildings in a variety of modern styles. It exemplified the transformation of capital cities in neocolonial Latin America. *Library of Congress, Prints and Photographs Division.*

outright. Foreign influence was so pervasive and powerful that Latin American historians call the years 1880–1930 their *neocolonial* period.

Despite many transformations, neither Latin America's subordinate relationship to European countries nor its basic social hierarchy—created by colonization—had changed. Hierarchical relations of race and class, in which those at the top derive decisive prestige and advantage from their outside connections, remained the norm. Where once Peninsular Spaniards and Portuguese had stepped ashore with their irritating airs of superiority and their royal appointments firmly in hand, now it was an English-speaking *míster* who arrived with similar airs of superiority and princely sums to lend or invest in banks, railroads, or port facilities. Whether in 1790 or 1890, elite Latin Americans reacted by swallowing hard and throwing a party for their guests. Ultimately, the "decent people's" own status and prosperity was linked to the outsiders, and they knew it. Ninety percent of their wealth came from what they sold to European and US markets, and their own social pretensions, their own airs of superiority at home, came from their Portuguese complexions, their Austrian crystal, their son's familiarity with Paris. Neocolonialism was a relationship between countries but also an internal phenomenon—and a familiar one—in Latin America.

## The Great Export Boom

Elite and middle-class Latin Americans had a lot to gain from Progress. First and foremost, they stood to profit from the great export boom, over half a century of rapid, sustained economic growth, never equaled in Latin America before or since. For example, Mexican exports, which still included silver along with sugar, coffee, and fibers, doubled and then doubled again in the late 1800s. In fact, the total value of Mexican trade grew by 900 percent between 1877 and 1910. By the early 1900s, Brazil was producing two thirds of the coffee drunk in the entire world. Coffee now utterly dominated Brazilian exports. Cuba depended even more on its single crop, but what a crop! Cuban sugar production reached an astounding five million tons by 1929. Then there was the saga of Chilean mining production— nitrates, copper, iron—hundreds of millions of dollars' worth by 1929. And on and on. The greatest prodigy of all was Argentina. Argentina exported twenty-one tons of wheat in 1876 and over one thousand times that much by 1900. And the country's exports continued to grow rapidly into the 1920s.

From Guatemala (coffee) and Honduras (bananas) to Ecuador (cacao) and Bolivia (tin), all the smaller countries of Latin American had their own versions of the great export boom of 1870–1930. The quantity of railroad track in the region— integral to the boom, because railroads were built primarily to carry exports—went from 2,000 to 59,000 miles between 1870 and 1900.

The direct beneficiaries of this export bonanza were the large landowners, whose property values soared with the approach of the railroad tracks. Beneficiaries, too, were the middle-class city dwellers—professionals, merchants, and office workers— who performed secondary functions in the import/export economy. For these people, Progress opened cultural horizons and brought material enrichment. Still, they constituted only a tiny fraction of the Latin American population. The middle class grew rapidly between 1880 and 1930, but even Argentina's middle class, perhaps the largest in the region by 1930, represented only a quarter to a third of the population. Mexico's smaller middle class was more typical of Latin America. Around 1900, a million or so middle-class Mexicans were clerking in offices, riding bicycles, and listening to US ragtime music. A small working class—a third of a million cooks, laundresses, shoe-makers, policemen, and so on—comprised the rest of the urban population. Meanwhile, eight million country people, mostly of indigenous heritage, lucky to have a single change of clothes, sweated on the sun-drenched land to produce Mexico's agricultural products. Thanks to Progress, their lot was actually getting worse.

The arrival of the railroad benefited the owners of large Mexican estates by raising property values. But it also drove a lot of peasants off the land, allowing the landlords to extend their holdings, make landless peasants their employees, and multiply their profits. Despite the official abolition of communal village property in the 1850s, many indigenous villagers had managed to hold on to their lands through the 1860s and 1870s. But now it seemed that wherever the tracks unfolded and opened a way for the locomotives to pass, hissing steam and belching smoke, peasant villages lost their lands to greedy hacienda owners who could foreclose on a mortgage or bribe a judge. Although Mexico was still a heavily rural country in 1910, only about 3 percent of the people owned land. Most rural Mexicans lived and worked as peons on large haciendas, some of them vast indeed. To take an extreme but illustrative example, just three families owned a third of the Mexican state of Colima.

The indigenous people of the Andes, too, lost their village lands in the neocolonial period. In general, the landless country people of Latin America, who for centuries had grown their own food and supplied their other needs as subsistence farmers, now had nowhere to plant their potatoes, manioc, corn, and beans. As export profits beckoned, the owners of haciendas and plantations acquired more and more land. They bought land that had been public property and evicted the families who had dwelled there without legal title, sometimes for generations. Because they worked their resident laborers harder and planted more of their acreage in export crops, the estate owners left their workers less time and space to grow their own food. Workers often got wages too small to support a family. To make ends meet, women and children who had formerly stayed

A PORTRAIT OF PRIVILEGE. This unidentified Mexican woman clearly belonged to the small class of people prosperous enough to imitate European fashions more or less perfectly when her picture was taken in the late nineteenth century. *Library of Congress, Prints and Photographs Division.*

close to home, cooking and mending and tending the family's chickens and garden, now had to join the field gangs who worked under the watchful eye of an overseer. And just for good measure, labor-hungry landowners pressed for and won "vagrancy" laws to harass people who got along without wages completely. Thus did the great export boom enrich landowners at the expense of the rural poor.

In Argentina, large numbers of Italian immigrants performed miracles of wheat production, but only in exceptional cases managed to acquire their own land. What incentive did the owners have to sell? Some of the immigrants returned to Italy, but most went to the cities, especially Buenos Aires. Rowdy, rootless gauchos also vanished from the countryside as wire fences and fancy English breeds of cattle and sheep transformed the open pampa. In 1876, the first refrigerator ship took Argentine beef to Europe. The trade in chilled beef was vastly more profitable than the older trade in beef jerky of prerefrigeration days. By 1900 refrigerator ships numbered in the hundreds.

Coffee boomed in the tropics, creating several kinds of neocolonial landscapes. In the deep red soils of São Paulo, Brazil, Italian immigrants tended coffee after abolition because freed slaves wanted nothing to do with plantations. To attract European immigrants to a job recently performed by slaves, the plantation owners had to make special concessions, such as allowing workers to cultivate their own crops in the spaces between the rows of coffee bushes. Italian agricultural workers in São Paulo proved unusually successful at making the export boom work for them. But, like the immigrant farmworkers in Argentina, they tended to move to the city eventually. Coffee also grew in the tropical sun and crisp mountain air of Colombia and Venezuela, Central America and the Caribbean. In Guatemala, El Salvador, and southern Mexico, indigenous people became workers on coffee plantations often owned by foreigners, especially Germans. Although usually a plantation crop (always bad news for agricultural workers), coffee could also be grown profitably on family farms. It contributed to the growth of a rural middle class in highland areas of Colombia, Costa Rica, and Puerto Rico. Tobacco—like coffee, a delicate crop that thrives in small-scale production—benefited small producers in Brazil and Cuba.

Sugar production and mining, in contrast, were always massive, industrialized operations that divided societies ruthlessly into rich and poor. By the late 1800s, great gleaming sugar refineries, with their high smokestacks and rail depots, stood like industrial monsters amid the cane fields of northeastern Brazil, on the Peruvian coast, and in the Caribbean. The owners of the sugar refineries, like the Brazilian senhores de engenho of the 1600s, utterly dominated the rural economy, and for the same reason. Immediate, reliable milling is crucial to the sugar harvest. The refineries set their price, and growers had no choice but to accept it. Factories in the fields turned cane cutters into industrial workers. Their wages were low, and they earned them only part of the year. Cane cutters spent part of each year unemployed—what Cubans called "the dead time." Mining in Mexico, Peru, Bolivia, and Chile constituted a similarly capital-intensive activity, carried out by powerful companies employing thousands of workers who had little bargaining power. Because of high capital requirements, installations such as refineries for Cuban sugar, oil wells pumping Mexican and Venezuelan crude, and deep-shaft mines in the high Andes were usually foreign-owned. In Peru, the massive, state-of-the-art mining complex of the US Cerro de Pasco Copper Corporation squatted at twelve thousand feet amid a cluster of tiny earth-colored huts where the indigenous miners lived—something like a twentieth-century version of Potosí.

In the rain forests of Amazonia, neocolonialism brought a rubber boom. The latex sap of the rubber tree was a raw material consumed especially in the United States for tires. Rubber harvesters lived isolated along riverbanks deep in the Amazon basin, tapping sap from rubber trees. In Brazil, the tappers were mainly refugees from droughts of the arid sertão lands of northeastern Brazil. In the Colombian, Ecuadorian, and Peruvian areas of the Amazon basin, many were semisedentary indigenous people, terrorized into wage labor they neither needed nor wanted. Rubber workers earned tiny wages, barely enough to pay for the food and supplies sold them by the rubber company. Meanwhile, the rubber trade produced vast profits for international traders and for the companies whose steamboats outfitted the workers and collected their rubber in periodic visits. By 1910, rubber accounted for a quarter of Brazilian export earnings. Rubber barons could literally find no way to spend all their money. (So why not send shirts to Paris to be properly laundered?) In Manaus, the one Brazilian city a thousand miles upriver, in the middle of the impenetrable forest, the rubber barons built an opera house and attracted touring opera performers—though not, as myth would have it, the immortal tenor Enrico Caruso. Meanwhile, the rubber boom ravaged indigenous people, their tribes decimated by alcohol and disease. Then, by the 1920s, rubber from Malaysia definitively undercut the price of Amazonian rubber. The rubber barons steamed away downriver, never to return, and the rubber tappers looked for another way to survive. Only the Manaus opera house stood as a silent reminder of Progress.

Bananas were a neocolonial nightmare for the palm-studded coasts of the Caribbean. US banana companies blossomed there in the 1880s and 1890s, becoming multinational corporations—among the first anywhere in the world. By the early 1900s, several merged into the United Fruit Company, a banana empire operating in Costa Rica, Honduras, Guatemala, Nicaragua, Panama, Colombia, and Venezuela. Banana companies far overmatched the governments of their small host countries in economic power. United Fruit made several Central American nations into "banana republics," where it could keep governors, cabinet ministers, even presidents in its deep corporate pockets. The banana companies acquired millions of acres for their plantations, millions more for future use, and millions more simply to head off possible competition. Sometimes, railroad builders used land along the tracks (given to the companies as an incentive) to start banana plantations. Sometimes, banana companies laid their own rails. Either way, fast transport of the delicate fruit was the sine qua non of the banana business.

Banana companies created company towns, inhabited by managers, engineers, and agronomists from the United States, along with their families, with miniature US neighborhoods of screen-porched houses on meticulously manicured lawns, virtually sealed off from the country around them. After delivering bananas to the United States, company ships returned with newspapers, clothes, movies, vehicles, and food, allowing these new colonizers to live as if they had never left home. These isolated banana *enclaves* contributed little to the development of their host countries. Companies like United Fruit reserved managerial positions for white US personnel and hired "natives" for the machete work. Governors and ministers benefited from cordial relations with company officials, of course. Whoever sold the banana companies land profited, too. The companies also paid some taxes, on terms invariably favorable to them. And when they pulled out—because of a banana blight or a new corporate strategy—all that these multinational installations left behind was ex-banana choppers with no job, no land, no education, and a lot of missing fingers.

No wonder that rural people migrated to the cities as agrarian capitalism took hold of the countryside. This flow was not yet a flood in 1900. Mexico City, today one of the biggest cities on the planet, still had only about 350,000 inhabitants at the turn of the twentieth century. Neither Bogotá nor Lima had many more than a hundred thousand. All of Latin America had a comparatively small and overwhelmingly rural population of around sixty-three million at this time. Still, cities were growing steadily, and those that attracted new inhabitants both from rural areas and from Europe grew spectacularly. At the fall of Rosas in 1852, the city of Buenos Aires had about a hundred thousand inhabitants. By the end of the neocolonial period, around 1930, it had two million. In 1900, it was already the largest city in Latin America at two-thirds of a million inhabitants. Rio de Janeiro, a magnet for Portuguese as well as Italian and Spanish immigrants, was the second biggest city of the region at just under half a million. Montevideo, Santiago, Havana, and São Paulo followed at around a quarter million each. By this time, virtually all the capital cities of the region boasted electricity, telephones, and streetcars. Buenos Aires, Mexico City, and Rio were building splendid avenues on the Parisian model.

Except for the top four or five, Latin America's neocolonial cities were not places of factories and smokestacks. Industrialization would come later to most of the region. Instead, cities and towns were chiefly commercial, administrative, and service centers. Now they bustled as landowning families spent the profits of the export boom.

Money from crops, livestock, and mines bought mansions, pianos, fine furniture, china, artworks, and eventually cars. All over Latin America, landowning families began the 1900s with an exhilarating sense of new cultural horizons. Their prosperity allowed them gradually to become urban people, leaving the hacienda or plantation under the supervision of a hired administrator or a country cousin. They went back only occasionally, for a few days' vacation, to sample rustic delicacies and amaze their faithful servants with tales of urban Progress.

Education was increasingly important for the sons and daughters of urbanized landowning families. Some studied engineering, architecture, agronomy, and medicine, but the favorite degree by far remained law. Indeed, the standard image of the

coffee    rubber
copper    guano
cacao    sugar
cattle    sheep
silver    wheat
oil    tin
bananas    yerba mate
henequen    nitrate
cotton    tobacco

**Neocolonial Export Products**

landowner's son in 1900 is that of the young doctor of law, probably bound for politics rather than legal practice. (All university
graduates were addressed respectfully as *doctor*.) Education and
city life went together. Rarely could an education, even a primary education, be gotten in the countryside. Thus, Argentina
and Uruguay, the most urbanized countries in Latin America,
were also the most literate. By 1900, a majority there could read.
Well over half the population in most countries was still illiterate, however. In Brazil, a heavily rural country that had almost
no rural schools, no more than two people in ten could read.

During these years, talented people of mixed racial heritage
continued gradually to infiltrate the white middle class. Because
education was such a scarce, prestigious commodity, nonelite
Latin Americans rarely got it—but when they did, it opened
doors.

Occasionally, the person walking through the door was a
literary genius, like novelist Joaquim Maria Machado de Assis,
still considered the greatest Brazilian novelist. Whatever their
attitude toward his *café-com-leite* ("coffee with milk") complexion, elite Brazilians expressed unreserved awe for his mastery of
the written word. Machado de Assis's mother had been a laun-
dress. He worked his way up as a typesetter, then a journalist.
In 1897, Machado de Assis became president of the prestigious
Brazilian Academy of Letters, where he presided over a distinguished (and very white) crowd of poets, statesmen, and scholars. Rubén Darío, a dark mestizo child prodigy from a small
town in Nicaragua, was another Latin American to receive universal tribute for his literary genius. Even amid the generally
racist neocolonial climate, Latin American respect for art, especially literature, conferred on men like Darío and Machado de
Assis a status then unequaled by any person of color in the
United States. Darío became one of the most influential poets
ever to write in the Spanish language. For the first time ever,
people throughout the Spanish-speaking world, *including Spain,*

recognized a Spanish American poet as the great master whose vision and style defined the highest artistic expression of their civilization.

These writers were exceptional men whose stories are not typical. Still, as part of a slow, steady process happening all across Latin America, talented mestizos were joining the middle classes of Latin American countries, finding more opportunities and meeting less prejudice than did socially ascendant black people in the United States. By the turn of the century, the Mexican middle class had become notably mestizo, and many other countries were not far behind.

Only in the mid-1900s would most countries of the region become predominantly urban. Until 1930, the balance of population and power rested in the countryside, where landowners controlled not only the national wealth, but also the electoral system. This phenomenon—by which a landowner in Chile or Brazil or practically anywhere in Latin America took his clients to the polls on election day to "vote them"—was the backbone of every strong government in the region. Such "managed elections" were essential to the political system of neocolonialism. On this point, the ruling liberals truly did not deserve their name.

## AUTHORITARIAN RULE: OLIGARCHIES AND DICTATORSHIPS

A funny thing happened to the liberals of Latin America during their big comeback of the 1860s and 1870s. Once in control, they forgot about the political freedoms they had demanded under the conservative caudillos. Democracy now took a distant second place, in their thinking, to the material Progress associated with export growth. Economic growth required railroads and export crops, and to get *them*, you needed law and order: firm, qualified government, not mass politics but "scientific" rule by the nation's supposedly "best and brightest," which amounted, in most cases, to its richest and whitest. The philosophy that justified their rule was *positivism*, a French social doctrine that prescribed authoritarian medicine to achieve order and progress and made European norms into universal standards. The new Brazilian republic put the positivist slogan "Order and Progress" on the national flag in the 1890s.

Governance did become more orderly. As the profits of the export boom rose, government revenues from import/export taxes rose, too. National armies and police forces received modern weapons and a new level of training, as country after country invited European military advisors. Now national presidents commanded far more firepower than any regional caudillo. Railroads and telegraphs speeded the deployment of troops to quell rebellions. Civil wars became less frequent as elite families busied themselves with the export boom. Higher government revenues afforded middle-class people new employment opportunities in the expanding bureaucracies and schools. Greater stability and prosperity attracted further investment from abroad, intensifying trade, and the cycle repeated itself. In most Latin American countries, frequent revolutions became a thing of the past by about 1900. Instead, stable *authoritarian* governments characterize the neocolonial period.

What about those—the huge majority—left out of the euphoria? Progress held little appeal for them—often hurt them, in fact—so why would they go along? For the most part, the majority had little say in the matter. The political influence of the rural majority was limited by income and literacy requirements for voting, and limited even more by the practice of managed elections. The authoritarian governments of neocolonial Latin America made electoral management into an art form.

Managed elections constituted a tug-of-war between rival patronage networks, a test of strength at many levels. At the national administrative level, those in power named electoral officials favoring their party. That practice radically tilted the election from the outset. At the local level, an election was still a no-holds-barred contest among factions who tried to cast as many ballots as possible—per person—while preventing the other side from doing the same. The countryside, where great landowners controlled the votes and the fighting power of many clients, was the managed election's natural habitat. As long as the great export boom lasted, most neocolonial governments had the landowners' solid support, delivering reliable electoral majorities. The judges and local authorities who administered the process also influenced the final tally. They kept the voter registration rolls and could disqualify their opponent's clients ("I'm sorry, sir, your name just isn't on the list") while allowing even dubious votes for the "right" candidate.

Everybody knew about the fraud. Opposition newspapers and representatives frequently denounced it. But many Latin American electoral systems had been subtly modified to facilitate "management" from above, so it was very hard to thwart. Mostly, people just endured the fraud and learned to live with it, coming to see managed elections as the normal way of the world.

After 1880, authoritarian governments preserved republican forms but actually functioned as dictatorships or oligarchies. Oligarchies (from Greek, meaning "rule by a few") represented a narrow ruling class. Within oligarchies, elections served to measure the strength of client networks. Even when ballots were not freely cast or fairly counted, they still showed who controlled what, and where—information that helped negotiate oligarchic power sharing. Dictatorships, on the other hand, centered on one all-powerful individual. Dictators might hold elections purely for the aura of legitimacy or to impress their foreign associates. Take landowner support and a good show of institutional legitimacy, add lucrative customs revenues and a dash of modern military technology, and neocolonial governments needed nothing else to rule—except, of course, for good relations with Europe or the United States or both.

This basic power structure facilitated a half century of economic transformation that benefited a quarter of the population at the expense of everybody else. Oligarchies and dictatorships provided *stability*, the virtue always most desired by foreign investors. That was the virtue that a former US secretary of state had in mind when, in a moment of diplomatic ardor, he called Mexican dictator Porfirio Díaz "one of the greatest men to be held up for the hero worship of mankind."

The rule of Porfirio Díaz (1876–1911), called the Porfiriato, was the very epitome of neocolonial dictatorships in Latin America. Díaz kept up constitutional appearances, but only his candidates ever won elections. He also had a circle of technocratic advisors steeped in the positivist "science" of government— the Científicos, they were called. As the value of Mexico's import/export trade expanded by roughly ten times during the Porfiriato, Díaz used the new revenues to strengthen the Mexican state. He curbed regional caudillos by crushing them or buying them off. He created public jobs for middle-class townspeople by vastly enlarging the bureaucracy. Díaz offered just two alternatives: *pan o palo,* meaning roughly "carrot or stick." For example, he subsidized the press to keep it friendly, then jailed journalists who spoke against him. Mexico acquired a national rail system and graceful, monument-lined avenues in its capital city. But as Mexico approached the centennial of Hidalgo's 1810 uprising, the Mexico City police had orders to hustle indigenous people away from downtown, so that the foreign visitors would not get "the wrong impression" of Mexico.

Interestingly, Díaz himself was part Mixtec. He was a man of the strongly indigenous south, an authentic war hero who rose in the ranks during the struggle against the French, whom he famously defeated on Cinco de Mayo (5 May 1862), a red-letter date in Mexican history. But, as with Benito Juárez, Díaz's indigenous roots added to his popular image as a national leader without making him, in any way, a defender of indigenous identities.

In the countryside, Díaz founded the famous *rurales* (mounted national police) to secure an environment for investor confidence. He also oversaw a massive sale of public lands, most of which went to speculators and others who already had large properties. Almost all the land remaining to indigenous villagers now passed into the hands of surveying companies. Díaz welcomed foreign investment in Mexican land, and foreigners soon owned about a quarter of it, as well as the silver and oil underneath. Oil gushed from newly opened wells on Mexico's gulf coast. Champagne gushed, too, as glasses were raised to toast the exemplary president of neocolonial Mexico with effusive praise in a variety of foreign accents. Still, Díaz knew that outside influence was a mixed blessing. "Poor Mexico," he quipped, "so far from God, so close to the United States."

Except for the champagne and managed elections, government in neocolonial Brazil was a very different affair. It was highly decentralized, exemplifying the possibilities of oligarchic— as opposed to dictatorial—rule. With the emperor gone, how could far-flung landowning families control Brazil's vast territory? The first Brazilian Republic (1889–1930) was a federation of twenty states with a weak central government. Its first principle, contrasting markedly with the Porfiriato, was local autonomy for each landowning oligarchy. Cattle ranchers, coffee and sugar planters, cacao and rubber barons from one end of Brazil to the other managed local elections to their liking. Various regional oligarchies negotiated control of each Brazilian state. Importantly, the new federal structure let each state keep its own export revenues. In effect, the country's state governors together determined who would be president. The two most powerful states were the current leading coffee producers, São Paulo and Minas Gerais, and they traded the presidency back and forth between them.

Because the São Paulo and Minas Gerais oligarchies wanted autonomy above all—and already had it—their federal presidents did very little. The republicans opened Brazil for business, so to speak, and then stood out of the way. One initiative of Brazilian neocolonial government is an exception proving the rule. In 1906, the Brazilian federal government began to buy and stockpile excess coffee, millions of tons of it, to prevent overproduction from lowering the price. In so doing, the coffee planters who controlled the central government used meager federal resources to bolster privileged interests. Huge stockpiles of coffee were burned when the system finally came crashing down.

Meanwhile, northeastern Brazil provided several examples of angry resistance to liberal Progress. In 1874–75, peasants rioted in marketplaces to defy the imposition of metric weights and measures that they were sure would cheat them. The excited crowds then burned the official records and archives that lawyers used to evict families without legal title to land. In the 1890s, bandits with Robin Hood reputations, backlanders of the arid sertão, became popular heroes and the subjects of ballads in northeastern Brazil. This dirt-poor region of Brazil also had a tradition of wandering holy men who fixed broken-down churches, revived traditional religious ardor, and occasionally gained fame as miracle workers. Between 1893 and 1897, thousands of fervent believers gathered around one Antônio the Counselor, who preached against modern materialism and the "godless republic." With astonishing speed, Canudos, the Counselor's backland base in the Bahian sertão, became the second largest agglomeration of people in the state, surpassed only by the state capital. Horrified by the specter of a fanatical prophet—the opposite of Progress—the Brazilian federal government launched one military expedition after another against the Counselor's "holy city" of Canudos, annihilating it along with most of its inhabitants, at least ten thousand of them. Here, according to *The Backlands* (1902), the famous chronicle of the event by a military engineer and brilliant writer, Euclides da Cunha, was yet another fiery battle between civilization (championed by the modern army, a hotbed of Brazilian positivism) and barbarism (represented by the Counselor and his pious followers).

The self-confident forces of Progress ruthlessly crushed Canudos just as, during these same years, they finally liquidated the Cruzob people of Yucatán's speaking cross (1901). To stand in the way of Progress and Civilization was madness, thought da Cunha, even as he also admired the backlanders' spectacular resistance to the repeated onslaughts of the Brazilian army. Da Cunha's book became a great classic of Brazilian literature, somewhat reminiscent of Sarmiento's *Facundo*, which told marvelous stories of the gauchos even while slating them for extinction. Progress was destiny, pure and simple—a notion da Cunha shared with most other educated Westerners around 1900. Neocolonial thinking, like neocolonial economics, was characterized by its links to things outside Latin America.

## LINKS WITH THE OUTSIDE WORLD

The influence of outside examples was not all bad, of course. The Latin American women who campaigned for voting rights in the 1910s and 1920s were clearly inspired by examples in Europe and the United States. Modern feminist movements arose in cities where outside influences were strongest. Meanwhile, in provincial towns and villages, patriarchy and the old honor code remained practically unchallenged. International influences are evident in the lives of feminist leaders, many of whom had non-Spanish, non-Portuguese surnames: Gucovski, Scheiner, Laperriere, Moreau—all from Argentina.

Or take Paulina Luisi of Uruguay, the first woman in her country to get a medical degree (1909). Her Italian name was typical of the heavily immigrant population of Montevideo. In 1906, still a student, the provocative Luisi was called an anar-chist for advocating use of a French sex-education textbook. Despite the flap, she commanded respect and was soon representing Uruguay in international women's conferences and traveling extensively in Europe. In 1919, she began the drive for women's voting rights in Uruguay. Her political tact showed when she was interviewed on that issue and delivered her feminist perspective while demurely knitting. In 1922, she became an honorary vice president of the Pan-American Conference of Women, held in the United States, and advised the leading Brazilian feminist, a much younger woman named Berta Lutz.

Berta Lutz's father was Swiss-Brazilian and her mother English. She liked to explore and catch frogs and became a biologist, something unthinkable for a Brazilian woman of her mother's day. She grew up in São Paulo, Brazil's progressive dynamo, but left there as a young woman for seven years' study in Europe. Returning to Brazil in 1918, she published a feminist call to arms. Brazilian women were "lagging behind" European and US women, she wrote. Given a chance, they could become "valuable instruments of the progress of Brazil." Lutz, too, attended the 1922 Pan-American Conference of Women, and she made special friends there with the pioneer US feminist Carrie Chapman Catt. In fact, it was during a visit with Catt following the Baltimore conference that Lutz sketched the constitution for an organization for the Brazilian Federation for Feminine Progress. Lutz and her organization deserve credit for Brazilian women's winning the vote in 1932, before Uruguayan, Argentine, and most other Latin American women.

Few today would question the positive influence of international feminism on Paulina Luisi or Berta Lutz. Indeed, the intense outside influence we now call neocolonialism was rarely identified as harmful during its heyday. The powerful vogue of Progress seemed universal. Liberals believed that Progress was European-oriented only because it started in Europe, then spread to the rest of the world. This idea was hard to shake off.

So, in ideology and values, as in trade and finance, neocolonialism meant the absorption of Latin America into an international system dominated by Britain and the United States. It is here, in friction with powerful outsiders, that Latin Americans began to feel the *colonial* in neo*colonialism*.

Until the late 1800s, it was definitely Britain that ruled the international roost in Latin America. British power had loomed over Latin America since the defeat of Spain and Portugal in the 1820s. Despite the overwhelming naval power of Great Britain for almost a century, British military exploits in Latin America were rare, however. Argentina bore the brunt of them, as during the independence era. Only the British seizure of a few cold and lonely South Atlantic islands—the Malvinas in Spanish, the Falklands in English—was of lasting consequence. Britain had little need of Latin American colonies. It controlled territories enough elsewhere: South Africa, India, Australia, Canada, and Jamaica, to mention only a few of the areas under British rule at the time. British commercial and financial expansion in Latin America, on the other hand, was relentless. By 1914, when Latin America's foreign investment and debt totaled close to $10 billion, over half belonged to Great Britain, with US and French investors in distant second and third places. British diplomats were mild-mannered when compared to their French and US counterparts, because British pounds sterling talked by themselves.

The ideological sway of Great Britain was also subtle but powerful. Undeniably, Great Britain was a center of the Progress and Civilization that so mesmerized Latin American liberals. Whereas France remained the Latin American ideal of literary and artistic culture, and Paris the fashion Mecca for "decent" women of the middle and upper classes, Great Britain was imitated in economics and politics. The British Parliament's Liberal and Conservative Parties, for example, were the model for most Latin American party systems. And while elegant

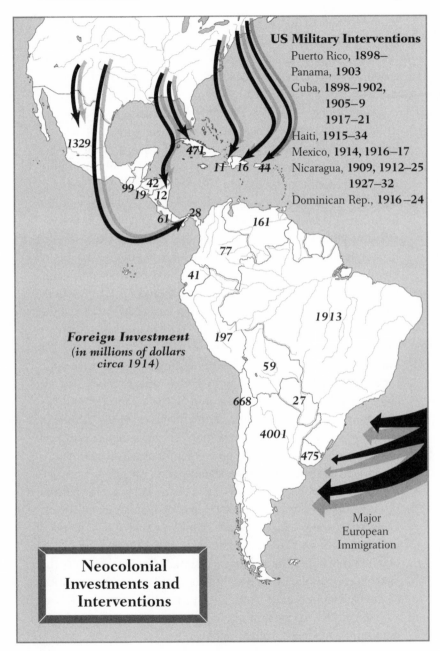

**US Military Interventions**
Puerto Rico, **1898–**
Panama, **1903**
Cuba, **1898–1902,**
**1905–9**
**1917–21**
Haiti, **1915–34**
Mexico, **1914, 1916–17**
Nicaragua, **1909, 1912–25**
**1927–32**
Dominican Rep., **1916–24**

*Foreign Investment*
*(in millions of dollars*
*circa 1914)*

Major
European
Immigration

Neocolonial
Investments and
Interventions

ladies looked to French fashion, "decent" gentlemen adopted British styles. Dark wool suits suitable for cool and misty Britain became excruciating in the tropics, but fashionable males wore them anyway, a measure of their devotion to the European model.

US influence in Latin America began to overtake British influence only in the 1890s. Admittedly, the United States had invaded and dismembered Mexico in the 1840s, and various US presidents and secretaries of state had coveted Caribbean islands. But the capitalist energies of the industrializing, railroad-building, Civil War–fighting, West-winning United States had been turned mostly inward until, in the 1890s, the US frontier officially closed and the country entered the worst depression of its hundred-year history, later overshadowed only by the Great Depression of the 1930s. According to the conventional wisdom, US factories had outrun the internal demand for US products, glutting the market. Like Great Britain earlier in the 1800s, the United States would now have to export manufactured goods in order to maintain industrial health at home. The US National Association of Manufacturers was formed to search for markets abroad, especially in Latin America and Asia. At the same time, some in the United States called for military expansion. Great Britain, France, and many other European countries, as well as Russia and Japan, had recently acquired colonies in Africa and Asia. These colonies provided raw materials and captive markets for our competitors, warned US imperialists, and "our backyard" in Latin America was the natural place for us to acquire colonies of our own. Also in the 1890s, US naval strategist Alfred Thayer Mahan wrote about the need for a powerful navy and a transoceanic canal linking the Atlantic and the Pacific. In the US presidential campaign of 1896, the victorious Republican Party called for that canal, for annexation of the Hawaiian Islands, strategically located halfway across the Pacific, and for intervention in Cuba, where patriots were fighting for independence against Spain.

In 1898, the United States declared war on Spain and invaded Puerto Rico and Cuba as well as the Philippine Islands, another Spanish colony. The war lasted only a few weeks, in part because Spain's decrepit forces were already weakened by years of patriot rebellion in Cuba and the Philippines. The Cuban rebellion had been organized by Cuban exiles in New York and coincided with a protracted circulation battle between two major New York newspapers. These papers created the term "yellow journalism" by using sensational stories of alleged Spanish atrocities to boost sales. US public opinion favored "rescuing" Cuba from Spanish tyranny. But the outcome of the war benefited US strategic and economic interests, not those of the people who were "rescued." The United States seized these islands from Spain and treated Cuban and Filipino patriots like bandits. Cuba remained a protectorate of the United States for thirty-five years. By a specific proviso, the Platt Amendment, written into the Cuban constitution, US Marines could intervene in Cuba whenever the US government thought it necessary. The Philippines, viewed as the commercial gateway to Asia, were governed directly by the United States until the 1940s. The Hawaiian Islands, too, were annexed to the United States in 1898. Only they and Puerto Rico were colonized permanently by the United States. Yet, this "splendid little war," as the secretary of state called it, permanently projected US military power into the Caribbean basin.

A future president of the United States, Theodore Roosevelt, enjoyed the war enthusiastically. His special cavalry unit, the "Rough Riders," boosted Roosevelt's political career. An admirer of Alfred Thayer Mahan, Roosevelt had been secretary of the navy during the 1890s. As president in 1903, he acquired a US base—along with rights to build and control a canal—in Panama. But his bravado in doing so offended many Latin Americans sympathetic to the United States. Until then, Panama had been part of Colombia. To fulfill Mahan's vision, Roosevelt helped separate Panama from Colombia and then bought the canal rights from the new Panamanian government only a few days later. This shády deal, for which the US Congress later apologized, was conducted with no native Panamanians present. Roosevelt did not worry much about this high-handedness. To him, Latin Americans, whom he customarily described as "dagoes," did not rate the consideration owed to equals.

Nor were Teddy Roosevelt's racist attitudes unusual. In fact, US attitudes toward the people of Latin America were colored by intersecting veins of prejudice. As US soldiers swept aside indigenous and Mexican claims to western North America during the 1800s, many in the United States saw US triumphs as preordained by racial and cultural superiority. In the early 1900s, having asserted military power in Mexico, Central America, and the Caribbean basin generally, the United States gradually overthrew Britain's old position of dominance in Latin American trade and diplomacy. This changing of the guard was completed by World War I (1914–18), with its devastating cost to Britain. International US hegemony spread southward over South America in the 1920s. Distant Argentina remained, for a few years, a last bastion of British influence on the continent.

US diplomats and businessmen, not to mention missionaries, had a more sanctimonious approach than their British counterparts, but their overall vision was similar. Rudyard Kipling, a respected British writer of the day, famously urged the United States to "take up the white man's burden" of "civilizing" non-Europeans during its post-1898 expansion. US diplomats saw precisely that role for themselves in Latin America. In the United States, visions of a "Manifest Destiny" of irresistible, inevitable US expansion into Latin America had stirred some people's imaginations for generations. "The Mexican is an indigenous aborigine, and he must share the fate of his race," proclaimed a US senator in the 1840s. Ideas about the racial inferiority of indigenous, mestizo, and black Latin Americans combined with old Protestant prejudices against Catholic Spain.

"This powerful [white US] race, will move down Central and South America," wrote the US Protestant visionary Reverend Josiah Strong, whose ideas of white supremacy were not unusual. According to Senator Alfred J. Beveridge, a key architect of US foreign policy, "God has marked the American people as His chosen nation to finally lead to the regeneration of the world." British imperialists had always been more pragmatic and less preachy.

The overbearing US sense of superiority went double in "our backyard." Since 1823, the reader may recall, US diplomats had proclaimed the Western Hemisphere off-limits to powers outside it. The Monroe Doctrine had remained mostly bluster for half a century. Still, along with a superior attitude, the idea that the Americas, North and South, share a special relationship became an enduring assumption of US policy toward Latin America. In 1905, Theodore Roosevelt provided the Monroe Doctrine with a corollary. The Roosevelt Corollary to the Monroe Doctrine made the US Marines a sort of hemispheric police force to prevent European military intervention in Latin America. European powers had repeatedly used gunboat diplomacy to extract payment for debts. Roosevelt thought that the US government should no longer tolerate European interventions. Yet, he believed, incompetent Latin American governments would occasionally need correction "by some civilized nation." During these same years, cartoons in US newspapers often showed Uncle Sam dealing with Cuba, Puerto Rico, Nicaragua, and other countries caricatured as naughty "little black Sambos." Uncle Sam was sometimes shown as a stern but benevolent teacher, reluctantly whipping these childish pranksters. Likewise, under the Roosevelt Corollary it became US policy to discipline Latin American countries militarily when "required" by international trade and finance. And it was required fairly often. By the close of the neocolonial period in 1929, 40 percent of all US international investments were in Latin America.

Meanwhile, US diplomats had created the Pan-American Union, an organization based on the ideal of free trade—and the reality of neocolonial inequality—among countries. The Pan-American Union was composed initially of Latin American ambassadors to the United States meeting as a hemispheric body headquartered in Washington, DC, chaired by the US secretary of state. At periodic Pan-American conferences, US secretaries of state promoted trade while Latin American representatives voiced dismay at US interventions in the region. Their unanimous protests came to a head at the Havana Conference of 1928.

By that time, Latin American diplomats had much to protest. In addition to the interventions in Puerto Rico, Cuba, and Panama already described, US soldiers had occupied Nicaragua (1912–33), Haiti (1915–34), and the Dominican Republic (1916–24). Sometimes, as in the Dominican Republic, these were mostly peaceful debt-collection operations that included some "messy police work" but also public health and sanitation projects. Sometimes, as in Nicaragua, they were more violent military interventions. By the late 1920s, US Marines were in a five-year shooting war with Nicaraguan patriot guerrillas. The guerrilla leader, Augusto César Sandino, accused the United States of "imperialism." He became a hero to many Latin Americans, much the way Fidel Castro later did, precisely because he stood up to the United States. Several US interventions installed leaders who became long-term dictators, corrupt petty tyrants, known for their greed and their obedience to US policy.

Shocked by the US takeover of Cuba and Puerto Rico, Latin America's greatest writers began to protest. Rubén Darío raged poetically against the "Godless" Roosevelt. The Cuban poet José Martí began a literary movement in defense of "Nuestra América" ("Our America"), which did *not* include the United States. Cuba's greatest patriot hero, called "the Apostle" of Cuban independence, Martí began to fight Spanish colonialism

at a young age. He was exiled from Cuba at sixteen and devoted his life to the cause of "Cuba Libre." He edited a magazine in Mexico and taught at the University of Guatemala. From 1881 to 1895, he wrote and worked for the Cuban patriot cause in New York City, while reporting on the United States for Latin American newspapers as far away as Buenos Aires. Martí knew the United States close up, but the most influential warning against the United States came from afar—from a Uruguayan essayist, José Enrique Rodó, whose book *Ariel* (1900) inspired an entire generation of Latin American teachers and intellectuals. Like Martí, Rodó respected the United States but found its utilitarian values alien. Rodó accused US culture of crass materialism and challenged Latin Americans to cultivate finer things—personified by the spirit Ariel. In other words, by the early 1900s, some respected voices had actually begun to question the US/European model of Progress.

They had a difficult task, however. The cinema, with its moving pictures that heralded a new era, would bind the Latin American imagination to Europe and the United States more firmly than ever. Moving pictures first arrived in Latin America in the 1890s, with little time lag. For example, in 1902, six years after representatives of the pioneering Lumière brothers showed Porfirio Díaz their flickering images of Paris, Mexico already had two hundred movie houses. Despite some early innovations, such as the world's first animated feature film, produced in Argentina, Latin American movie screens soon succumbed to a US cinematic invasion that would last through the 1900s. The main US advantage was—and would remain—its huge home market. Hollywood had privileged access to half the world's movie screens, located in the United States. Hollywood soon dominated the world's most expensive art form because it could afford the highest production values and the most glamorous stars. Soon Hollywood began to define what people expected in a movie. As in other respects, US influence increased while Europe lost ground during World War I. After the war, 95 percent of the movies Latin American audiences were watching came from Hollywood.

By the 1920s, the warnings of Darío, Martí, and Rodó against US influence had sunk in. Latin Americans widely admired Sandino in his fight against the US Marines, and a tide of nationalism rose in country after country. Nationalist sentiments did not fit the neocolonial mold, and they generated political energies capable of breaking it. The limitations of the mold were becoming unpleasantly evident. Although neocolonial Latin America had *grown* economically, it had *developed* much less. Export agriculture had boomed for half a century, but industry was still lacking. Landowners, foreign investors, and the middle classes generally had profited, but many ordinary Latin Americans, especially rural people, suffered a decline in their standard of living. Governments were more stable, but rarely more democratic—and often less so. Many of them seemed totally in thrall, first to Great Britain, then to the United States.

Then the neocolonial mold was shattered totally by an international event akin, in its impact, to the Napoleonic Wars. The New York stock market imploded in 1929, the international system of trade and finance came crashing down around everyone's ears, and the world slid gradually into two stormy decades of Depression and war. Demand for Latin American export products plummeted. From Mexico to Brazil to Argentina, the importation of Progress screeched to a halt. The external supports of neocolonialism had disappeared, and its internal supports would soon crumble, as nationalists toppled oligarchies and liberal dictators from the Rio Grande to Tierra del Fuego.

# New Immigration to Latin America

Buenos Aires conventillo. *Courtesy of Archivo Nacional, Buenos Aires.*

The period 1870–1930 saw one part of Latin America totally transformed by a new kind of immigration, roughly equivalent, in size and impact, to the earlier forced immigration of enslaved Africans. The new immigration was principally a mass movement of laborers from southern Europe, displaced by economic

| Country of Origin | Millions of Immigrants |
|---|---|
| Italy | 4.2 |
| Spain | 3.0 |
| Portugal | 1.2 |
| Germany | 0.3 |
| France | 0.3 |
| Russia | 0.3 |

Magnus Mörner, *Adventurers and Proletarians: The Story of Migrants in Latin America* (Pittsburgh: Univ. of Pittsburgh Press, 1985), 50.

changes at home, seeking a better life in the New World. This immigrant flow paralleled similar immigration to the United States, peaking in the years before World War I. The new immigration gave Argentina, Uruguay, and southern Brazil a separate identity as the continent's most European-style societies.

The countries of the Southern Cone (those already mentioned, plus Chile) got nine-tenths of the European immigrants. Why? Although they usually ended up in cities like Buenos Aires or São Paulo, these immigrants generally envisioned themselves farming at first. Unfamiliar tropical environments— most of Latin America is tropical, after all—did not attract them as farmers. The lands of the Southern Cone, on the other hand, would grow European staples like wheat and grapes. Then too, as agricultural workers, the European immigrants had good reason to fear Latin American systems of slavery and debt peonage, and the far south of the continent was relatively free of these. With no fully sedentary indigenous people and no profitable plantation crop, the sparsely settled lands of the Southern Cone had escaped the worst legacies of colonial exploitation. Now, thanks to the new immigrants, these poorest parts of the old Iberian empires would become the richest part of Latin America in the 1900s.

Argentina was the main destination. During these years, over five million European immigrants poured into the fertile provinces around Buenos Aires. The great city itself became a South American version of Chicago, with half its population composed of European immigrants in 1914. In that year, 30 percent of the Argentine population was foreign-born, overwhelmingly Italian and Spanish but also Irish, Jewish (from Russia and eastern Europe), German, Austrian, French, English, and Swiss. New arrivals in the city often lived in *conventillos*, decaying colonial mansions that had been partitioned into tiny rooms. These immigrants tended not to form US-style ethnic neighborhoods, so Buenos Aires conventillos housed diverse collections of people. A social historian of Argentina describes the census information for a Potosí Street conventillo in the early 1900s:

> The 207 inhabitants of this conventillo filled thirty rooms and took up the same floor space which one well-to-do family of ten to fifteen members and five to ten servants would have occupied. Some nuclear families lived in individual rooms: a Spanish washerwoman in her sixties with four children, the oldest of whom was widowed and lived here with his six-year-old Argentine-born son; an Italian shoemaker with his wife and three children, all born in Italy; a French mason and his French wife (a washerwoman), and their four children, all born in Buenos Aires; a widowed Spanish washerwoman and her five children, the three oldest born in Uruguay and the youngest two in Buenos Aires. More common was the group of men, some single and others married to wives they had left in Europe, who had banded together to form a single room.[*]

[*]James R. Scobie, *Buenos Aires: Plaza to Suburb, 1870–1910* (New York: Oxford Univ. Press, 1974), 51.

Many of these immigrants had farmed, as renters or share-croppers, before deciding that metropolitan Buenos Aires offered better opportunities. In the bustling early 1900s, they were becoming Argentine, dancing the tango and invent-ing the Italian/Spanish slang called *lunfardo* in which tango lyrics came to be written, imparting a special character to the city of Buenos Aires—and to its smaller Uruguayan twin, Montevideo.

Southern Brazil was second to Argentina as an immigrant destination in 1870–1930. It welcomed Italians aplenty, Portu-guese too, as well as Spanish and German and eastern Euro-pean Jewish immigrants. The Brazilian cities of Rio de Janeiro and, above all, São Paulo, attracted immigrant flows similar to those arriving in Buenos Aires and Montevideo. Distinc-tive to São Paulo, on the other hand, was the arrival of many Japanese. On the coffee plantations of rural São Paulo, Ital-ian farmworkers arrived to work as sharecroppers, but, as in Argentina, these immigrants soon headed for the city. Far-ther south, however, in the Brazilian states of Paraná, Santa Catarina, and Rio Grande do Sul—also in southern Chile—immigrants were granted land. There, distinct ethnic colonies emerged. Germans, for example, frequently kept apart, speak-ing German, farming European crops, and building spic-and-span little settlements that have maintained their cultural distinctness down to the present day. Despite their distinct-ness, however, these immigrants, too, have gradually inte-grated themselves into Brazilian and Chilean national life.

Other Latin American countries received a sprinkling of immigration. The largest-scale flow outside the Southern Cone was Spanish immigration to Cuba, which continued to fill Havana and other Cuban cities with Spanish store clerks, artisans, and laborers even after Cuban independence. Mean-while, people of Middle Eastern descent (often lumped together as "turcos," or "Turks," in Latin American slang) owned retail businesses all over the continent. By 2000, three of their descendants had become presidents of Argentina, Colombia, and Ecuador. A man of Japanese descent had become president of Peru.

**DISTRIBUTING ARMS.** Nationalist movements transformed Latin America in the mid-1900s. This mural, painted on the walls of Mexico's Department of Public Education in 1928 by Diego Rivera, exemplifies the militant nationalist mood. Rivera depicted his wife, Frida Kahlo, among those distributing arms to Mexican revolutionaries. The hammer and sickle in the background signals Rivera's Marxist inspiration, but nationalism was not necessarily a movement of the left or the right. © 2010 *Banco de México Diego Rivera Frida Kahlo Museums Trust, Mexico, D.F. / Artists Rights Society (ARS), New York. Photo Credit: Schalkwijk / Art Resource, NY.*

| 1910 | 1929 | 1930s | 1937–45 | 1945 |
|---|---|---|---|---|
| Mexican Revolution begins | Stock-market crash undermines neocolonial order | Import Substitution Industrialization | Estado Novo in Brazil | Gabriela Mistral wins Nobel prize |

# 7.

# NATIONALISM

For nations to be united internally, they have to know who they are; they need a clear and positive sense of national identity. Four centuries of Latin American transculturation—the creative process of cultural give and take—had given rise to a multitude of differences in speech, in customs, in attitudes. Intertwined with the process of transculturation, the process of race mixing had created national populations that were also distinctive.

During the colonial period, European rulers had assigned American difference a negative meaning—an essentially "political" act. Then independence-minded Creoles reversed that attitude in their nativist rhetoric of 1810–25 ("Americanos, you are the true sons of the soil!"), again as a power move, a matter of politics. But nativism faded after the Spanish and Portuguese were expelled, except when occasional foreign intervention revived it. The new nationalism that swept the region in the 1900s was another wave of the earlier nativist spirit, now with a strong economic agenda.

Who were the new nationalists, and what were they after? The nationalists very often were urban, middle-class people, recent immigrants or of racially mixed heritage. They had benefited less than landowners from the export boom. They rarely could travel to Europe or the United States, rarely could afford to import all the "Progress" they wanted. Neocolonial elites had created glass bubbles of European culture in Latin American countries, but middle-class nationalists, too numerous to fit inside those bubbles, committed themselves to a larger, more ambitious, and above all, *more inclusive* vision of change. The nationalists would shatter the neocolonial bubbles, breathe Latin American air, and feel pride when young factories made it smoky, because industrialization was the practical goal they most desired.

Unlike the neocolonial elites, they would also feel comfortable in Latin American skins. Nationalism fostered collective self-respect by positively reinterpreting the meaning of Latin American racial and cultural difference. The nationalists declared psychological independence from Europe. No longer slaves to European fashion, Latin Americans would create styles of their own, especially in painting, music, dance, and literature. True, they would still watch Hollywood movies and listen to US jazz, but they also would teach Paris to tango and New York to rumba.

Nationalism's wide appeal—reaching far beyond its "core constituency" of middle-class urban people—gave it a special power. Four centuries of colonial and then neocolonial exploitation had left a bitter, divisive legacy in Latin America. Independence in the 1820s had created the outlines of countries, but not cohesive national societies. Neocolonialism, with its official racism and its railroads connecting exportable resources to seaports, but not connecting major cities to each other, had done little to advance national integration. The nationalists' simple truths—that everybody belonged, that the benefits of Progress should be shared, and that industrial development should be the priority—offered an important principle of cohesion. Nationalist critiques of imperialism also provided a clear, external focus for resentment—foreign intervention, both military and monetary. And a shared enemy is politically useful. Like all rhetoric, nationalist rhetoric sometimes rang hollow, and nationalism had its dark side, too, as we shall see. Yet, nationalists who rejected the premise of white superiority and directed practical attention to long-neglected matters of public welfare clearly had a new and exciting political message. Nationalism attracted the ardent support of people across the social spectrum—something that liberalism had never really done. No wonder the advent of nationalism marks a clear watershed in the history of the region.

Latin American nationalism celebrates the unique—a particular historical experience, a particular culture. This *ethnic* nationalism is more like the German or French variety than like US nationalism, which tends to focus on a set of shared political ground rules and ideals. The US version is sometimes called *civic* nationalism. Consequently, signs of ethnic identity—folk costume, for example, or traditional foods—take on a nationalist importance in Latin America that they lack in the United States. In addition, ethnic nationalism tends to emphasize the idea of race—often, the idea of racial purity. German Nazism of the 1930s offers an extremely unpleasant example.

Latin American nationalism, on the other hand, emphasizes mixed-race, *mestizo* identities. The racial optimists of the neocolonial 1890s, persuaded by doctrines of "scientific racism" emanating from Europe and the United States, believed that national populations could—and should—be whitened over time, through immigration and intermarriage. And these were the optimists! The racial pessimists claimed that race mixing inevitably caused degeneration. Thus, people of color who made up the Latin American majority were to be excluded or, at best, *phased out* from the neocolonial vision of the future.

In contrast, Latin American nationalists celebrated the mixing of indigenous, European, and African genes. Each country's unique physical type, argued some nationalists, was an adaptation to its environment. Back in neocolonial 1902, Euclides da Cunha had called Brazil's mixed-race backlanders "the bedrock" of Brazilian nationality, yet he still thought them inferior to Europeans. A generation later, in the 1930s, the idea of inferior races was dying a well-deserved death in Latin America—officially, if not in racist hearts—and mestizo nationalism had made the difference. In Cuba, for example, the poet Nicolás Guillén celebrated two metaphorical grandfathers, the slave and the conquistador, in his poem "Ballad of the Two Grandfathers" (1935), some lines of which may be translated as follows:

> They're shadows only I can see,
> my two grandfathers escorting me.
> With his bone-tipped lance,
> his wooden drum with rawhide head
> —my black grandfather.
> With his ruffled collar,
> his grey and warlike armor,
> —my white grandfather.
> The black one with his bare feet
> and stony-muscled torso.
> The white one
> with his pupils of Antarctic glass . . .
>
> In the night they dream,
> and dreaming, roam,
> —the two of them.
> And in me, they come together.

As a metaphor for his mixed descent, the two grandfathers of Guillén's poem defined his racial identity and, in a larger sense, constituted a myth of descent for Cuba as a mestizo (or mulatto) nation. Guillén's poetry had a musicality that was intended to echo percussive African rhythms, and some poems

**WHITENING IN THREE GENERATIONS.** *Redemption of Ham*, by Modesto Brocos y Gomez. This 1895 Brazilian canvas illustrates the outmoded neocolonial idea that European immigrant blood would "whiten" Latin American populations. Three generations—a black grandmother, a mulatta mother, and her white child—are intended to show the whitening that resulted from the women's finding lighter-skinned partners. The father of the child, a Portuguese immigrant, is seated to one side. Nationalist thinking on race did away with the official goal of whitening and made African and indigenous roots a point of pride. *Courtesy of Museu de Belas Artes, Rio de Janeiro.*

phonetically imitated black Cuban speech. These choices signaled a profound rejection of the Eurocentric aesthetic typical of earlier periods of Latin American history. And Guillén, while he became the most acclaimed exponent of Afro-Cuban

**BROWN PRIDE.** *The Coffee Grower* (1934) by the internationally recognized Brazilian painter Cândido Portinari is a confident and powerful figure in no need of "whitening." Like many nationalists, Portinari artistically celebrated the dignity of the working class. *Sao Paulo Museum of Art.*

poetry, was hardly unique. Instead, he was part of a much broader literary and artistic current that also included the Négritude movement of the French Caribbean. Furthermore, a string of fine contemporary novelists—Cuba's Alejo Carpentier, Peru's Ciro Alegría, and Guatemala's Miguel Ángel Asturias—used African and indigenous themes to put their countries on the literary map. Not only did these nationalist authors deny the premise of European racial superiority; they raised the idea of race mixing to a special position of patriotic honor. And they did so even as Hitler's Nazis were successfully promoting the doctrine of white supremacy in Europe.

## NATIONALISTS TAKE POWER

You might guess where the nationalist eruption started—a country where neocolonialism had done its worst, where nationalism drew energy from repeated foreign invasions, where people of mixed race were now the majority, a country that had already elected a president with no European blood—Mexico. The centennial of Hidalgo's 1810 rebellion saw the outbreak of the twentieth century's first great social revolution, the Mexican Revolution (with a capital R).

By 1910, Porfirio Díaz had dominated Mexico for thirty-four years, and he was getting old. Reformers backed the presidential candidacy of Francisco Madero, a slim gentleman from northern Mexico. Madero wanted only for Díaz to share more power among the Mexican elite, but the dictator refused. Madero's appeal broadened when Díaz jailed and then exiled him. Now Madero got radical. He talked of returning lands unfairly taken from indigenous communities. Among many others, people of an indigenous community called Anenecuilco had lost land to encroaching sugar plantations during the years of neocolonial Progress. A leader of Anenecuilco, one Emiliano Zapata, allied his own uprising with Madero's national movement. Zapata's image—broad sombrero and black mustache, cartridge belts across his chest, riding a white stallion—became an icon of the Mexican Revolution. But Emiliano Zapata represents only one of many local leaders of rebellions that broke out all over Mexico. Unable or unwilling to fight them, Díaz left for Parisian exile in 1911.

Suddenly, Mexico was full of "revolutionaries" with vastly differing backgrounds and goals. They had agreed only on the need to oust Díaz. Who would rule now? Madero tried first but failed. He was removed by a general—with an approving nod from the US ambassador to Mexico—and assassinated in 1913. Years of upheaval followed in 1914–20, as various forces fought it out, their armies crisscrossing the Mexican countryside with women and children in tow. New weapons of the World War I era, especially machine guns, added their staccato music to the dance of death. In the northern state of Chihuahua, and then nationally, Pancho Villa built an army of former cowboys, miners, railroad workers, and oil field roustabouts very different from the peasant guerrillas of southern movements like Zapata's. A third movement, better-connected, more urban and middle-class, finally gained the upper hand and drafted a new, revolutionary constitution in 1917. These so-called Constitutionalists, fairly typical of the nationalist core constituency throughout Latin America, may be called the winners of the Mexican Revolution. Their political heirs controlled the destiny of Mexico for the rest of the 1900s.

The Constitution of 1917, still Mexico's constitution, showed strong nationalist inspiration. Article 27 reclaimed for the nation all mineral rights, for instance, to oil, then in the hands of foreign companies. It also paved the way for villages to recover common lands (called *ejidos*) and for great estates to be subdivided and distributed to landless peasants. In principle, Article 123 instituted farsighted protections (although practice would vary) such as wage and hour laws, pensions and social benefits, the right to unionize and strike. The new constitution also sharply limited the privileges of foreigners and, as a legacy of earlier Mexican radicals, curbed the rights of the Catholic Church. The Mexican church now lost the rest of its once-vast wealth. It could no longer own real estate at all. Its clergy, their numbers now limited by law, could not wear ecclesiastical clothing on the street nor teach primary school. Anticlerical attitudes exemplify the revolutionaries' commitment to destroy traditions associated with old patterns of cultural hegemony. Leaders who emerged from the Constitutionalist movement strengthened their rule in the 1920s. They did away with both Zapata and Villa, crushed Mexico's last renegade caudillos, and fought off a challenge from armed Catholic traditionalists in the countryside. (These devout counterrevolutionary peasants were called *Cristeros* from their habit of shouting "Long live Christ the King!") Finally, the Constitutionalists created a one-party system that would last, in various permutations, until the late twentieth century.

This party was first called National, then Mexican, and finally Institutional. But for seven decades it remained a Revolutionary Party. Its official heroes were Madero, Zapata, and Villa, its official rhetoric full of revolutionary and nationalist images. Despite incalculable destruction and horrendous loss of life (a million people died), the Revolution had been a profoundly formative national experience. It had created powerful new loyalties and would loom on the imaginative landscape of Mexican politics for generations. Two US interventions during the years of fighting—a punitive invasion against Villa, who had raided a town in New Mexico, and a US occupation of the port of Veracruz—only added nationalist luster to the Revolution. The new government also brought some material benefits to the impoverished rural majority. A road-building program lessened their isolation, and some land was distributed—though not nearly enough for everyone. Major initiatives in public education began to reduce the country's 80 percent illiteracy rate. The Mexican minister of education in the 1920s was José

Vasconcelos, one of the hemisphere's leading cultural nationalists, who celebrated the triumph of what he called (colorfully,
but confusingly) the Cosmic Race, meaning mestizos.

The great Mexican painters Diego Rivera and Frida Kahlo,
who married in 1929, illustrate Mexico's revolutionary nationalism. Diego Rivera was huge, ugly, magnetic, and brilliant.
He was a muralist, a public painter whose works covered walls
and ceilings. He painted like a tornado for days straight, eating,
even sleeping on the scaffold. Rivera's crowded murals depict,
above all, Mexico's indigenous heritage. He worked from 1923
to 1928 painting Vasconcelos's Ministry of Public Education
with scenes of open-air schools and indigenous peasants dividing land won by the Revolution. In 1929–30, he painted Mexico's National Palace (built by heirs of the conquerors!) with
images of Aztec Tenochtitlan's colorful bustle, images that
show the Spanish conquest as a greedy, hypocritical bloodbath.
In Rivera's mural, Cortés, resembling a troll, looks on as the
conquerors slaughter, enslave, and count gold. Rivera's nationalist message is vivid—and likely to remain so: he painted al
fresco, on wet plaster, so that his murals became part of the
walls themselves.

Frida Kahlo, by contrast, painted small self-portraits, one
after another. She painted especially while bedridden. Surviving
polio as a girl, she had a horrible traffic accident that led to dozens of surgeries. Her body, like Aleijadinho's in colonial Brazil,
was literally disintegrating while she created. Her paintings
explore a private world of pain, but also humor and fantasy. "I
paint my own reality," she said. European surrealists began to
admire her in the late 1930s, but recognition elsewhere, including Mexico, came later. Frida expressed her nationalism in personal ways—fancy traditional hairstyles, pre-Columbian jewelry,
and the folk Tehuana dress of southern Mexico (floor-length, to
conceal her leg withered by polio). She especially enjoyed wearing these clothes in the United States, where Diego painted in

the 1930s. Frida loved Mexican folk art, like the papier-mâché skeletons that decorate Day of the Dead celebrations.

The nationalism of Diego Rivera and Frida Kahlo was widely shared in Mexico during the 1920s and 1930s. Everything *national* had become fashionable—folk music (*corridos*) and dance (*jarabes*), traditional dishes (*tamales* and *moles*), old-style street theater (*carpas*), and artisan objects (like Frida's papier-mâché skeletons). Mexican movies featuring musically macho *charros* like Jorge Negrete, a Mexican version of the US singing cowboy, now competed with Hollywood. The nationalism of many Mexican revolutionaries had Marxist overtones. Diego and Frida, for example, joined the Communist Party and offered their home to the exiled Russian revolutionary leader Leon Trotsky, who lived with them for several months.

Far away, in Argentina and Uruguay, nationalism showed a different face. In this most urbanized, literate, and middle-class part of Latin America, the core constituency of nationalism was stronger than in Mexico. So the nationalists of Argentina and Uruguay were able to take over without a revolution. Uruguay, in particular, soon had one of the most progressive governments in the world.

During the 1800s, Uruguay had been just another war-torn minirepublic battered by more powerful neighbors. Its political struggles were entangled with those of neighboring Argentina. Then Uruguay's economic growth during the post-1880 export boom paralleled Argentina's phenomenal performance. As in Argentina, Uruguay's delirious prosperity was controlled through managed elections. The country's great nationalist reformer José Batlle y Ordóñez began as a tough, traditional politician. Batlle used his first presidency (1903–7) mostly to vanquish political rivals. But having established broad support in the heavily immigrant middle and working classes of Montevideo, he used his second term (1911–15) to launch the reform movement known simply by his name: Batllismo.

Batllismo was not about race or cultural uniqueness. It was more a civic and *economic* nationalism. Batllismo meant concerted state action against "foreign economic imperialism." It brought an unprecedented level of government involvement to the Uruguayan economy: tariffs to protect local businesses; government monopoly over public utilities, including the formerly British-owned railways and the port of Montevideo; government ownership of tourist hotels and meat-packing plants; and lots of state-owned banks to spread credit around. In accord with Batlle's determination that "modern industry must not be allowed to destroy human beings," Uruguay became the hemisphere's first welfare state, complete with a minimum wage, regulated working conditions, accident insurance, paid holidays, and retirement benefits. Public education, a matter of special pride in Uruguay since the 1870s, received further support, and the university was opened to women.

Batllismo transformed Uruguay forever, but the reforms depended, at least in part, on prosperous times to fund its ambitious social programs. In addition, this was an urban movement that left rural Uruguay virtually untouched. Batllismo was also aggressively anticlerical, making Uruguayan society among the most secular in the hemisphere. Traditional Catholic Holy Week, formerly a somber time of religious processions, became Tourism Week in modern Uruguay. To eliminate caudillo rule once and for all, Batlle even tried to abolish the one-man presidency in favor of an executive council. Ironically, many saw Batlle himself as a caudillo—but a "civil caudillo," unlike the military caudillos of the 1800s.

Across the Río de la Plata, in Argentina, another "civil caudillo" representing urban interests overthrew the country's landowning oligarchy by means of (believe it or not) an election in 1916. "The revolution of the ballot box," they called it. Hipólito Yrigoyen, the winner of that election, led an essentially middleclass reform party with considerable working-class support, the

Radical Civic Union. When the Radicals won the election of 1916, jubilant crowds pulled Yrigoyen's carriage through the streets of Buenos Aires while flowers rained from balconies.

The Radicals quickly entrenched themselves, creating the first truly mass-based political party in the history of Latin America. Not by any means above engaging in patronage politics, the Radical Civic Union distributed plenty of pensions and public employment to its supporters. Meanwhile, the reforms it enacted were less impressive than Uruguay's. The Radicals talked economic nationalism, but the role of foreign capital in Argentina did not diminish. Yrigoyen's one significant act of economic nationalism was the creation of a government agency to supervise oil production.

Still, Yrigoyen's presidency marked an important change, not so much because of what he did, but because of what he represented. Poorly dressed and lacking in social graces, Yrigoyen was a man of the people. He hated the elegant elite of Buenos Aires, and they hated him back. Yrigoyen framed politics in moral terms, as a kind of civic religion. He never married and lived a reclusive life of legendary frugality in a simple dwelling that his enemies called the presidential "burrow." A famous anecdote exemplifies his disdain for the trappings of power. A friend, it is said, asked for a personal souvenir. Yrigoyen gestured vaguely toward a cardboard box overflowing with medals and honors. "Help yourself," he replied.

Ordinary Argentines could visit the president to ask for some humble bit of patronage. Yrigoyen cared little about Europe and also maintained an Argentine diplomatic tradition of resisting US hemispheric initiatives. During World War I, despite US pressure, he insisted on Argentine neutrality. The greatest stain on his record is his violent repression of organized labor during the "Tragic Week" of 1919 and the strike of Patagonian sheep herders in 1921. Yrigoyen was succeeded by another member of the Radical Civic Union, but he returned to the presidency himself in 1928, now senile, hardly fit to steer Argentina through the turbulent 1930s. Although he soon lost popularity and had to leave office, all Buenos Aires turned out for Yrigoyen's funeral a few years later.

Batlle and Yrigoyen were individual leaders of towering importance, not generals on horseback, but caudillos nevertheless. Nationalist politics was mass politics that often focused on such leaders. Another was Víctor Raúl Haya de la Torre, who led Peruvian nationalists mostly from exile.

Haya de la Torre was first exiled from Peru in 1920 for leading student protests against Peru's pro-US dictator. In Mexico, whose revolution strongly impressed him, the young radical intellectual founded an international party, the Popular American Revolutionary Alliance (APRA), as a kind of collective self-defense against economic imperialism in Latin America. Haya de la Torre preferred the term Indo-America, to highlight the region's indigenous roots, exactly the way Mexican muralists such as Rivera did. This nationalist emphasis on indigenous roots is called *indigenismo*. Another young Peruvian intellectual of the 1920s, José Carlos Mariátegui, imagined an indigenous socialism combining Inca models with Marxist theory. But Peru, when compared to Mexico, remained more ethnically split: the highlands heavily indigenous, the coast more black and white. Consequently, indigenismo was less successful as a unifying force in Peru.

APRA did not go far as an international party. Still, by threatening to make indigenismo more than theory or fiction, the movement had a powerful impact on Peru. APRA terrified conservatives. The party's mass rallies filled the streets with poor and middle-class people who roared their contempt of the oligarchy, their fury at imperialism, and their loyalty to the "Maximum Leader," Haya de la Torre. In 1932, APRA revolted after "losing" a managed election. The army crushed the uprising with mass executions, and APRA was banned from Peruvian

**INDIGENISMO.** *The Indian Mayor of Chincheros* (1925) by José Sabogal, Peru's principle indigenista painter, shows a community leader holding his staff of office in an idealization of traditional indigenous life. *José Sabogal, The Indian Mayor of Chincheros: Varayoc, 1925, Museo de Arte de Lima.*

politics. But the popularity of the outlawed party and its perpetually exiled leader only increased as years passed.

Ciro Alegría, a fervent, high-ranking APRA militant, was
one of the many nationalists who had to flee Peru. While living
in Chile, he began to write fiction inspired by indigenismo.
Peruvian novelists had explored indigenismo for decades, since
the time of Clorinda Matto de Turner. Still, it is appropriate
that the greatest indigenista novel, Alegría's *Wide and Alien Is
the World* (1941), emerged from the ranks of APRA. Writers
like Alegría defended indigenous people, but the main practical
goal of indigenismo was changing its subjects to fit the wider
world. Perhaps it is not so odd that Alegría wrote his book for a
New York publishing contest. He won and became one of the
best-known of the many Latin American writers cultivating
non-European roots in the 1930s and 1940s.

Nationalists did not take power everywhere in Latin America, but nationalism showed its political potency even where it
did not rule. In many countries conservatives managed to co-
opt nationalist influences or hold them in check. That was the
case in Colombia, where nationalists tried to outflank traditional rural patron-client networks by unionizing urban workers
and appealing directly to their self-interest. The conservatives'
hold on Colombia was too strong, however, to allow nationalist
reformers to gain much headway. Rural oligarchies held their
ground, region by region, while popular discontent accumulated in the enormous following of a fiery popular leader, Jorge
Eliécer Gaitán. Gaitán rose to national fame denouncing a
massacre of banana workers who worked for a U.S. multinational corporation, and his angry condemnations of power and
privilege put the word *oligarchy* into Colombia's everyday vocabulary. Two decades later, discontent would finally explode in
violence.

Meanwhile, effective nationalist reform had to wait in other
countries as well. One was Venezuela, despite (or perhaps

because of) the country's oil wealth—all of it flowing through concessions to foreign companies. As a result of the freely bubbling black gold and easy money, Venezeula's rulers were able to avoid the popular outreach that essentially defined nationalist movements. Such outreach was often carried out by communist and socialist grassroots organizers, new players on the political stage of Latin America. Chile saw plenty of that kind of outreach, however, especially during the thirteen-day "Socialist Republic" associated with a flamboyant leader known as Marmaduke Grove, but Chilean nationalists of the Right vied quite successfully against those of the Left, and no single government consolidated power. In Cuba, the overthrow of an unpopular neocolonial-style dictator in 1933 was carried out by a wide nationalist coalition that included inspirational university professors and left-wing students, as well as noncommissioned army officers and enlisted men led by one Sergeant Fulgencio Batista. Batista was a poor man who had been a cane cutter and whose mulatto coloring represented, to some extent, the same nationalist aspirations symbolized by Nicolás Guillén's "Ballad of the Two Grandfathers." But Batista wanted power, above all, and he bowed so compliantly to US instructions that he was allowed to run Cuba as a client state of the United States for decades, his nationalist gestures reduced to mere window dressing.

Nationalism made the most striking changes when stable governments were able to combine mass mobilization with economic transformation. That transformation involved a rejection of the basic neocolonial model of export-oriented economic growth, which brings us to the Great Depression.

## ISI AND ACTIVIST GOVERNMENTS OF THE 1930S

The Great Depression of the 1930s finished the demolition of neocolonialism and energized nationalist movements throughout Latin America. In the years following the 1929 crash of the New York stock market, the volume of Latin America's international trade contracted by half in a violent spasm. Governments that depended on the export boom collapsed everywhere.

As the 1930s progressed, however, an important phenomenon occurred, a positive side effect of the collapse of international trade. The name of this phenomenon—import-substitution industrialization—is a mouthful, and people usually prefer ISI for short. But the name says a lot. Earnings from exports had gone down, down, down, and with them, the ability to import manufactured products. The ISI process occurred as Latin American manufacturers filled the market niches left vacant by vanishing imports. Those who believe that trade is always mutually beneficial should ponder a startling fact: The 1930s interruption of trade—the interruption that idled so many factories in the United States and Europe—*had the opposite effect* in parts of Latin America, where industrialization took off in these same years. ISI gave the nationalist critics of economic imperialism a persuasive case against the old import/export trade.

ISI had really begun before the 1930s, most notably when World War I interrupted the import/export system in 1914–18. Buenos Aires, São Paulo, Rio de Janeiro, and Mexico City were already becoming major industrial centers. Overall, though, Latin American industries remained minor-league players. Until the 1930s, they could not compete with export sectors like agriculture or mining. Now that changed, and Latin American industrial production increased substantially. Nationalists made industrialization a point of pride. For them, industrialization meant moving out of the neocolonial shadow and controlling their own national destiny. The nationalist governments of the 1930s and 1940s therefore engaged in Batllista-style economic activism: setting wages and prices, regulating production levels, manipulating exchange rates, and passing protective labor laws. They also promoted direct government ownership of banks, public utilities, and key industries.

Unfortunately, not all Latin Americans got the benefits of ISI. As a rule, the larger the national market, the more likely import-substituting industries will thrive. Therefore, the most populous countries of the region—Brazil, Mexico, and Argentina—were the main beneficiaries. Chile and Uruguay, despite their small populations, also underwent considerable ISI. Their comparatively high living standards provided more prospective consumers per capita. But small countries with predominantly poor rural populations could not absorb the products of many factories. So ISI meant little in Ecuador or Bolivia, Nicaragua or Honduras, Paraguay or the Dominican Republic.

Nor did ISI bring all varieties of industrial growth, even to the big countries. Light industry (producing mass-consumption items like soap, matches, beer, biscuits, shoes, aspirin, and cheap cloth) responded most to the market opportunities of ISI. Heavy industry (producing "durable goods" like cars, radios, and refrigerators) responded less. Heavy industry required equipment that simply had to be imported. And it required steel. A national steel industry meant joining the big leagues. Only Brazil, Mexico, Argentina, and Chile did so during the 1940s.

Brazil—with over twice as many inhabitants as any other Latin American country in 1930, but still heavily rural and dependent on agricultural exports—offers an excellent example of ISI in action. Within two decades, industry would surpass agriculture as a percentage of Brazilian GDP. Although market forces explain most of this gain, economic nationalism played its part as well. The story of nationalist politics in Brazil centers once again on an individual leader, by far the best known and most beloved of all Brazilian presidents—Getúlio Vargas.

Those in search of US analogies might well call Getúlio Vargas the Franklin D. Roosevelt of Brazil. Note that, from a

Latin American perspective, FDR and his relative, Theodore Roosevelt, stand worlds apart, never to be confused. The first Roosevelt seemed an enemy to Latin Americans, the second a friend. Vargas's first period in office (1930–1945) parallels FDR's multiterm presidency, except that Vargas later returned, for a total of nineteen years as Brazilian president. Vargas, like FDR, made famous use of the radio and vastly expanded the national government. Both men were masterful politicians, but physically unimposing: FDR paralyzed by polio, Vargas short and jolly. Both exuded a contagious optimism. Both died in office— Vargas, memorably, by his own hand.

The Brazilian "coffee kingdom," Latin America's largest oligarchic republic, had begun to crumble during the 1920s. Considering Brazil's oligarchic politics hopelessly corrupt, rebellious young army officers, collectively known to history as the *Tenentes* (lieutenants), staged desperate symbolic uprisings. One was a bloody gesture of defiance on Rio's glamorous Copacabana beach in 1922. A bit later, other Tenentes formed a thousand-man armed column and marched for two years and countless miles through the Brazilian backlands trying to drum up support for their revolutionary nationalist vision. Meanwhile, the coffee economy lurched from crisis to crisis in a permanent state of overproduction. By 1927, the government's coffee valorization program was fighting a losing battle. Its vast stockpiles of unsold coffee only continued to accumulate. Then came the Depression, and the price of coffee dropped to less than a third of its already low price on the world market.

The rise of Vargas magnificently illustrates the political consequences of 1929. The following was an election year, and Vargas, governor of Rio Grande do Sul, a rising state but not a coffee producer, ran against the official candidate of São Paulo, a representative of the pro-coffee interests that had dominated Brazil for two generations. Although the electoral managers produced an official victory for King Coffee's candidate, the old king had lost his grip. This time, opposition forces forcibly disputed the election results. With the support of the army, Vargas seized the presidency. This "Revolution of 1930" became a clear turning point in Brazilian history.

For seven years, Vargas ruled as a more or less constitutional president over a country suddenly filled with new political energies. No more would conservative liberalism alternate with liberal conservatism. All sorts of new ideologies were afoot. The "revolutionaries" of 1930 had included both frustrated liberals opposed to King Coffee and the idealistic young Tenentes, strong nationalists who despised liberals. The Tenentes absorbed the new radical ideologies of the day. Some of the most famous Tenentes joined the Communist Party, making it the heart of the Alliance for National Liberation (ALN). With the ALN, the radical left became a real power contender in Brazil for the first time. Meanwhile, on the far right, a group calling themselves Integralists drew inspiration from European fascism. The Integralists saluted each other with out-thrust arms, used a symbol (the Greek letter sigma) slightly reminiscent of the Nazi swastika, and wore colored shirts, like Hitler's brownshirts or Mussolini's blackshirts, when they acted tough in the streets. Their shirts were patriotic Brazilian green.

Vargas deftly negotiated the political tangles of the early 1930s, playing liberals, conservatives, communists, Tenentes, and Integralists against each other. Then, in 1937 he seized dictatorial power with the support of the army and went on the radio to announce a nationalist institutional makeover for Brazil: the *Estado Novo,* or New State. The Estado Novo was a highly authoritarian government, in which all legislative bodies were dissolved, political parties were banned, and mass media were censored. Vargas scrapped liberal-inspired federalism and sent centrally appointed "interventors" to direct state governments. The police of the Estado Novo operated with brutal impunity. Yet, despite all this, Vargas remained popular. Why?

Vargas was pragmatic, flexible about his means, more interested in results than basic principles—another trait he shared with FDR. Always, too, he was a nationalist. Nationalism was the common ground of his multiclass alliance and the animating spirit of the Estado Novo. From far left to far right, everyone, it seemed, was a nationalist now. These were the 1930s, after all, when nationalist movements were on a roll around the world.

Everything was "*national* this" and "*national* that" in the Estado Novo. Vargas even ceremoniously burned Brazil's state flags to symbolize the unchallenged primacy of the national government. The Estado Novo spawned dozens of government boards, ministries, and agencies, a bit like the "alphabet soup" agencies of FDR's New Deal, to further the nation's common goals and welfare. National councils and commissions were created to supervise railroads, mining, immigration, school textbooks, sports and recreation, hydraulic and electrical energy, and so on. The Estado Novo founded a National Steel Company and built a massive steel mill between the two most industrialized cities, Rio and São Paulo. Its National Motor Factory turned out engines for trucks and airplanes. It prohibited foreign ownership of newspapers. And in the far south of Brazil, where German, Italian, and other European immigrants had established agricultural colonies and maintained a separate culture and language, the Estado Novo exerted new assimilationist pressures. Immigrants were told to speak Portuguese and integrate themselves into the national society.

Like Mexico's Revolutionary Party, the Estado Novo celebrated race mixing, and it encouraged Brazilians to embrace their African heritage. In 1933, the positive qualities of racial and cultural "fusion" had been promoted in a landmark study, *The Masters and the Slaves*, by a young anthropologist named Gilberto Freyre. Freyre argued that Brazil's African heritage, far from constituting a national liability, as in racist theories, had created Brazil's distinctive national identity and imbued all Brazilians, whether or not they knew it, with aspects of African culture. Brazilians seemed eager for Freyre's unifying message, and a whole field of Afro-Brazilian studies suddenly arose with official encouragement. During these years, too, the spirited Afro-Brazilian samba became accepted as the country's cultural signature, vigorously promoted by the mass media of the Estado Novo.

Carmen Miranda—a singer, dancer, and actress whose trademark was headgear apparently made of fruit—rode the nationalist samba wave to movie stardom first in Brazil, which now had its own movie industry, and later in the United States. Carmen Miranda embodied paradox. In Brazil, her movie roles filled the niche—*national* musicals featuring *national* music—that the charro singing cowboys did in Mexico. But her later US movie-star image was a generic, gesticulating, "hot Latin" caricature that today seems far from nationalistic. She created this persona to suit US rather than Brazilian taste. Still, her outrageous costume, often blamed on Hollywood, was pure Rio de Janeiro; a carnival-kitsch version of traditional Afro-Brazilian Bahiana dress. Her samba moves were carefully studied from Bahian teachers. But Miranda was not Afro-Brazilian herself. In fact, she was Portuguese, although she grew up in Brazil. Still, her dancing made her Brazilian—both according to her ("Tell me," she said, "if I don't have Brazil in every curve of my body!") *and* according to the Brazilian public that applauded her in the 1930s. Miranda made nine sold-out South American tours. In 1940, after performing for FDR at the White House, she returned to a hero's welcome in Rio de Janeiro. But her popularity in Brazil plummeted when Brazilians heard her sing in English.

Across Brazil, a process of cultural self-discovery was underway. A landmark festival, São Paulo's Modern Art Week of 1922, inaugurated an innovative nationalist current in the Brazilian arts. Among those associated with the São Paulo modernist movement was Heitor Villa-Lobos, who integrated Brazilian folk melodies into his classical compositions, just as Chopin and Liszt had done with Polish and Hungarian folk melodies for similar nationalist reasons a century earlier. Under Vargas, Villa-Lobos worked on a national program of musical enrichment, arranging huge concerts for tens of thousands. Today Villa-Lobos is by far Latin America's best-known classical composer. Another leading light of São Paulo's Modern Art Week was writer Oswald de Andrade. "Tupi or not tupi, that is the question," declared Andrade, with typically Brazilian tongue-in-cheek lightheartedness, in his influential *Cannibalist Manifesto* of 1928. Recalling certain Tupi dietary customs, Andrade suggested that Brazilian artists metaphorically "cannibalize" European art—consume it, digest it, then combine it with native and African influences to invent a new art unique to Brazil. Meanwhile, storytellers of northeastern Brazil were creating a great narrative tradition with strong nationalist roots. Among them was Jorge Amado, today Brazil's best-known novelist. Amado's books are almost always set in Bahia, where Brazil's African roots are especially deep. Like Diego Rivera, Frida Kahlo, and many other nationalist artists and writers, Amado became strongly committed to a revolutionary Marxist vision during the 1930s.

The government of Vargas, too, eventually moved leftward, as we will see. In the 1930s and 1940s, though, Vargas's policies were hard to place on the left-right spectrum of political ideologies. Nationalism, not socialism, was the vision he used to reconcile the demands of industrialists and industrial workers. The Estado Novo made industrialization a priority, and its extensive labor legislation disciplined the labor force, which the factory owners wanted, but also protected it, which the workers needed. The Estado Novo created government-affiliated labor unions by the hundreds, but it did not allow them to strike.

Instead, worker grievances were to be adjudicated by the government. It was a paternalistic system, not controlled by the workers themselves. Still, it constituted an improvement over earlier years, when worker protests had been simply "a matter for the police." An impressive array of social legislation—from health and safety standards to a minimum wage, a forty-eight-hour work week, retirement and pension plans, and maternity benefits—was put in place for industrial working-class and urban middle-class people.

Like Argentina's and Uruguay's, Brazil's nationalist movement was urban-based and urban-oriented. Only in Mexico, where peasants in arms had helped make a revolution, did nationalism transform rural society too. The period of greatest transformation was unquestionably 1934–40, during the presidency of Lázaro Cárdenas.

Whereas Vargas, like FDR, came from a rich landowning family, Cárdenas had humble village beginnings. He had fought ably in the Revolution and then become governor of his home state, Michoacán, in rugged and conservative western Mexico. Thirty-nine years old when be became the Revolutionary Party's presidential candidate, Lázaro Cárdenas was known for his loyalty to the cause, but not for his initiative. He surprised everyone by seizing the reins of power and galloping out to infuse the whole country with his vision of a better, fairer Mexico. He started this process during his campaign for election. As the Revolutionary Party's official candidate, he ran unopposed, yet he campaigned like an underdog, ranging across sixteen thousand miles of Mexican countryside, visiting remote villages—on horseback, if necessary—as no presidential candidate had ever done before. Cárdenas did not forget about the villages of Mexico after becoming president, either.

During his six years in office, he distributed almost forty-five million acres of land, twice as much as in the previous twenty-four years put together. He gave his support to labor organizations and, unlike Vargas, defended their right to strike. Government support of striking workers even led to a major international confrontation in 1938. These workers were employed by British and US oil companies that operated along the northeastern gulf coast of Mexico. When the companies and the strikers submitted their dispute to government arbitration, the arbitrators awarded the workers an increase in pay and social services. The foreign owners refused to pay, however. The Mexican Supreme Court reviewed and upheld the decision, but still the foreign companies stonewalled. The foreign owners were shocked when Cárdenas then decreed the expropriation of the oil companies in accord with Article 27 of the Mexican constitution. Few measures have ever been more popular with the Mexican people, who voluntarily contributed part of their meager earnings to help the government compensate the foreign owners. Even the Catholic Church, despite its long and bitter conflicts with the revolutionary government, rang its bells in jubilation when the oil expropriation was announced. Mexico's "declaration of economic independence," as it became known inside the country, gave rise to a national oil company, PEMEX. The railroads had already been nationalized, less noisily, in 1937.

Great Britain severed diplomatic relations as a result of the oil expropriation, and the US oil companies clamored for intervention, but FDR had other ideas. The world seemed a dangerous place in the 1930s, and FDR thought the United States badly needed allies in Latin America. As world war loomed on the horizon, he did everything possible to cultivate Latin American goodwill. In his inaugural address, he announced a "Good Neighbor Policy" toward Latin America. The idea was not totally new in 1933. Republican US presidents of the 1920s had already begun to abandon the aggressive interventionism of earlier years, finding that it created more problems than it solved. In 1933, however, at the seventh congress of the Pan-

American movement, FDR's representatives publicly swore off military intervention. In addition, Cuba and Panama were no longer to be "protectorates" where US Marines could come and go at will. The result was a remarkable change in the mood of US–Latin American relations. FDR then took advantage of improved relations to advance hemispheric security arrangements in successive Pan-American conferences during the late 1930s and early 1940s. Carmen Miranda, now living in the United States, made "Good Neighbor" movies, and so did Walt Disney; an example is the 1945 animated feature *The Three Caballeros*, in which Donald Duck joins forces with a Brazilian parrot and a Mexican rooster.

If the nationalization of Mexico's oil industry in 1938 was the acid test of the Good Neighbor Policy, it passed. Relations between Latin America and the United States became friendlier than ever before or since. After the United States entered the war, all the countries of Latin America eventually joined as allies. The small states of Central America and the Caribbean, closest to the United States in all senses, signed on immediately. Sadly, however, some of the quickest to join the war effort were former "beneficiaries" of US military intervention, now in the hands of pro-US dictators. Some of these were outrageous petty tyrants, like Rafael Trujillo of the Dominican Republic, about whom FDR supposedly admitted: "He may be a bastard, but he's *our* bastard." *Ours rather than the enemy's* was the point. Chile and Argentina—much farther away from the United States and diplomatically more aloof, with many immigrants from "the other side," Germany and Italy—were the last to join the US war effort. Brazil, in contrast, became the most helpful ally of all. The "bulge of Brazil," reaching far east into the Atlantic, had major strategic importance in the Atlantic war, and Vargas allowed the construction of US military bases and airstrips there. In addition, a Brazilian infantry division went to fight in Italy alongside US troops. Mexican fighter pilots, for their part, flew missions in the Pacific, doing much to mend relations between Mexico and the United States.

World War II also gave further stimulus to ISI—more, even, than had the Depression—not only in Brazil, but everywhere. Government spending for war production brought US industry humming back to life—although now building tanks and bombers instead of cars and buses. US demand for Latin American agricultural exports also recovered. Foreign earnings in hand, the Latin American middle classes were ready for a shopping spree, but consumer goods could not be bought in the United States or Europe because of the war. So, with demand up and foreign competition still out of the picture, Latin American industries continued to flourish. In 1943, for example, Brazil's exports totaled about $445 million, a $135 million trade surplus. For the first time ever, many Latin American countries had favorable balances of trade with Europe and the United States.

In 1945, at the end of World War II, the nationalists could take credit for leading the major countries of Latin America successfully through stormy times. Great things seemed just over the horizon. If their industrialization continued at the rate of the prior decade, Brazil, Mexico, Argentina, and possibly others would soon get the heavy industries characteristic of the world's most developed countries.

At the same time, a sweeping transformation of public culture suggested that Latin America's bitter legacy of racial hierarchy and political exclusion was fast disintegrating. The hallways of Mexico's palace of government—truly "corridors of power"—now proudly displayed Diego Rivera's huge murals depicting the achievements of indigenous Mexico and the evils of Spanish colonization. The black samba dancers of Rio de Janeiro were now acclaimed as exponents of Brazilian national culture, and their carnival parades received state subsidies. Across the board, Latin Americans were taking pride in themselves and each other. The advent of the phonograph, radio, and cinema had made Argentina's great tango singer, Carlos Gardel, an idol throughout Latin America. Audiences loved the handsome Gardel's tangos so much that they sometimes interrupted his movies to make the projectionist rewind and repeat a song. Gardel was on a triumphant international tour in 1935 when his plane crashed on a Colombian mountainside, tragically ending his still-ascendant career. Then, in 1945, Gabriela Mistral, a Chilean poet, became the first Latin American to receive a Nobel Prize. In literature, as in painting and music, Latin America was finally world-class.

Yet great problems remained. For one thing, nationalism, ISI, and the growth of an urban middle class had left some parts of Latin America virtually untouched. Central America provides a good example. The internal markets of Central American countries were too small to support much industrialization. So old-style landowning oligarchies had not, for the most part, ceded control to more progressive nationalist coalitions on the isthmus between Panama and Guatemala. In the years when nationalists like Cárdenas were breaking the back of Mexico's landowning class, old-fashioned coffee-growing oligarchies still ruled much of Central America.

In Guatemala, many coffee growers were Germans who had little interest in the country's national development. Guatemala's ruler throughout the years of the Great Depression and World War II was a liberal authoritarian of a classic neocolonial cut, Jorge Ubico, who came to power promising "a march toward civilization" and whose main concern was promoting the cultivation and exportation of coffee. Ubico wanted Guatemala to be the closest ally of the United States in Central America, and during his presidency the United Fruit Company became the country's single dominant economic enterprise. El Salvador, a miniature version of the old Brazilian "Coffee Kingdom," represented the worst-case scenario. There, a grim dictator, Maximiliano Hernández Martínez, a dabbler in the occult, defended El Salvador's King Coffee so brutally that 1932 became known in Salvadoran history as the year of "The Slaughter." Most of the victims—more than ten thousand—were indigenous people. To be an "Indian" became so dangerous in the 1930s that indigenous Salvadorans gradually said good-bye to their ethnic identity. They hid their distinctive clothing, spoke only Spanish, and tried to blend in. Ironically, in the same years when indigenismo became an official creed in nationalist Mexico and elsewhere, the native heritage of stubbornly neocolonial El Salvador practically ceased to exist.

The United States generally put a lid on nationalism in Central America and the Caribbean. US co-optation of Fulgencio Batista's nationalist impulse in Cuba has already been mentioned. In a number of countries, the rulers of this period actually owed their jobs to US intervention. Nicaragua's Anastasio Somoza and the Dominican Republic's Rafael Trujillo had been placed in power, indirectly, by US marines. Both deployed a bit of nationalist imagery, but both distinguished themselves above all, for their greed, corruption, obedience to the United States, and determination to retain power at all cost. Trujillo renamed the capital city after himself and erected a large electric sign that proclaimed the motto "God and Trujillo." His most nationalist undertaking was the massacre of Haitian immigrants.

Even in Latin American countries where nationalism was a more serious force, rhetoric often outran reality. Despite the popularity of indigenismo and mestizo nationalism, racist attitudes lingered everywhere in Latin America. The poet Gabriela Mistral never forgave the Chilean elite that made her feel inferior early on because of her mestizo coloring. Also, urbanization had outrun existing housing and city services. Shantytowns, constructed by rural migrants in search of industrial jobs, sprawled on the outskirts of major Latin American cities.

Hopefully, these would be temporary; in the meantime, blackouts and water shortages became routine. Outside of Mexico, the Latin American countryside had felt few of the improvements brought by nationalism. More industrial jobs were needed for the migrants who arrived day by day in the shantytowns. Meanwhile, Latin American industries remained technologically far behind those of Europe and the United States. They had prospered under the special conditions of ISI during the Depression and World War II, but they would have to improve rapidly to be competitive in the postwar period.

# Populist Leaders of the Twentieth Century

Juan and Eva Perón.
*Courtesy of UPI,
Bettmann/Corbis.*

The mid-twentieth century was a time of charismatic leaders in Latin America. Generally they were electrifying speakers with a nationalist message. They became *populists* by directing their message to poor and lower-middle-class voters. Populist versions of nationalism dominated Latin America's political scene after World War II. Populists invariably cultivated a folksy style, often a paternalistic one; "Father-knows-best" paternalism is generally a conservative trait. On the other hand, populists often used radical rhetoric, blasting oligarchies and economic imperialism. Their behavior in office is very hard to categorize on a left-right political spectrum. But in the cold war days of 1948–89, any leader who talked a lot about workers was likely to be viewed as a leftist, or even as a communist, by US diplomats. The result was a lot of confusion. Recognizing this confusion is essential to interpreting the turbulent politics of the cold war in Latin America, our next stop.

Peru's Victor Raúl Haya de la Torre, the creator of APRA, qualifies as a populist. When he ran for president in 1932, the frightened Lima elite called him a communist, but the Peruvian communists criticized him just as much. Haya's real issues were nationalist ones—cultural pride ("Indo-America") and anti-imperialism ("Foreign firms extract our wealth and sell it outside our country"). Although he never became president of Peru, Haya de la Torre established a powerful bond with Peruvian voters that lasted a quarter century. Populist leaders like Haya de la Torre awakened the kind of personal loyalties inspired by caudillos in the 1800s.

Ecuador's José María Velasco Ibarra, another famous orator, worked similar magic. His self-bestowed title of "National Personification" exemplifies the idea, used by many populists, of a mystical identification with the masses. "Give me a balcony, and I will return to the presidency," he famously declared, and it was no empty boast. From the 1930s to the 1960s, Velasco Ibarra's nationalist rhetoric got him elected president of Ecuador no fewer than five times, always from a slightly different position on the left-right spectrum. Usually, the army expelled him before the end of his term.

Colombia's Jorge Eliécer Gaitán was perhaps the most fiery orator of them all, although, like Peru's Haya de la Torre, he never reached the presidency. When Gaitán stepped to the microphone before a Colombian crowd, he often reminded them of his own poor upbringing and early humiliations, and they loved him for it. He did not have to remind them of his dark mestizo coloring, for it was plainly visible and, anyway, never forgotten by anyone—least of all by the light-skinned elite. Gaitán's assassination in 1948 triggered one of the greatest urban riots ever to occur in Latin America—the *Bogotazo*, an upheaval that shattered the Colombian capital, took two thousand lives, and etched itself in the mind of every Colombian living at the time.

MEXICO'S LÁZARO CÁRDENAS, who reenergized Mexico's institutional revolution in the 1930s, was another populist. Cárdenas was less a high-flown public speaker than a non-stop grassroots campaigner, who mingled comfortably with the common people and received crateloads of letters from humble petitioners, just as FDR did in the United States. In fact, Cárdenas spent little time in Mexico City, preferring to travel tirelessly around the country, hearing the grievances and requests of humble petitioners who came hat in hand, then dispatching his presidential decisions from tables set up in dusty village squares.

BRAZIL'S EX-DICTATOR GETÚLIO VARGAS, creator of the Estado Novo, made a comeback in the 1950s, as we shall see. And he came back as a left-leaning, vote-winning populist. Vargas exemplifies the puzzle of populism. Was he really a worker's candidate, defending the little guy, or was he using pro-labor rhetoric opportunistically? The answer is yes, or rather, both. The Estado Novo had persecuted the Communist Party. It had been paternalistic in many ways. But Vargas's nationalist policies had made him truly popular among the Brazilian poor. In fact, a radiantly smiling Vargas, described as "father of the poor," became a principal theme in Brazil's *literatura de cordel* (popular narrative poems sold in cheap pamphlets on the street), a good gauge of positive lower-class attitudes.

ARGENTINA'S EVITA AND JUAN PERÓN were probably the greatest and most controversial populists of all. Their story is told in the next chapter. The bedrock of their Peronist movement was the loyalty of Argentine workers to the calm, fatherly figure of Perón and to his glamorous consort, a loyalty that has never gone away. The Peróns won this loyalty in part by raising the workers' standard of living. But there was more to it than that. Like Vargas, Perón had a famous smile that seemed to function as a blank screen on which people projected their own hopes and dreams. Officially, the Peróns espoused a political "third position"—not the left or the right—but their movement eventually split on left-right lines.

**CUBAN REVOLUTIONARIES OF 1959.** *LA ABUELA,* **BY RAUL CORRALES.** The Cuban Revolution was a truly popular movement that helped put a Marxist tilt on nationalism throughout Latin America. Marxist ideology offered a persuasive explanation of Latin American problems as well as a clear prescription for direct revolutionary action. Leaders Che Guevara and Fidel Castro quickly became heroes for young revolutionaries in many countries.

| 1946 | 1952 | 1954 | 1959 | 1961 |
|------|------|------|------|------|
| Perón elected president of Argentina | MNR takes power in Bolivia | Overthrow of Arbenz in Guatemala | Cuban revolutionaries march into Havana | Bay of Pigs invasion |

# 8.

# REVOLUTION

After World War II, Latin American industrialization lost momentum. The 1930s nationalist dream of economic independence proved difficult to achieve in the postwar world. Meanwhile, population growth accelerated as improvements in sanitation and health radically lowered the death rate. Argentina, Cuba, Colombia, and Brazil had been the world's fastest-growing countries since 1900. In 1900, there were 61 million Latin Americans; in 1950, there were 158 million and, only ten years later, already 200 million. Urban population rocketed. Buenos Aires, Rio de Janeiro, São Paulo, Mexico City, Havana, and Santiago all surpassed a million inhabitants after World War II. By 1960, Lima, Caracas, Bogotá, and Recife did, as well. Soon Latin American countries became among the most urbanized in the world. Latin American economies expanded, too, but not enough to meet the basic needs—much less the hopes and dreams—of the added millions.

Carolina Maria de Jesús had more dreams than most. In 1947, when she built herself a shack of used lumber, cardboard, and flattened tin cans in a São Paulo shantytown, she was thirty-three years old. She had come to the city seeking a better life. A single mother, she provided for her children by collecting waste paper, which she carried in a burlap bag and sold

**SHANTYTOWN DWELLERS.** As migrants poured into Latin American cities in the mid-twentieth century, many found no housing, so they constructed shanties in vacant lots. This shantytown is in an unglamorous part of Rio de Janeiro, Brazil. *The Granger Collection, New York.*

for about twenty-five cents a day. Her life resembled her neighbors' lives, except for her second-grade education. She could read and write, and her literacy gave her imagination wings. She found usable notebooks in the trash and wrote about her life and her aspirations. She had filled twenty-six notebooks when, in 1958, a reporter discovered her and published an extract of her diary. Brazilian middle-class readers were stunned to read words written in a shantytown. Her diary became a best-seller in Brazil and was eventually translated into thirteen languages. It became her ticket out of the shantytown. But millions of others stayed, eating putrid food, dying from preventable diseases, miserable and desperate.

Many in Latin America began to believe that truly revolutionary change was needed. Meanwhile, Latin American nationalists began to see their wartime "good neighbor" as, once again, their old imperialist adversary. Nationalism was at the heart of their anti-US attitude. Frequently, nationalism joined in a powerful combination with another ideology, Marxism. But not all Latin American nationalists became Marxists in the postwar period, by any means. Nationalist leaders who made a vigorous outreach to the common people without being Marxists were often called populists.

## POST–WORLD WAR II POPULISM

Populism was basically a leadership style, one that focused on mass politics and winning elections. The postwar period saw significant strides in Latin American democracy as voting was opened to women, the voting age was lowered to eighteen, and literacy requirements were struck down. Many countries made voting a legal obligation. In Brazil, a majority voted to make Getúlio Vargas president again in 1950—despite his clearly demonstrated dictatorial inclinations—because his government had raised the hope of material betterment for so many. In the postwar period, the nationalists who had come to power all over Latin America depended, as few governments before them, on the freely expressed suffrage of large numbers—basically a coalition of middle-class people and industrial workers.

Pleasing this coalition was harder than pleasing a handful of landowners here, a handful of landowners there, and trusting electoral management to do the rest, as neocolonial rulers had done. To win elections in the postwar period, the nationalists adopted populist political tactics, such as flying candidates around the country for huge rallies and making ample use of radio. The populists bashed the old rural oligarchies and their imperialistic accomplices outside the country. Populist appeals were calculated to attract working-class voters with a vision of radical improvement of living conditions, without scaring away middle-class voters with images of class warfare. Nationalism helped give a sense of unified purpose to the new coalition.

Populist politics kept power away from the *old* coalition— the combination of oligarchic and foreign economic interests— that had governed most of the region before 1930. The economic power of landowners and international financiers had been eclipsed when the great export boom went bust, but they were poised to make a comeback when the import/export system revived. The old coalition still exercised decisive influence over voting in the countryside. So Latin American nationalists had to win—and win big—in the industrializing cities.

Meanwhile, Latin American industrialization began to slow alarmingly after World War II. With imported consumer goods back on the shelves, the window of opportunity closed for ISI. US consumer goods were again available to satisfy pent-up demand. To compete, Latin American manufacturers needed *capital* goods: new machinery for their factories. Trade surpluses in the war years had provided buying power to acquire industrial machinery from Europe and the United States. But Europe was rebuilding its own factories destroyed by the war, and that rebuilding created a shortage of capital goods on the world market.

US economists, backed by unanimous US business and diplomatic pressure, recommended a return to pre-1929-style import/export trade. Latin American countries, explained the US economists, should do what they did best: concentrate on their "comparative advantage" as low-wage producers of raw materials and foodstuffs. That would help the world's industrial countries, in turn, do what *they* did best: produce all the gadgets (for instance, cars and electronics) and cultural goods (such as movies and clothing styles) that defined modernity.

According to liberal economic theory, the result would be an improved standard of living for everyone. According to Latin American nationalists, on the other hand, the result would be a return to neocolonialism. For them, industrialization had become the bottom line of national development, the only thing that could level the economic playing field between Latin America and the already industrialized countries.

This "developmentalist" interpretation found an influential voice in the Economic Commission for Latin America (ECLA), set up by the United Nations. The guiding light of ECLA was an Argentine, Raúl Prebisch, who became the most influential Latin American economist ever. His economic analysis focused on Latin America's "peripheral" position (exporting raw materials) within a global economy increasingly dominated by an already industrialized "center" (the United States and Europe). For most Latin American economists, Prebisch's center-periphery, or *dependency*, model replaced the liberal theory of comparative advantage as a guide to action. The problem, they believed, was not how to find comparative advantages on the periphery, but how to escape from it and join the industrialized center.

During the postwar years, then, Latin American nationalists faced a set of stiff challenges: urgent social needs, a counterattack from their old political adversaries, a weakening economic base, and the hostility of the United States. Populist politics was, in large measure, a response to these challenges. Events in Argentina, Brazil, and Mexico illustrate variants on the populist theme.

Argentina, the richest, most industrialized, urban, and literate country in Latin America during this time, also had the most dynamic nationalist movement: Peronism. The Argentine military had controlled the country during the 1930s, acting sometimes as nationalists of a right-wing sort, but more often as guardians of the old social hierarchy. Juan Perón, for whom the Peronist movement is named, was a nationalist army officer who, as secretary of labor, won a strong following among Argentine workers. Fearing Perón's influence, the government removed him, but on 17 October 1945, an immense demonstration of workers converged on downtown Buenos Aires to demand his return. Ever after, Peronists solemnly commemorated 17 October as Peronist Loyalty Day, and their enemies annually groaned about it as Saint Perón's Day. Perón gave the frightened Argentine elite a lot to groan about after his election by a wide margin in 1946.

Perón's presidency of Argentina (1946–55) witnessed the rapid unionization of the country's industrial workforce. For decades, the industrial working class would remain the mainstay of the Peronist movement. Perón and his wife, Eva Duarte— Evita to the millions who adored her—raged, in good nationalist fashion, at the traditional landowning oligarchy, a class unloved by urban people in general. Evita played a large role in mobilizing the Peronist movement. Her dramatic gestures in favor of Argentina's poor helped the movement to broaden its populist constituency beyond organized labor.

A glamorous actress of radio soap operas when she met Perón, Evita had been poor and socially ostracized as a girl. She, too, had come to Buenos Aires from "the sticks," at the same time as had so many Peronist workers. She felt she understood them. She certainly spoke their language. Even her lavish wardrobe, with a Eurochic far from Frida Kahlo's peasant garb, suited the Argentine workers' taste. Evita's flashy style invited them to savor her triumph: "I'm one of you. And I haven't forgotten you. My glory is yours, too." Her greatest pride, she declared, lay in deserving "the love of the humble and the hatred of oligarchs." She created a Social Aid Foundation where she liked to hand out charity personally.

Evita helped win the vote for Argentine women in 1947 and advocated equal pay for equal work. But her slavish adoration of Perón reeked of patriarchal tradition, and she believed that a woman's highest aspiration should be marriage and mother- hood: "We were born to be homemakers, not to go around in the street." Evita never used the word "leader" to describe her- self. "*He* is the leader," she said of her husband. "I am only the shadow of his superior presence." In her impassioned speeches, more powerful than Perón's, Evita presented herself as a medi- ator, a "bridge of love between Perón and the people." Evita died suddenly of cancer in 1952, amid wrenching demonstra- tions of public grief. The picture on page 248 shows Evita's last public appearance, shortly before her death.

Nationalism guided Peronist economics, and the United States protested vociferously. The Peronist government tried to end foreign ownership of, well, almost everything in Argentina. In addition to public utilities, it bought or expropriated the country's important meatpacking plants, banks and insurance companies, and, most famously, the extensive British-owned railway system. At the same time, it expanded social services and the bureaucracy to administer them. The centerpiece of the Peronist program was a five-year drive for industrialization- or-bust, subsidized at the cost of the agricultural export sector. What happened, however, was more bust than industrial- ization. A severe economic downturn and an unpopular tiff with the Vatican undermined the movement's middle-class support.

The military exiled Perón in 1955. But Peronism, by improving workers' lives, restoring their dignity, and, above all, giving them hope, had won a permanent place in many Argentine hearts. Perón could activate Peronist loyalties even from exile. In 1957, for example, a quarter of the electorate voided its ballots in response to his remote control. The Peronists could not quite govern, but nobody else could rule without them. A rocky road lay ahead for Argentina.

Brazilian history ran more or less parallel, except that Brazil's populist coalition was not as strong. Brazil's urban working and middle classes, in a country more rural and more dependent on export agriculture, remained proportionately much weaker than Argentina's. Still, the Vargas years had created momentum—and the Vargas years were not over. When the Brazilian military ushered Vargas out of office in 1945, the nationalist leader had already prepared a populist comeback by founding not one, but two political parties. Vargas returned to the presidency in 1950 as the victorious candidate of one of these, the Brazilian Workers' Party. But he accomplished little. In 1954, he committed presidential suicide, quite literally. His suicide note ranted against dark "forces and interests" that "sucked the blood of the Brazilian people" and frustrated his nationalist goals. The dramatic death of Vargas produced an awesome outpouring of public grief, similar to the Argentine reaction at Evita's death two years previously.

Brazil's populist coalition bumped ahead under other presidents. But development fever upstaged the commitment to the impoverished millions like Carolina Maria de Jesús. The new capital at Brasília, conceived as an ultramodern design of massive, widely spaced apartment blocks, was constructed with vast outlays of government resources at the expense of surging inflation. Its location in the sparsely populated interior of the country optimistically signaled a new frontier. Its design was decided by an international competition and reflected the futuristic urban planning of Le Corbusier. Brasília's strikingly original public buildings, such as the partly subterranean cathedral, made their creator, Oscar Niemeyer, the best-known Latin American architect of the century. This "space-age" urban mirage took shape in the late 1950s, during the poignant years of hardship described in Carolina de Jesús's diary. Inaugurated in

1960, Brasília is the perfect symbol of the post-Vargas moment in Brazil.

The perfect symbol of the moment in Mexico, on the other hand, was the PRI: the Institutional Revolutionary Party, with an accent on *Institutional* rather than *Revolutionary*. The military had now been definitively subordinated to the PRI, and Mexico had a one-party system of admirable stability—but questionable democracy—in which each outgoing president handpicked the next PRI candidate. And the PRI candidate never lost. The only thing "revolutionary" about the PRI now was a nationalist devotion to the Mexican Revolution's heroes and slogans. But the Mexican Revolution, if defined as a fight for social justice and a vindication of the downtrodden masses, was dead in the postwar period.

Mexican industrial growth continued, however. Landowner power had been definitively shattered, and the PRI held the political loyalty of the many who had benefited from land reform. Because the government marketed food grown on the restored common lands called *ejidos*, it could hold food prices down and thereby, in effect, subsidize urban living standards. Although the Mexican Revolution had been largely a rural uprising, its ultimate winners were urban people. Industrialization continued. The Mexican currency held rock-steady, in contrast to roaring inflation elsewhere. As in Brazil, the economic pie grew overall, but the redistribution of wealth stopped. The majority of Mexicans would not see great improvement in their welfare during the PRI's half-century rule.

## ONSET OF THE COLD WAR

The 1950s were a time of frustration for most Latin Americans. The United States, now definitively replacing Europe as the ultimate model of Progress, displayed a brilliant postwar prosperity, with living standards previously unimaginable.

Glossy magazines and movies showed Latin Americans what they were missing. The good life, proclaimed US media, meant having a refrigerator, even a car. But, for most Latin Americans, to have a refrigerator was a stretch—and a car, absurdly out of reach. Having modeled "the good life" to this attentive and yearning audience, the United States offered little help in getting there.

Now a superpower, preeminent in the world, completely unchallenged in the hemisphere, the United States no longer seemed a good neighbor. Latin American disenchantment with the United States began in 1947, with the announcement of the US Marshall Plan. The Marshall Plan spent vast sums rebuilding Europe to jump-start postwar prosperity and limit the appeal of communism. Among the major recipients of Marshall Plan aid were the US enemies of World War II. Former Latin American allies of the United States, also struggling for prosperity, thought they rated similar help; but Latin America got only about 2 percent of US foreign aid between 1946 and 1959. Latin American diplomats raised the issue at hemispheric meetings, but US priorities lay elsewhere. Western Europe, with the Soviet armies nearby and vigorous communist parties in several countries, was judged the danger zone, followed by Asia. Latin American issues hardly concerned US policymakers.

So, instead of aid, Latin Americans got a lean diet of diplomatic pressure from the United States. In 1947, the United States convened hemispheric nations to sign the Rio Pact, a permanent Pan-American defensive alliance. In 1949, China's communist revolution triumphed, and Soviet Russia tested an atomic bomb. Now the Cold War began in earnest.

The US population was thirsty for coffee, hungry for bananas, and ready, having shifted away from arms production (although the "military-industrial complex" formed a permanent pillar of the postwar economy), to provide consumer goods in return.

The few more-sophisticated, heavier industries that now began to appear in Latin America were often subsidiaries of US multinational corporations. They routinely installed used machines that had been retired from their US plants, equipment already obsolete in the United States. The result, logically enough, was factories planned *not* to be competitive with those in the United States—a bitter pill for nationalists bent on economic independence. According to the ECLA analysis, this kind of industrialization only reinforced the economic subordination of Latin America. For US policymakers, on the other hand, the expansion of the multinational corporations was a natural development of global capitalism. Free-market capitalism was viewed as "American," and US prosperity depended on it, at home and abroad. Any kind of Latin American economic nationalism was therefore "un-American," something to be combated.

In the grip of an anticommunist witch hunt at home, the US State Department began to regard virtually any Latin American opposition as a sign of "creeping communism." The principal venue of US anticommunist diplomacy was the Organization of American States (OAS), a beefed-up version of the Pan-American Union, no longer managed exclusively by the United States but always dominated by it. Rather famously, a chorus of unsavory dictators such as Rafael Trujillo in the Dominican Republic, "Papa Doc" Duvalier in Haiti, and Anastasio Somoza in Nicaragua followed the US line in the OAS, overwhelming any opposition (on a one country–one vote basis) from larger nations like Mexico, Brazil, and Argentina. In 1954, the OAS issued the Declaration of Caracas, saying that all Marxist revolutionary ideology was necessarily alien to the Western Hemisphere. Therefore, Marxist revolutionary movements, composed of peasants, workers, and university students, would be treated as foreign invasions. US diplomats had begun to view Latin America strictly through Cold War goggles. Everywhere, they saw red—or, at least, "pink."

In Venezuela, for example, US diplomats endorsed the dictator Marcos Pérez Jiménez, who had hosted the 1954 meeting of the OAS, because they thought Pérez Jiménez was at least better than the nationalists of Venezuela's Democratic Action Party. Democratic Action had convincingly won Venezuela's free election of 1947, but it was too "pink" by half for the US State Department. On the other hand, the dictator Pérez Jiménez, who made both Democratic Action and the Communist Party illegal, seemed reliably friendly to US oil companies, now in the midst of a major Venezuelan oil boom. Like Trujillo, Duvalier, and Somoza, Pérez Jiménez was unsavory—but nonetheless acceptable as one of "our bastards."

Guatemala's OAS representative voted alone against the anticommunist Declaration of Caracas, calling instead for Latin American solidarity against US pressures. Here—infuriatingly, for US diplomats—was the "pinkest" Latin American government of the hemisphere. To combat it, the US State Department abandoned its 1933 pledge of nonintervention in the internal affairs of Latin American countries. Instead of sending in US Marines, however, it inaugurated an indirect form of military intervention—the "proxy" force, recruited among the local enemies of the targeted government. Proxy forces were armed and trained, usually in secret, by another new player of the cold war era, the Central Intelligence Agency (CIA).

Following a string of grim dictators, Guatemala had enjoyed an exciting and hopeful "decade of spring" between 1944 and 1954. Two democratic elections had seated nationalist presidents, one after another, by wide margins—unprecedented events in the country's history. The first of these reformist presidents was Juan José Arévalo, a formerly exiled university professor who returned to oversee legislative advances such as social security, a new labor code, and a new constitution. Although hardly radical, he described his philosophy as "spiritual socialism," troubling words for US diplomats and for officers of the

United Fruit Company, with large banana plantations in the country. When the nationalist government urged better pay for Guatemalan workers, accusations of "communistic" behavior sounded in Washington.

Then came the second reformist president, an idealistic thirty-seven-year-old army officer named Jacobo Arbenz. Arbenz went beyond speeches and legislation to push for big changes on the ground. In this country where half the people were illiterate Mayan peasants, treated more or less like animals by the owners of the coffee plantations, who retained great influence, Arbenz started to confiscate large estates and divide them up for peasant cultivators. In addition, his government expropriated land from United Fruit, along with Guatemala's foreign-owned railway. The cries of communism now became intense, both in the United States and in Guatemala.

The Arbenz government was doing no more than other nationalist governments (and the United States in the radical 1930s) had done before it. But Guatemala was small, close, and previously obedient to the United States. Furthermore, just as the US diplomats suspected, Marxist ideas were becoming increasingly persuasive to nationalists in Guatemala. Arbenz had embraced them, and so had many of the shop-floor activists who propelled the country's unionization and the grassroots organizers who carried out the land reform. Some became members of the Communist Party, and many believed, along with millions of other Latin American nationalists, that the United States was their imperialist enemy, bent on bleeding them dry. A number of important US policymakers, including Secretary of State John Foster Dulles, had a personal interest in the United Fruit Company's banana empire. The same was true of 1954 CIA chief Allen Dulles, John's brother.

Most Guatemalan generals were far more conservative than Arbenz. Revolutionaries within the Arbenz government wanted to arm a people's militia as a counterforce to the army. They arranged for an arms shipment from Czechoslovakia, then part of the Soviet-controlled Eastern bloc, the last straw for US policymakers. Shortly thereafter, a US proxy force invaded from Honduras. Instead of fighting the invasion force, which was puny, the Guatemalan army joined it, ousting Arbenz. The State Department then announced a landmark victory for "democracy" in Guatemala. But the post-Arbenz military rule of Guatemala turned out, by all accounts, to be utterly murderous. As the decades passed and the grisly death toll mounted, US diplomats began to view the intervention of 1954 as a tragic overreaction. To see why, let us compare Guatemala to Bolivia, another mostly indigenous country with similar problems and about equal population.

Bolivia's National Revolutionary Movement (MNR) took power in 1952, just as the Arbenz government moved into its final phase. The MNR was entirely as nationalist as the government of Arbenz. In addition, the MNR showed clear Marxist influences. But because Bolivia is farther away from the United States, because US business interests were less affected by MNR expropriations, and because the Moscow-oriented Communist Party clearly lacked clout in Bolivia, the US State Department decided to remain "constructively engaged" with the MNR. Instead of arming a proxy force, it sent US aid.

Bolivian wealth rested on tin mining, much of it controlled by three incredibly opulent Bolivian families who lived in Europe. It was said that the young heir of the Patiño family, the richest clan of all, got an allowance larger than the country's budget for public education. The MNR received support from the miners' unions and their militias, who made deafening displays of their sentiments by tossing lit sticks of dynamite, a tool of their trade, the way mischievous boys elsewhere throw firecrackers. The MNR nationalized the tin mines and conferred substantial improvements in wages and benefits on the miners.

Indigenous Bolivians, whose peasant communities had been losing their land steadily for generations, now took the initiative, and the MNR supervised a substantial land reform. Almost sixty thousand poor families got title to a parcel of land to farm. Another important move of the revolutionary government—mindful of events in Guatemala, no doubt—was to reduce the power of the Bolivian army to a shadow of its former self.

Revolutionary change took a toll on middle-class living standards, however. Peasants with title to land now fed their own families better, so they sent less food to urban markets, raising prices there. Improved conditions for miners cut into the profits of Bolivia's main export earner. Furthermore, because tin refining continued to be done outside the country, where refiners kept the price of tin as low as possible, the mines began to operate in the red. Consequently, more conservative elements within the MNR gained influence, and US aid strengthened their hand. In the long run, the US policy of "constructive engagement" with the Bolivian revolution proved more effective than the Guatemalan-style intervention. Bolivian peasants and miners still got the land and wages they deserved, and the country's government steered clear of Soviet Russia.

As the 1950s advanced, the battle lines of the Cold War began to affect everything that happened in Latin America, even literature. Literature has always been political in the region, and during the Cold War, most authors sided with the left.

Take Nobel laureate Pablo Neruda. The most popular poet of twentieth-century Latin America, Neruda was lusty, expansive, democratic, and plainspoken. His *Twenty Poems of Love and One Desperate Song* (1924) are among the most widely recognized and recited in the Spanish language. Neruda's greatest theme was "América" itself—mostly Spanish America—but he roamed the world over. Like Gabriela Mistral, Chile's earlier Nobel Prize–winning poet, Neruda held a series of diplomatic posts, serving as consul in Asia, Europe, and the Americas between 1927 and 1945. This sort of tribute to literary talent is a Latin American tradition. Neruda's heart was with "the people," which meant, in mid-twentieth-century Latin America, siding with the revolutionaries. After World War II, he returned to Chile and devoted himself to revolutionary politics. In 1945, Neruda was elected senator for Chile's Communist Party. The great poet's reputation was at its height as the Cold War settled over Latin America in the 1950s and 1960s.

Argentina's Jorge Luis Borges, another literary giant with an international reputation, makes an interesting contrast to Neruda. Like Neruda and many other Latin American authors, Borges had strong international affiliations. He spent a few years in Switzerland, studied briefly at Cambridge, and translated works from German, French, and above all, English. Borges loved the English language and even wrote some poetry of his own in English. But the Argentine Borges was a retiring and bookish man, far different from the carousing, rambling Neruda. Born in Buenos Aires, Borges seldom left there for long. And for most of his life, he was blind. His world was a private, shadowy theater of *Fictions* and *Dreamtigers*, the titles of two of his books. For Borges, rustic gauchos and the brawling poor neighborhoods of Buenos Aires were literary motifs. He liked them as themes for an Argentine national literature, but he was no "man of the people" and he sympathized with the military in its long struggle against Perón. Nevertheless, Borges created short stories so startlingly innovative and imaginative that he became, if anything, more influential in literature than Neruda. Many believe that Borges never won the Nobel Prize only because of his unpopular right-wing views.

## THE CUBAN REVOLUTION

After the 1950s, Latin American nationalists increasingly adopted a Marxist perspective on history and a revolutionary vision of the future. Influential poets, novelists, artists, folk-singers, and social scientists—not to mention outspoken students at public universities throughout the region—expressed the Marxist revolutionary vision. And they did so just as anti-communism became the overriding imperative of US policy toward Latin America.

The rise of Marxist ideology among Latin American nationalists had little to do with Soviet Russia, a remote, unhelpful, and uninspiring ally. Nor was the Marxist dream of a perfect future without inequalities or injustice more convincing in Latin America than elsewhere. It was Marxist historical analysis that made persuasive sense to Latin American nationalists bent on dismantling neocolonialism. The Marxist view of capitalism, highlighting class exploitation, seemed an apt description of Latin American experience. The Leninist theory of imperialism—suggesting that a privileged class within the dominated countries would profit from collaboration with the outsiders' imperial plan—also seemed quite accurate in Latin America. In the 1950s, Marxism was becoming associated with nationalist struggles for decolonization and self-determination around the world. And if the imperialist United States hated and feared Marxism, many Latin Americans found that simply a further incentive to study it.

The Marxist diagnosis of Latin America's big problems was injustice—not a wrong policy here, a bad decision there, but injustice woven into the fabric of a society founded on conquest and dedicated, over the centuries, to maintaining inequalities. The prognosis was grave. Rapid population growth and urbanization were creating massive shortages of the most basic social necessities. Children on the street, whole neighborhoods built on garbage dumps—the toll in diminished lives was (and is) unspeakable. The recommended treatment was revolution, not reform. And by revolution, Marxists meant not simply a new, better government overthrowing a corrupt old one, but rather a full reshuffling of the social deck, pulling down the well-to-do and powerful who had enjoyed their privileges for so long in the presence of misery—worse, *at the expense of* misery—and redistributing the wealth among everybody. Social revolutionaries did not hesitate to confiscate fortunes extracted from generations of slaves and indebted peons. And they believed that US multinationals were only a new version of the Spanish and Portuguese empires, siphoning riches from what one influential book called *The Open Veins of Latin America*. Aspirin would not cure this cancer, believed the Marxist revolutionaries. The situation called for major surgery.

An Argentine medical student, later famous as "Che" Guevara (his real name was Ernesto), reached this conclusion in the early 1950s. Rebellion ran in Che's family. His mother before him had gained a radical reputation by brazenly smoking cigarettes in public. Che thought that Latin American poverty was linked to, and maintained by, an imperialist international economic system of awesome power. The victims of that system, among whom Che included all the countries of Latin America, could free themselves only by acting together. He began to show his "internationalist" vocation by cycling for thousands of miles to see for himself the poverty and oppression of the indigenous peoples of the Andes. Then, hearing of inspiring reforms underway in Arbenz's Guatemala, Che went to participate. From Guatemala, he escaped to Mexico when US-backed army officers toppled Arbenz in 1954. Che was now a bona fide Marxist revolutionary, "a soldier of America," as he told his father when he left home, and he considered the battle against capitalist imperialism *his* battle, anywhere in the world.

In Mexico, Che met Fidel Castro, a different kind of revolutionary, an intense nationalist immersed in the political traditions and struggles of his own county, Cuba. Castro was the son of a sugarcane-growing family who, as a law student in the late 1940s, was inspired by the idealistic, mildly socialist, and above all, keenly anti-imperialist themes of the student movement. In Cuba, as in Latin America as a whole, 1950s anti-imperialist attitudes focused almost exclusively on the United States, and nowhere were anti-imperialist feelings stronger than among Cuban nationalists. When US diplomats orchestrated the formation of the OAS in 1948 in Bogotá, Colombia, Castro traveled there to attend a parallel anti-imperialist meeting of student activists. In opposing the United States, the internationalist Che and the nationalist Fidel saw eye to eye.

The two met in Mexico because Fidel, along with his brother Raúl and others, had been exiled from Cuba. Their crime was resisting the US-backed military dictatorship of yet another of "our bastards," one Fulgencio Batista. In 1953, shortly after an elected Cuban government was overthrown by Batista, the Castro brothers led a disastrous attack on the dictator's army. But their gesture of defiance, which cost the student rebels many lives, proved popular with the Cuban people. Fidel and Raúl Castro were let out of prison and shipped off to Mexico as a sign of dictatorial benevolence. Within a couple of years, in late 1956, they were ready to launch their next pinprick attack on Batista, whom they regarded—because of his US backing and his staunch support of US anticommunism in the OAS—as an agent of imperialism.

The eighty-two invaders—many of them idealistic, middle-class youngsters—crowded aboard an incongruous assault vehicle, an old yacht with the unwarlike name, ironically in English, *Granma*. Their landing in Cuba did not go well, partly because local peasants alerted the army, and only a handful of the *Granma's* assault force survived to make history. In the meantime, they made legend, beginning with the magical number of remaining fighters—twelve, the number of Christ's disciples, symbolic of the guerrillas' physical vulnerability and spiritual superiority. Fidel, Raúl, and Che—now amounting personally to a quarter of the invasion force—made it into the Sierra Maestra mountains of eastern Cuba, where they successfully played a deadly game of hide-and-seek with the army for the next two years. A series of highly sympathetic articles about them appeared in the *New York Times*. Even the US government began to qualify its support of Batista, and resistance to the dictator inside Cuba became virtually unanimous. Seeing no future, Batista suddenly left the country on the last day of 1958, and the bearded guerrillas of the mountains met a tumultuous welcome in Havana.

To show that their revolution had only just begun, they did not shave or take off their khakis. The revolutionaries dispensed rough justice against the dictator's henchmen, trying and executing 483 of them in three months. At interminable mass rallies and equally interminable televised speeches, Castro explained his vision of a new Cuba. The revolutionary government retained a high level of popular support. Anyone watching the nationalist revolutions that had swept over Latin America in the twentieth century knew what to expect: measures against "economic imperialism," possibly including expropriation of foreign companies, and, above all, land reform. Land reform began almost immediately, in May 1959.

Which side would the new Cuban government be on in the Cold War? That was the US State Department's main question, overshadowing even the very considerable US economic interest in Cuba. The creation of "a Communist beachhead ninety miles from our shores" would be intolerable in their eyes. Was Castro a communist?

Never—not as a student radical in the 1940s, nor as a guerrilla leader in the 1950s—was Castro close to the Moscow-line Cuban Communist Party. Nor had the Communist Party played any substantial part in the overthrow of Batista. But when Fidel went on television for his five-hour chat on the structural changes of a "real revolution," the Marxist inspiration of his vision was obvious. The only thing that could reassure people in the United States, it seemed, was a demonstration that the Cuban Revolution would be aligned with the United States against international communism. In their own terms, the Cuban revolutionaries were being asked to betray everything they had fought for: to side with "economic imperialism" against the forces of "national liberation." Fidel and Che never even considered it.

And Castro had a way of rubbing in the point. On a 1960 trip to New York, he delivered a four-hour lecture in the United Nations on the topic of US imperialism. At a Harlem hotel, he met with Malcolm X and other critics of US policies at home and abroad. In February of the same year, he began to arrange an alternative Russian market for Cuban sugar, long sold almost exclusively in the United States, and in June he bought Russian oil, offered at an advantageous price. When Cuba's US-owned oil refineries refused to process this "red" crude, Fidel expropriated them. In July came the US government's response: an end to US purchases of Cuban sugar, responsible for three quarters of Cuba's export revenue. In August, the revolutionary government struck back by expropriating more US-owned property, from sugar mills and mines to telephone and electric companies. In the second half of 1960, the United States declared an embargo on all trade with Cuba, and word reached Havana of a proxy force being trained and equipped by the CIA to invade the island.

This time, however, the proxy technique failed miserably. Despite their hopes, the anti-Castro Cubans who landed at

the Bay of Pigs in 1961 sparked no internal rebellion. The new
Cuban army was a direct outgrowth of Castro's revolutionary
army of 1956–58 and totally loyal to him. It quickly defeated
these invaders. But they seemed unlikely to be the last invaders. The Cuban military alignment with Soviet Russia, what
US policymakers had so dreaded, now took shape as a defense
against new invasions from the United States.

In mid-1962, high-flying US spy planes called U-2s began to
photograph nuclear missile installations under construction,
and in October they got a clear picture of a missile. A few days
later, US President John F. Kennedy issued an ultimatum to
the Russians: withdraw the missiles "or else." The world held
its breath. The Cuban Missile Crisis was one of the most dangerous moments in the Cold War. Finally, the Soviets agreed
to remove their missiles in return for a US agreement not to
invade Cuba. Aside from petty harassment by the CIA—
involving such escapades as an exploding cigar and schemes to
make Fidel's beard fall out—the military threat from the United
States had ended.

The debilitating effects of the US embargo, however, would
go on for decades. The intention was to cut off not only US
trade, but also all trade between Cuba and countries allied
with the United States. Cuban trade with the rest of Latin
America was strangled thanks to the US grip on the OAS. Sanc-
tions applied even to Cuba's trade with neutral countries. Any
vessel that docked in Cuba would be unwelcome afterward in
US harbors. As a result, Cuba's external trade shifted decisively
to distant countries aligned with Soviet Russia.

Cuba was expelled from the OAS despite the opposition of
the largest Latin American countries. Here, again, was the
power of the many small countries that always voted with the
United States in the OAS. Gradually, Cuba became a center for
resistance to US policy in Latin America and a training ground
for Marxist revolutionaries. Moscow had decided that, in most

of Latin America, conditions propitious for a social revolution did not yet exist. But Che Guevara had developed a new theory of guerrilla warfare based on the Cuban experience in the Sierra Maestra mountains. Revolutionary conditions could be created, thought Che, by small, committed guerrilla groups like the *Granma* expedition. These groups would establish *focos*, focal points of guerrilla activity to jump-start a larger revolution. Che himself vowed to repeat the Sierra Maestra experience on a continental scale—to make the Andes "the Sierra Maestra of South America." His ill-fated Bolivian mission, which began in 1966, was meant to do just that.

Che traveled to Bolivia disguised as a balding Uruguayan businessman and launched his continental revolution with a mere fifty guerrillas—thirty Bolivians and various international (especially Cuban) volunteers. This time, though, the tiny but idealistic revolutionary force did not triumph. Che himself suffered from prolonged asthma attacks that incapacitated him and disheartened his followers. The Bolivian peasants were suspicious of the guerrillas, and none joined the movement. Meanwhile, the Bolivian army picked them off one by one, until only a handful remained; still, when he was finally captured, interrogated, and executed in 1968, Che had become a hero throughout Latin America, not so much for what he did as for how he died trying.

Che had left Cuba partly because of his own frustrations there. Che was a theorist and visionary who believed that, for true socialism to function, money should be abolished and people should work for ideals. But as revolutionary president of Cuba's national bank, then minister of industry in the early 1960s, he found those changes easier to envision than to implement. Che had been foremost among those insisting that the sugar-heavy Cuban economy must diversify and industrialize. He had shaped the revolution's first assault on the problem of underdevelopment, an impatient "crash" industrialization

plan. Grand promises of aid came from Soviet-aligned countries in Europe and also from China. The Soviet government
alone pledged to build a hundred factories in Cuba, but it soon
changed its tune. Like the United States, Soviet Russia really
preferred to exchange its own manufactured products for Cuban
sugar. Could the revolution harness sugar—that old dragon,
devourer of generations of slaves and other impoverished
workers—for the common good? Maybe so, thought stubbornly
optimistic Cuban revolutionaries in the late 1960s. The sugar
plantations, along with nearly everything else, now belonged to
the Cuban state, making them the property of the Cuban people. So, in the years after Che's death, Castro pursued a startling
new economic goal—a ten-million-ton sugar harvest.

As the revolutionary government worked feverishly to
increase production, middle-class people reluctantly volun-
teered to blister their hands chopping sugarcane on the week-
ends. Dissent was not permitted. When a well-known poet
was publicly silenced, the news produced unease among revolutionary sympathizers inside and outside Cuba.

Many outsiders were rooting for the Cuban Revolution. In
then-communist East Germany, university student Tamara
Bunke, later better known by her guerrilla pseudonym, Tania,
felt that the Cuban Revolution was also her fight. Tania was
born and grew up in Buenos Aires, where the Bunke family had
fled to escape the Nazis during the 1930s, returning to Germany
after World War II. When Che Guevara led a trade mission to
East Germany in 1960, Tania was his interpreter. Inspired by the
revolution's project to transform Latin America, she traveled to
Cuba and threw herself into work brigades, the militia, the literacy campaign—but she wanted something more heroic. By
1964, she got it, going to Bolivia alone as a secret agent to lay the
groundwork for Che's last, doomed campaign. By 1967 she was
dead, along with almost all the others. In death, she became a
hemispheric symbol of revolutionary commitment and self-

**POLICE VERSUS STUDENTS.** Guatemalan students battle police during a street demonstration in 1962. Many university students, along with artists, intellectuals, and unionized workers, were inspired by the Cuban Revolution during the 1960s. *AP Photo.*

sacrifice, much like Che himself. From Argentina to Mexico, baby girls were named Tania in her honor.

There were musical reverberations of revolution throughout Latin America, too. Folk music with protest themes became the international sound track of revolutionary organizing. Undercover in Bolivia, Tania had posed as a folk music collector. The spiritual mother of this "new song" movement was a Chilean woman, Violeta Parra. Parra was not of the sixties generation. In fact, she was old enough to be the mother of the young protest singers who gathered around her in the 1960s. Several were, in fact, her children. Parra, a superb lyricist herself, was steeped in Chilean folk music. Her music was more personal than revolutionary, and personal despair led her to commit suicide in 1967, the same year of Tania's death. But to the sixties generation, her music represented an authentic Latin American spirit of protest.

Parra killed herself with characteristic flair in a *carpa*, a tent set
up in the tradition of traveling folk performers. The young musi-
cians whom she had inspired soon scattered. Ultimately, Havana
would be the international center of the "new song" movement.

By the late 1960s, the Cuban Revolution had become a potent
symbol for young people all over the hemisphere. All but the
most committed Latin American anticommunists felt immense
satisfaction at seeing a Cuban David stand up to the US Goli-
ath. For Latin American socialists—including more and more
students, union leaders, and young people in general—the
Cuban Revolution had a lot to show. It had vastly increased educational opportunities, making decisive strides toward full literacy and exemplary public health. It had improved housing in
long-neglected rural Cuba. It had championed the full equality
of black Cubans, who before the revolution had been legally
banned from some beaches to suit the race prejudice of US
tourists. Cuban movies and poster art, particularly, communi-
cated the promise of a vibrant, creative revolution throughout
Latin America. Cuba's Casa de las Americas offered the region's
most prestigious literary prize. Cuban nationalists, so long frustrated by Spain's long rule in Cuba and the humiliating Platt
Amendment, gloried in the revolution. For them, Cuba's international prominence helped compensate for what the revolution
did *not* offer.

The Cuban Revolution did not offer the individual liberties so
central to liberalism, such as the right to speak against the government and to travel outside the country. These received a low
priority in revolutionary thinking. Only a small minority in Latin
America could afford to travel outside the country anyway, reasoned the revolutionaries. If revolution was major surgery, the
operating room would need tight discipline. Why permit anyone
to disrupt the team spirit? Restoring hope of a decent life to
the destitute majority seemed worth infringing the personal
liberties of the most fortunate citizens.

To anticommunists, especially in the United States but also in Latin America, the surgery of social revolution created a Frankenstein's monster—unnatural, powerful, and frightening. Communism challenged not only individual liberties but also older, even more traditional values like patriarchy and social hierarchy. Anticommunists regarded the revolutionary vision as "brainwashing" or the consequence of a viruslike contagion. And suddenly, from the perspective of US anticommunists only recently attentive to events south of the border, the contagion was here, in "our backyard"—"just ninety miles from our shores," in fact. The stage was set for conflict.

# COUNTERCURRENTS:
## Liberation Theology

Mass in the rural Andes. *Photograph by Severo Salazar.* © *Panes Pictures/*
TAFOS

The Catholic Church played no part in the Cuban Revolution, which totally marginalized religion and turned churches into public auditoriums. Historically, the Catholic Church had been, above all, a powerful bulwark of the status quo and therefore a prime target of revolutionaries. But churchmen could be revolutionaries, too. Father Miguel Hidalgo and Father José María Morelos had shown that during Mexico's independence struggle. Friar Bartolomé de las Casas, the early advocate for indigenous people, had led the way in the 1500s.

In the 1960s, Latin America's radical priests again followed the lead of Las Casas. Father Camilo Torres was one. A son of the Colombian upper class, Torres taught Latin America's most "subversive" academic discipline, sociology, at the National University. Sociologists were seen as "pink" because they talked a lot about social class, a favorite Marxist category of analysis. Torres did sound like the Cuban revolutionaries when he demanded "fundamental change in economic, social, and political structures," something he believed Colombia's traditional Liberal and Conservative Parties could never accomplish. Torres desired revolution, which he saw as "the way to bring about a government that feeds the hungry, clothes the naked, teaches the ignorant, and puts into practice works of charity and brotherly love." Father Torres joined a guerrilla army and died fighting in 1966.

Religious revolutionaries of the early 1960s saw Latin America's problems much as the Marxist revolutionaries did. Only a few joined guerrilla armies, however. Most believed that faith and good works were more powerful than guns. They took inspiration from the work of Paulo Freire, the region's greatest teacher of literacy, then at work among the peasants of impoverished northeastern Brazil. Freire argued that peasants were intelligent adults eager to empower themselves. He believed that methods used with schoolchildren were not appropriate in helping poor adults learn to read. For illiterate adults, learning to read and write meant taking greater charge of their own lives. So Freire developed a method of interactive learning and, to describe it, coined the term "consciousness-raising."

In 1968, when the Conference of Latin American Bishops held a landmark meeting in Medellín, Colombia, the bishops discussed the usefulness of Freire's approach. They agreed that the church should take "a preferential option for the poor," and they discussed the formation of Christian "base communities," in which believers would gather to read and discuss the Bible in something like one of Freire's literacy groups The bishops also talked of liberating people from the "institutionalized violence" of poverty. This was not violence in the ordinary sense. Rather, Latin America's Catholic bishops had begun to see hunger, ignorance, and rampant disease as tragically preventable damage to human lives. Governments that failed to prevent that damage were committing institutionalized violence. Its victims often saw the damage they suffered as something natural, an inevitable part of being poor. Consciousness-raising in Christian base communities could unmask institutionalized violence and strip away its seeming naturalness. Here were Catholic teachings designed to undermine, rather than reinforce, Latin America's ancient patterns of hierarchy and hegemony. This new message said nothing about suffering patiently through life to gain heavenly compensation. Instead, it called for soup kitchens, day care co-ops, neighborhood organizing, and demands for government responsibility. In a region well-known for religious fervor, the result might be powerful. That, at least, was the hope of priests and nuns who lived and worked in poor neighborhoods.

"Liberation theology" became the general name for the movement that had crystallized at the 1968 bishops' conference. Liberation theology immediately stirred enormous interest, both for and against. Conservatives pointed to Father Camilo Torres and cried "Communism!" In fact, the religious revolutionaries did have something in common with the Marxist ones. They shared a sense of emergency and the basic premise that Latin America required sweeping, fundamental change. They were equally committed to relieving the plight of the poor. Both believed that existing power structures were stacked against them. Despite the many disagreements between Marxist and Christian ideologies, these revolutionaries could logically see each other as potential allies.

A conservative reaction began immediately within the Catholic Church itself. Exponents of liberation theology have been passionate and eloquent, but never a majority. By the late 1970s, a new pope, John Paul II, threw the power of the Vatican fully against them. John Paul's formative experience as a Catholic leader in communist Poland made him inexorably opposed to Marxism, and he believed that Latin America's religious revolutionaries had crossed the line. The Vatican's campaign began at the 1978 Conference of Latin American Bishops held in the Mexican city of Puebla. It included the systematic appointment of Latin American bishops hostile to liberation theology and even the official "silencing" of liberation theologians. Likewise, the pope visited Nicaragua in 1983 to support a conservative archbishop against Sandinista revolutionary leaders who were Catholic clergy and exponents of liberation theology. (The Sandinista revolution will be discussed in the next chapter.) "Silence!" shouted the pope three times at the angry pro-Sandinista crowd, in a memorable moment of direct confrontation. Gradually, the liberation theology movement lost momentum in the 1980s before even 1 percent of Latin Americans had participated in a Christian-based community.

**MOTHERS OF THE PLAZA DE MAYO.** The return of *niños desaparecidos*, "disappeared children," is what these Buenos Aires protestors demanded, day after day, in front of the presidential palace during the 1980s. Carrying banners and poster-size photos of the children whom they wanted back alive, the courageous mothers had to settle more often for news of their children's abduction and clandestine murder by the Argentine military during its "dirty war" against Marxist guerrillas called Montoneros. *Photograph by Enrique Shore, Woodfin Camp and Associates Inc.*

| 1964 | 1973 | 1978 | 1984 | 1990 |
|------|------|------|------|------|
| Military coup in Brazil | Military coup in Chile | Puebla conference of Latin American bishops | *I, Rigoberta Menchú* published | Sandinista electoral defeat |

# 9.

# REACTION

After the Cuban Revolution exploded like a flare in the night sky, a beacon of hope for some and a signal of danger for others, the Cold War came to Latin America in full force. The Cuban government did what it could—not very much, offering training but rarely money or arms—to aid Marxist revolutionaries in other countries of the region. Soviet Russia never played a major role outside Cuba. Still, the US State Department saw any Marxist revolutionary movement as a Soviet proxy force. US policy encouraged a violent counterrevolutionary reaction that spread over the region in the 1960s and 1970s.

Admittedly, Marxism and the Cuban example were very prominent; that was no figment of the US State Department's imagination. Furthermore, Latin American Marxists did believe that Soviet Russia was on their side. But images of the USSR figured little in the appeal of Latin American Marxism. Almost never did the Marxist revolutionaries of Latin America organize because of Russian prompting or depend on Russian aid, much less operate on Russian instructions. There simply were no Soviet proxy guerrilla forces in Latin America equivalent to those created by the US government. Nationalism remained the bedrock of revolutionary feeling. Among most Latin

American revolutionaries of the day, to accept Marxism meant basically one thing: to side with the weak and impoverished masses against the rich minority and the US multinational corporations.

On the other side stood those who thought revolution spelled disaster. Latin Americans took this position for various reasons. The upper class and most of the middle class were logically anticommunist because they feared losing their privileged status. But traditional patronage networks involved many poor people in the anticommunist cause as well. Sometimes, the anticommunists successfully branded Marxist ideas as foreign to Latin America by tirelessly exaggerating the international connections of revolutionary movements. And after all, Marxism, like liberalism in the early 1800s, really was an imported ideology, and poor and culturally conservative people—of whom there are many in Latin America, especially in the countryside—might not think that radical university students spoke for them.

## NATIONAL SECURITY DOCTRINE

The most important US anticommunist allies, by far, were the armed forces of Latin America. The working alliance between the US military and Latin American armed forces, dating from World War II, had become an explicitly anticommunist alliance after the war. It involved permanent US military aid for Latin American armies, as well as training at the US military's School of the Americas, where the basic curriculum could be summed up as counterinsurgency—how to fight guerrillas. The overall logic of the anticommunist alliance, sometimes called "national security doctrine," ran as follows: Latin American armed forces are key US allies in defense of the "free world," and counterinsurgency is their special role. The strategic naval and air power of the United States will handle any communist invaders from outside the hemisphere. Latin American armies, for their part, should turn their guns inward against "the internal enemies of freedom": revolutionary organizers in factories, poor neighborhoods, and universities.

It is easy to see what Latin American generals liked about their alliance with the US military. The US alliance increased the power of Latin American armies within their own countries. Furthermore, national security doctrine offered a glorious mission—defending the "free world" or even "Western civilization"—and this mission won them rich and powerful friends as a fringe benefit.

The creation of the military alliances was complemented in the 1960s by a new US aid policy. In a clear reaction to the Cuban Revolution, US President John F. Kennedy announced—belatedly, in 1961—a sort of Marshall Plan for Latin America, to be called the Alliance for Progress. The basic idea of the Alliance for Progress was exactly that of the Marshall Plan: to reduce revolutionary pressures by stimulating economic development and political reform. "Those who make reform impossible will make revolution inevitable," declared Kennedy, in reference to the danger of communism in Latin America. US aid to Latin America increased. But making substantial changes in whole societies is harder, and much more expensive, than supplying guns and counterinsurgency training. The Alliance for Progress quickly ran out of steam. By the 1970s, Latin American generals believed that the region would inevitably fall to communist revolution unless they prevented it.

For military officers steeped in national security doctrine, the Cuban Revolution had been a call to battle stations, and, in their view, the situation grew more dire as the 1960s advanced. Spray-painted revolutionary slogans seemed to cover every available wall. Marxism was becoming the predominant political philosophy among Latin American artists, social scientists, and nationalist intellectuals in general. The 1960s New Cinema

of Brazil and other countries gained critical acclaim with gritty
films designed, according to one filmmaker, "to make the people aware of their own misery." Revolutionary Cuba's upstart
film industry soon became one of the best and most influential
in Latin America. The vogue of Marxist thought could be felt
with particular intensity at public universities. A novelistic
"Boom" had made Latin American literature famous throughout the world, and its prestigious authors spoke for revolution.
Colombia's Gabriel García Márquez, for example, traveled
often to Cuba and shared a warm friendship with Fidel Castro. The García Márquez novel *One Hundred Years of Solitude*
(1967), arguably the best-known Latin American novel of the
century, climaxes with a massacre, as government machine
guns fire into crowds of workers on strike against a US banana
company. The real event, involving the United Fruit Company,
took place in 1928 near the Colombian author's home. Other
Boom authors, such as Mexico's Carlos Fuentes and Peru's
Mario Vargas Llosa, shared the general admiration for revolutionary Cuba in the 1960s. Even the Catholic Church, long a
pillar of tradition and hierarchy, developed a dissenting wing
that aligned itself with the revolutionaries, as we have seen.
When radios played the Beatles singing "Back in the USSR you
don't know how lucky you are," even the youth counterculture
seemed, in military eyes, to conspire against national security.

Perhaps a siege mentality explains the gruesome violence
committed from the 1960s to the 1980s by Latin American militaries against their "internal enemies." Whatever explains it,
military use of secret kidnapping, torture, and murder as counterinsurgency techniques became widespread. With the "free
world" depending on them to combat the "red tide," Latin American militaries targeted anyone suspected of sympathizing with
the guerrillas—student protesters, labor leaders, peasant
organizers—snatching them off the streets and "disappearing"
them forever without legal record. "This is war," explained the

generals. They were doing what they had to, they said, to defeat communist guerrillas. By the 1960s, these were often urban guerrillas. Urban guerrillas lived and fought in big cities, where they could menace the government, strike at army headquarters, or kidnap and ransom an industrialist to finance their operations. By the same token, with their enemies literally around the corner, urban guerrillas were extremely vulnerable. Their only protection was secrecy. To find guerrilla hideouts, Latin American security forces subjected prisoners to a variety of horrors, including repeated rape over a period of weeks, electric shocks to nipples and testicles, permanent blindfolding, and psychological torment such as being forced to witness the torture of a loved one. Many in Latin America believe that such techniques were taught at the US School of the Americas. One thing is certain: National security doctrine maintained the climate of emergency used by torturers to justify their acts.

US policy called for democracy but helped trigger dictatorship. National security doctrine encouraged Latin American armed forces to take an increasingly active role in national life, promoting economic development and public health, for example. As they gained this kind of experience, some officers began to consider civilian politicians an unnecessary hindrance. Civil liberties such as the right to denounce torture hindered the military's freedom to smash its enemies by any means necessary. To save democracy from the Marxists, the generals destroyed it themselves in a series of preemptive strikes.

The government of one Latin American country after another was now taken over by executive committees composed of generals and admirals. These were called *juntas*, like the provisional governments founded in Spanish America after Napoleon imprisoned the king of Spain in 1808. The military juntas of the 1960s, 1970s, and 1980s tried to keep things under collective institutional control, avoiding the emergence of an unpredictable Perón. The nonpersonalist nature of the new military dictatorships led political scientists to speak of "bureaucratic authoritarianism." By the mid-1970s, a plague of bureaucratic authoritarianism had swept through South America, and constitutional civilian governments survived in only a few countries.

## MILITARY RULE

Brazil offers a perfect example. Brazilian military leaders, who had fought alongside US forces during World War II, enjoyed close ties to the United States. The US response to the Cuban Revolution put the Brazilian military on "red" alert, and the generals saw danger everywhere. To their dismay, even the decidedly unrevolutionary Brazilian president, elected in 1960, pinned a medal on Che Guevara to signal diplomatic independence from the United States. This president eventually resigned, but his vice president, who was on a visit to Red China at the time of the resignation, was even worse in military eyes. Limiting his powers, they watched his every move.

They did not like what they saw. The new president was João Goulart, a political protégé of Getúlio Vargas. Labor minister in the last Vargas government, Goulart had inherited leadership of the Vargas constituency, Brazil's nationalist coalition of the urban middle and working classes. But that coalition had unraveled after the Cuban Revolution, when frightened middle-class voters bolted to the right. So Goulart redoubled his outreach toward urban workers, his rhetoric sounding more radical each day. Foreign investors feared expropriation. In a climate of sharp and unpredictable political confrontation, the economy stalled completely.

Meanwhile, the land-hungry Peasant Leagues of desperately impoverished northeastern Brazil began to admire the Cuban model, and Brazilian landowners resolved to fight land reform tooth and nail. The military feared that Goulart might build a new revolutionary coalition of workers and peasants, capable of steamrollering all resistance. So, with the knowledge and collaboration of the US ambassador and the US military atta-ché in Brazil, and with US naval support offshore standing by, Brazilian generals seized control of the country. The US ambassador interpreted the coup as the "single most decisive victory for freedom in the mid-twentieth century." But the Brazilian military ruled undemocratically for twenty years following their 1964 coup.

Brazil had no tradition of military rule per se. So military leaders carefully maintained the outward appearance of constitutional government. If laws got in their way, they decreed a change in the laws. They decreed that their enemies had no political rights for ten years. They decreed that there were only two legal political parties, which Brazilians joked about as the "Yes" party and the "Yes, sir" party. Opposition emerged anyway. Before dissolving the congress, an unconstitutional act, the generals decreed amendments that let them dissolve it legally. When urban guerrillas organized in the late 1960s and early 1970s, the military attacked them—and anybody around them or suspected of supporting them—with out-of-uniform "death squads." Meanwhile, they kept meticulous files on official prisoners, files that even recorded their interrogation under torture. Eventually, an archbishop sympathetic to liberation theology and basic human rights was able to compile copies of these files to document military abuses.

The Brazilian military had various currents within it. Moderate constitutionalists were in control from 1964 to 1967, but as protest mounted, hard-liners with more dictatorial inclinations took over. The hard line dominated the government from 1968 to 1974, after which popular protest temporarily subsided and the regime relaxed somewhat. Along with generals who took their cues from the United States, there were right-wing nationalists who talked freely of making Brazil into a world power. The nationalists paid special attention to road-building and development projects in the Amazon basin, through which Brazil's borders run, believing that otherwise, the country might lose this vast territory.

The Brazilian military had a nationalist commitment to industrialization, too. It drove relentlessly toward a new level of heavy industrialization, the manufacture of durable consumer goods. Middle-class protest subsided in the early 1970s, partly because the economy had begun to grow explosively. For a few years, the government spoke proudly of a Brazilian economic "miracle." Growth it certainly was; a miracle it was not. The military government had created conditions in which new industries could thrive at the expense of Brazil's poor majority. Not tied to a broad electoral coalition, the military could hold down wages and "disappear" anyone who complained. It could attract international capital with a "safe climate for foreign investment," meaning low wages, no strikes, few restrictions, and no expropriations. And it could freely channel resources into developmental priorities like mining, transportation, steel production, and oil refining.

Heavier industries used less of Brazil's abundant unskilled labor, and their products were aimed mostly at a middle-class market. Therefore, most people in Brazil, where the middle class is a minority, benefited little or not at all from the "miracle" of the early 1970s. Military policies put more money and credit not in the hands of the poor who most needed it, but in the hands of better-off people likely to buy cars, electronics, and domestic appliances. In a country half-malnourished, the malnourished half got only one tenth of the income gains between 1964 and 1974. Instead, the bulk of those gains went to the richest tenth of Brazilian society. Some miracle! The cake had to rise, said the generals, before it could be sliced. But they really had no plans for distributing this prosperity. Instead, they pursued their vision of Brazilian greatness by constructing some of the world's biggest, and most environmentally devastating, hydroelectric dams—also highways, bridges, and airports.

Then the miracle was over. Oil prices had been rising steeply since the early 1970s, and Brazil imported a lot of oil. For a while, sudden oil profits, the so-called petrodollars, flowed from oil-rich countries like Saudi Arabia and Iraq into international banks, then out of the banks as low-interest, short-term loans into oil-poor countries like Brazil. The Brazilian military government borrowed billions of petrodollars to maintain its developmental drive. They also borrowed petrodollars to import expensive petroleum, in a vicious circle. A more creative reaction was the program to make cane-alcohol fuel for cars, fuel that eventually powered a quarter to a third of Brazilian motor vehicles. Then, in the late 1970s, the second shoe dropped when international interest rates rose dramatically. Brazil's foreign debt mushroomed. By the early 1980s, Brazil had the world's largest foreign debt.

Brazilian industries now produced cars, buses, and trucks with all-Brazilian components. However, when the value of Brazil's manufactured exports surpassed the value of its coffee exports in the early 1970s—a historic moment for economic nationalist dreams—it happened partly because so many Brazilians could not afford the items being exported. Ironically, half-malnourished Brazil was now one of the world's leading exporters of food. Beginning in 1978, massive strikes of workers in São Paulo, the country's industrial heart, announced the revival of popular opposition to the military's regressive social policies. After saving Brazil from the "Cuban threat" very early on, the military had used economic growth to justify its continued authoritarian rule. Now, in the early 1980s, with an economic meltdown and an awakening opposition on its hands, the military was finally ready to bow out.

The legacy of military rule was worse, much worse, in Argentina and Uruguay, scene of a "dirty war" fought by the armed forces against urban guerrillas. Argentina and Uruguay could not be more unlike Brazil at this time, in their high over-all standard of living and their unequaled indices of literacy and life expectancy. Yet this did not save them from the crisis unleashed by the Cold War.

Whereas in the early 1960s Brazilian generals were dreading what might happen if industrial workers and peasants joined forces, Argentine generals were dreading what already *had* happened—Perón. The exiled leader was still directing the now outlawed Peronist movement personally, and the industrial workers of Argentina still revered him. Perón had never been a Marxist, but during the Cold War any working-class movement looked suspicious to anticommunist eyes. A few years after oust-ing Perón in 1955, the Argentine military had stepped aside and allowed civilian rule to resume, but whenever it allowed the Peronists to compete in elections (1962, 1965), the military came hurrying back to annul a Peronist victory. Then, in 1966, two years after the military takeover in Brazil, the Argentine armed forces set up their own version of a bureaucratic authoritarian state, with similar goals: to eliminate the revolutionary threat, hold down wages, and encourage foreign investment. The Argentine military government also mirrored Brazil's official anticommunist repression, but with ghoulish intensity.

Not easily repressed, Argentine revolutionaries drew strength from their Peronist heritage and from deeper socialist and anar-chist roots. The Argentine military, on the other hand, did not benefit from economic growth comparable to the Brazilian "mir-acle" of these years. Without carrots to distribute, it relied on the stick. The killing began in the late 1960s and escalated through the 1970s, making the Brazilian record of military torture and murder appear child's play by comparison. A number of tenacious Marxist guerrilla movements, their members often young, urban, middle-class, and university educated, fought against the Argentine military government. Many Montoneros, the best known guerrillas, came from Peronist families and still considered themselves Peronists, although their ideology had swerved left. The military responded with death squads that "disappeared" probably more than twenty thousand people, murdered them—after interrogation and torture—and disposed of their bodies secretly, disclaiming any knowledge of their victims' whereabouts.

This dirty war continued even after the military finally permitted Perón's return to Argentina, where he became president in 1973. Sick and in his late seventies, Perón himself now appeared less dangerous than the supposedly Peronist guerrillas. Unfortunately, he died almost immediately. His second wife, Isabel, a former nightclub dancer who had been made vice president, now stepped into the role of Evita, as a political leader in her own right, but she had none of Evita's charisma. The Peronist movement split apart utterly, and Isabel Perón was replaced by a new military president in 1976. Now the counterinsurgency operations moved into homicidal high gear, and the military finally succeeded in exterminating its guerrilla enemies. The generals proudly announced the triumph of "Judeo-Christian civilization," but, as the Argentine economy continued its twenty-year pattern of fits and starts, only Argentina's 1978 home-team victory in the World Cup soccer championship bolstered their popularity. Encouraged by government secrecy, most Argentines tried not to notice the dirty war.

But in the late 1970s, mothers carrying photographs of their "disappeared" children began to protest in the main square of downtown Buenos Aires, the Plaza de Mayo. The military called them crazy. Not wanting to know the grisly truth, people looked the other way. *Las Madres de la Plaza de Mayo*, as they became known, did not give up. They used white scarves embroidered with the names of their disappeared children as a kind of uniform. Middle-aged schoolteachers, social workers, sales clerks—desperate to do something, anything—they became the conscience of a nation, living proof of the military's secret, dirty war. The Argentine military, which loudly proclaimed its mission to defend traditional values such as respect for motherhood, could not touch Las Madres de la Plaza de Mayo, although it called them *las locas*, "the crazy women of the Plaza." Gradually, the whole world recognized and honored the truth of their crazy accusations. This did not bring their children back, but it was something.

Across the Río de la Plata, in Uruguay, military repression took a similar path. Unlike their Argentine counterparts, the Uruguayan generals had no Peronist movement to fear. Compared with Argentina, Uruguay had been notably placid since World War II. Between 1951 and 1966, Uruguayans even implemented Batlle's earlier proposal for an executive committee in place of a one-man presidency. Despite economic problems, Uruguayan standards of living remained the envy of the hemisphere. Then a group called the Tupamaros tried to precipitate a revolution, just as Che attempted to do in Bolivia.

Formed in 1964, the Tupamaro urban guerrilla movement was directly inspired by the example of the Cuban Revolution. The Tupamaros recognized the absence of revolutionary conditions in Uruguay. Not relying on spontaneous combustion, they hoped to spark a hope, set an example, and ignite a larger conflagration in surrounding countries. The Tupamaros carried out daring, brilliantly planned operations designed to impress public opinion. One of their most flamboyant stunts was tunneling into a prison to free captured comrades. In 1967, the Uruguayan president declared martial law to fight the Tupamaros. The military began a gradual takeover, completed in 1973. It then annihilated the Tupamaros, who, as urban guerrillas in a country with only one city to speak of (Montevideo), were quickly cornered once torture penetrated their cover. The dark curtain of bureaucratic authoritarianism descended on this once privileged society. By the end of the 1970s, Uruguay had more political prisoners, relative to its size, than any other country in the world.

## Dictatorship Almost Everywhere

The sad fate of stable, democratic Uruguay shows how the Cold War ravaged even countries not prone to insurgency or dictatorship. Chile is the best example of all. No other Latin American country could equal Chile's record of constitutional government. For years, Chilean democracy had negotiated major ideological differences. The Chilean Communist Party was one of the oldest and strongest in the hemisphere. It had participated in electoral coalitions with various other parties of the left since the 1930s. This was the kind of Communist Party that frustrated Che Guevara because it did not advocate armed revolution.

In the Chilean presidential election of 1958, a socialist-communist coalition got almost one third of the vote. Their candidate was Salvador Allende—like Che, a medical doctor and a Marxist. Allende was not an advocate of armed revolution, however. He was committed to Chilean constitutional traditions. In the 1964 election, Allende ran again and did even better, despite the fact that the CIA bankrolled his chief opponent. Alarmed by Allende's popularity, the US State Department made Chile a model of the Alliance for Progress aid program— but to no avail. In the 1970 presidential election, Allende won. The coalition called Popular Unity now had its constitutional chance to show what it meant by "a Chilean road" to socialism.

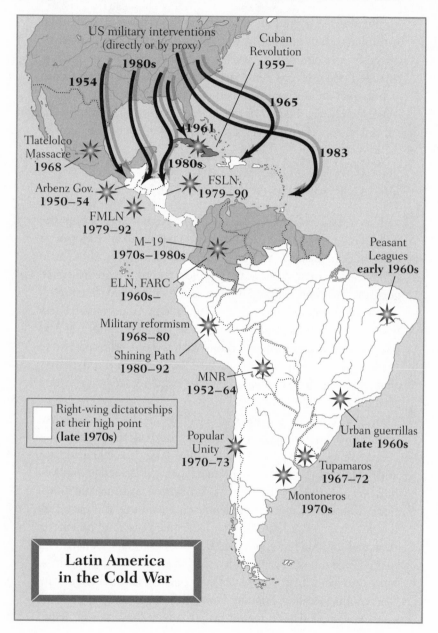

US military interventions
(directly or by proxy)
**1980s**
**1954**

Cuban
Revolution
**1959—**

**1965**

**1961**

**1983**

Tlatelolco
Massacre
**1968**

**1980s**

Arbenz Gov.
**1950—54**

FSLN
**1979—90**

FMLN
**1979—92**

M–19
**1970s—1980s**

Peasant
Leagues
**early 1960s**

ELN, FARC
**1960s—**

Military reformism
**1968—80**

Shining Path
**1980—92**

MNR
**1952—64**

Popular
Unity
**1970—73**

Urban guerrillas
**late 1960s**

Tupamaros
**1967—72**

Montoneros
**1970s**

Right-wing dictatorships
at their high point
**(late 1970s)**

**Latin America
in the Cold War**

But ambitious dreams of social transformation—nationalization of Chilean copper, coal, and steel, along with most banks,
not to mention land reform—outran Popular Unity's electoral
strength. Allende had won the three-way election with a plural-
ity of 36 percent. The two losers, both more conservative than
Allende, had garnered 63 percent between them, and they were
now united, more or less, in opposition to the Popular Unity
government. Allende's enemies found a powerful ally in the
CIA, which pumped money to the candidates opposing Popular
Unity. The CIA now adopted a "firm and continuing policy," as
one agency directive quite explicitly put it, "that Allende be
overthrown by a coup." The US State Department used all its
leverage to cut off international credit to Allende's government.
As Popular Unity imposed price freezes and wage increases to
raise the living standards of the Chilean poor, triple-digit inflation roared. Very prosperous Chileans (industrialists, lawyers,
physicians, and architects) as well as moderately prosperous ones
(shopkeepers and various small entrepreneurs such as independent truckers) fought the initiatives of Popular Unity, sometimes
with CIA support.

Meanwhile, the Popular Unity government retained the
strong backing of urban workers whose hopes for the future
had soared. Many supporters, in fact, thought Popular Unity
too timid. Workers moved directly to take over factories that
the government had been slow to nationalize. Some urged
strong measures against reactionary organizations. But Allende
insisted, as always, on working within constitutional restraints.
He had some reason for optimism. The expropriation of the
copper industry had, in fact, been widely popular, and in the
1971 midterm elections, Popular Unity won by a bigger margin
than ever.

Then Chilean army tanks rolled into the streets on 11 September 1973. Refusing safe passage out of the country, Allende
went to his office and died under attack by his own armed

**THE CHILEAN COUP.** Positioned on a rooftop, Chilean soldiers fire on the palace of government during the military overthrow of President Salvador Allende in 1973. The coup leader, General Augusto Pinochet, took over Chile with US support. *OFF/AFP/Getty Images/Newscom.*

forces. Here, in the estimation of US Cold Warriors, was yet another victory for democracy.

The Chilean coup turned out to be the bloodiest such takeover in the history of Latin America. Thousands of supporters of Popular Unity, from folksingers to peasant organizers to university professors, were herded into the Santiago soccer stadium, many never to be heard from again, their bodies shuttled to secret mass graves. As in Brazil, Argentina, and Uruguay, thousands fell victim to a well-organized program of official but clandestine torture and murder. Closing the legislature, the military governed by decree for seventeen years. For most of that time, it had the firm support of the US State Department. The exception was the presidential term of Jimmy Carter, who emphasized human rights as a criterion of US foreign policy.

Although ridiculed as unrealistic by the Cold Warriors, Carter's policy definitely inhibited the military blood fest in Chile and Argentina, and juntas all over Latin America heaved a sigh of relief when Ronald Reagan, a confirmed Cold Warrior, took office as US president in 1980.

The Chilean dictatorship was basically a bureaucratic authoritarian regime, except that the original leader of the 1973 coup, General Augusto Pinochet, had a leading role unparalleled in Brazil or Argentina. Sadly, exceptional Chile had for once become the epitome of a Latin American trend.

Peru, on the other hand, constitutes an interesting exception to the trend, because its military government was not driven by anticommunist reaction. Peruvian officers announced revolutionary intentions that were explicitly not communist but also not capitalist. Their program showed a sincere desire to serve Peru's poor majority, and it amounted mostly to old-fashioned nationalism: a truly ambitious agrarian reform in a country of vast rural poverty, nationalization of oil and other industries, and indigenista themes, such as raising Quechua to the formal status of co–national language with Spanish. Other aspects, such as promotion of employee-owned companies, were more novel. Overall, Peru's military government, which lasted from 1968 to 1980, was hard to categorize in Cold War terms. Although a dictatorship, it was not guilty of heinous human rights violations.

The revolutionary government of Cuba, which expressed strong support for the Peruvian regime, could be described the same way in the 1970s and 1980s. It remained authoritarian, and the army, long headed by Fidel Castro's brother Raúl, constituted one of its chief pillars. But the revolutionary state worked steadily to improve the lives of Cuba's poor majority, and it never committed the wholesale mayhem so characteristic of anticommunist military governments.

Mexico, on the other hand, bucked the military trend completely. Marxism had influenced a generation of Mexican students no less than elsewhere. But revolutionary socialism was nothing new in Mexico, so its anticommunist reaction was less fearful, less violent. The rhetoric of the PRI—officially a "revolutionary party," after all—had employed socialist motifs off and on for decades. In the 1930s, Mexico had seen real land reform and the expropriation of major foreign-owned industries. Precisely for this reason, the PRI retained considerable revolutionary legitimacy and, through its massive patronage, kept a firm grip on industrial workers, urban middle classes, and country people alike. Buoyed by an oil boom, too, the PRI could absorb any challenge in the 1960s and 1970s. Its one famous sign of momentary panic, as Mexico prepared to host the Olympic Games in 1968, was a wanton massacre of protesting university students in the Tlatelolco district of Mexico City. As for Mexican generals, they had not been key political players for decades. And in the United States, dire warnings about "Red" Mexico were already half a century old and not very scary. US governments had long since learned to live with a "revolutionary" Mexico.

## THE LAST COLD WAR BATTLES: CENTRAL AMERICA

By the mid-1970s, the revolutionary tide had turned in Latin America. Reactionary anticommunist dictatorships, in turn, began to recede. Bureaucratic authoritarian governments collapsed in the late 1970s and 1980s because of their own mistakes and excesses—the creation of colossal debts, hyperinflation—but also because their anticommunist crusades had already succeeded. What excuse, now, for dictatorship? In Argentina, the military government made a desperate bid for nationalist glory by identifying a new, external enemy—Great Britain. Initially, the military got considerable public support for its 1982 war with Great Britain over the Falkland, or Malvinas, Islands. But the gambit backfired when ill-equipped, poorly trained Argen-

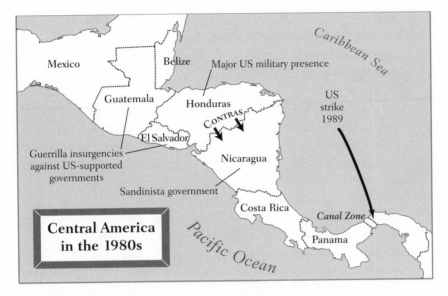

Central America in the 1980s

tine soldiers quickly surrendered. Nothing disgraces military rulers like military defeat. In 1983, Argentina had real elections and sent the armed forces back to the barracks.

Uruguay got a civilian president in 1984, Brazil in 1985. Peru, Ecuador, and Bolivia had already returned to constitutional rule, too, by that time. Meanwhile, revolutionaries and reactionaries in Central America fought what turned out to be the last major battles of the hemisphere's thirty-year Cold War.

Central America, with its volcanoes, tropical forests, and steep cascading rivers, had barely felt ISI. All Central American countries depended heavily on a few agricultural exports, especially coffee and bananas. Their populations numbered only a few million, and their capital cities had only a few hundred thousand inhabitants each. In Central America, urban workers and middle classes had not curbed the power of landowners, who still controlled the national wealth. Therefore, rural oligarchies still dominated Central America in the 1970s, half a century after nationalist movements overthrew them elsewhere. The fate of the Arbenz government in Guatemala, the first major hemispheric battlefield of the Cold War, points out another barrier to Central American nationalism—the habit of US intervention in "our backyard." Throughout the Cold War years, Central America was plagued by greedy tyrants who enjoyed US support because of their furious anticommunism.

Furious anticommunism certainly characterized the rulers of Guatemala. Guatemalans had groaned under ruthless military or military-controlled governments ever since 1954. The landowners of Guatemala and El Salvador lived in dread of massive peasant uprisings. In the 1970s and 1980s, the Guatemalan armed forces carried on a dirty war against rural guerrilla armies and urban opponents such as student activists and labor leaders. To deprive the guerrillas of support, indigenous peasants were herded into new "model" villages that served as rural concentration camps. "Low-intensity conflict" became the US strategists' new term for all this. The term has its logic, from the perspective of a desk at the Pentagon, but for the families of the "disappeared" college students whose bodies turned up in garbage dumps, for indigenous people like Rigoberta Menchú, whose mother and brother were tortured and murdered by the Guatemalan army, these conflicts were not lacking in "intensity."

Rigoberta Menchú was a Quiché Mayan woman whose community wished only to raise its crops and follow its traditional customs. Rigoberta's father became a peasant organizer and her brothers joined the guerrillas. Rigoberta herself was influenced by liberation theology and became a spokesperson for her people. In 1992 she won the Nobel Peace Prize for calling world attention to the atrocities of Guatemala's dirty war. The story of her life, *I, Rigoberta Menchú* (1984), became essential reading for anyone interested in the "low-intensity conflicts" of the Cold War. It was later shown that she had merged her own story with other people's, but no one could deny the existence of the horrors she described. The Guatemalan death toll spiraled toward two hundred thousand, and the military perpetrated 95 percent of the atrocities, just as her story suggested.

Costa Rica, at the other extreme of Central America in all senses—geographical, social, and political—largely escaped the crossfire of the Cold War. Because Costa Rica had few indigenous inhabitants before the conquest—and, more to the point, because those few were then liquidated by the conquerors—this whitest of Central American countries was less burdened by exploitative colonial hierarchies. Consequently, it was less politically explosive, too. Besides, one of Costa Rica's more innovative presidents had taken the precaution of abolishing the army in the 1940s.

In between Central America's geographic and demographic extremes was Nicaragua, land of the famous anti-imperialist Augusto César Sandino, whose guerrilla war against the US Marines had won the rapt attention of nationalists all over Latin America in the 1920s. Since the 1930s, Nicaragua had been ruled by a single family, the Somozas. The Somozas personified the perverse side effects of US anticommunism in Cold War Latin America. The Somoza dynasty had its origins in the US intervention against Sandino, when the first Somoza, Anastasio, whose main qualification was that he spoke good English, headed the Nicaraguan National Guard. Somoza invited Sandino to parlay, had him assassinated, and then used the National Guard to take over Nicaragua. Various Somozas ran the country almost as a private estate during the 1940s, 1950s, 1960s, and into the 1970s. They were sturdy anticommunist allies who also preserved enough democratic window dressing to satisfy US diplomats. Symbolically, the Somoza mansion stood near the

US Embassy on a hill overlooking Managua, the Nicaraguan capital. Rumor had it that an underground tunnel connected the two buildings. Anastasio Somoza's son, also Anastasio, who ruled the country in the 1970s, was a West Point graduate and head of Nicaragua's US-trained, US-equipped National Guard. Meanwhile, the Somoza family wealth swelled to include about a fifth of Nicaragua's best land, the country's airline, and other such trifles.

By 1961, Nicaragua had a revolutionary movement formed in Havana, but also inspired by Nicaragua's own strong anti-imperialist traditions. Like Cuba and Mexico, Nicaragua had long suffered US intervention, and nationalist resentments ran deep there. Remembering Sandino's earlier anti-imperialist struggle, the revolutionaries of the 1960s called themselves the Sandinista National Liberation Front (FSLN). For almost two decades, the Sandinistas alone resisted the Somozas. Then, in 1978, the dictator Anastasio Somoza overplayed his hand, assassinating Joaquín Chamorro, publisher of a conservative opposition newspaper. Chamorro's death finally united Nicaraguans of the left and the right against the Somozas. A widespread rebellion began, and the veteran Sandinistas assumed leadership. Eventually, the uprising swept away the National Guard despite its arms and training. Somoza fled Nicaragua for Miami. His fate illustrates the international dimensions of the conflict. In search of a comfortable exile, the unpopular Somoza accepted the hospitality of Paraguay's anticommunist strongman, Alfredo Stroessner, one of the world's most durable and repressive dictators. But Somoza had hardly unpacked his bags in Asunción when Argentine guerrillas, who considered him their enemy too, found him and put an antitank rocket through the windshield of his bulletproof Mercedes Benz.

Back in Nicaragua, the Sandinistas took charge, shouldering aside Violeta Chamorro, widow of the murdered publisher, who represented the late-blooming anti-Somoza forces of the right. The Sandinistas had nonnegotiable revolutionary plans. Their Cuban inspiration was reflected in their campaigns for full literacy and public health. Hundreds of Cuban teachers, medical personnel, and sanitary engineers arrived to help. France, Spain, and West Germany sent substantial aid, too. US President Jimmy Carter also gave cautious support, but he was soon replaced by Ronald Reagan. From Reagan's perspective, Nicaragua was just another square on the Cold War chessboard. As long as the Sandinistas identified themselves as revolutionary friends of Cuba, nothing else mattered. The Cold War language of Reagan found a mirror image in Sandinista rhetoric about that "scourge of the human race," the United States. Confrontation was in the cards.

Following their defeat in 1979, Somoza's trusty National Guard had regrouped in Honduras under CIA supervision. The Argentine military government, triumphant in their dirty war, sent trainers for this new US proxy force called the Contras, for *counter*revolutionaries. Through the 1980s, the Contras raided Nicaragua from bases on the Honduran side of the Honduran-Nicaraguan border. Reagan called them "Freedom Fighters" and supported them unwaveringly. Honduras filled with US military personnel, supply dumps, and air bases. The Contras gained recruits among Nicaraguans disaffected by the Sandinista revolution. Contra raiders could wreak havoc and cripple the economy, but they could not hold Nicaraguan territory.

Havoc was enough, however. The Sandinistas had to concentrate their time and money on defense. US forces mined Nicaragua's harbors to cut off its trade with other countries. Gradually, the Nicaraguan economy disintegrated. By 1988, Nicaragua had quintuple-digit inflation. In 1990, the Sandinistas lost an election on which they had staked everything. In a stunning defeat, the young Sandinista guerrilla leader Daniel Ortega took second place to Violeta Chamorro, who became the first woman ever elected president in Latin America. In the 1990s, Nicaragua remained divided, a circumstance dramatized by Chamorro's own family, which included several prominent Sandinistas as well as opposition leaders. At one point, two of Chamorro's sons edited the country's two main newspapers, both the Sandinista *Barricada* and the anti-Sandinista *Prensa*.

The uprising against Somoza, and then the Contra war, had killed tens of thousands of Nicaraguans. El Salvador suffered even more. Like Nicaragua under the Somozas, tiny El Salvador had a totally undemocratic anticommunist government through the 1960s and 1970s. If Nicaragua had a classic dictatorship, El Salvador had an equally classic landowning oligarchy, called the "fourteen families" or, sometimes, "the forty families." The precise number matters less than the general fact of oligarchic rule by the few.

The misery of the rural poor had made El Salvador a social pressure cooker by the 1970s. Long before coffee, Spanish conquest and colonization had pushed El Salvador's indigenous people off level agricultural land onto then-unwanted volcanic slopes, where they reestablished their communities. But those fertile slopes, once terraced, were perfect for coffee. So when coffee cultivation began in the 1870s, prospective coffee planters wanted the slopes also. Liberal reforms then privatized the indigenous people's newly valuable community lands, and, little by little, in fair deals and unfair ones, coffee planters bought them. Indigenous Salvadorans became agricultural peons on estates that had once been their own lands. Workers were many—tiny El Salvador is among the most densely populated landscapes in the Americas—and wages low. Very gradually, the rural poor began to starve. During the 1920s, the Salvadoran Communist Party became one of the strongest in Latin America, but its attempt to lead a major uprising was savagely crushed in "the Slaughter of 1932." Military and military-controlled governments then followed one another in El Salvador for almost half a century, all staunchly anticommunist and allied with the United States. In the 1960s, El Salvador became a showcase of the Alliance for Progress, but little improved in the countryside.

Then, in the 1970s, the Salvadoran church began to take liberation theology's "preferential option for the poor." In effect, the country's highest Catholic authority decided that anticommunism itself was an unholy cause. Archbishop Oscar Romero was a quiet man, named to head the Salvadoran church because he seemed conservative to the Vatican. But anticommunist death squads changed his heart by targeting priests and nuns who worked with the poor. "Be a Patriot, Kill a Priest" was the anticommunist slogan. Moved by the butchery of his clergy and flock, the archbishop spoke against the army. The anticommunists viewed this as a dangerous heresy. One day in 1980, a political assassin gunned down Archbishop Romero in front of the altar as he celebrated Mass.

As with Nicaragua's FSLN, Salvadoran revolutionaries drew on history in naming the Farabundo Martí National Liberation Front (FMLN). Farabundo Martí was a martyred hero of the Salvadoran left, a communist organizer of the indigenous uprising of 1932. In addition, Martí had served with Sandino in Nicaragua against US forces there. In the 1980s, the FSLN tried to return the favor by helping the FMLN against the US-backed Salvadoran army. But the Sandinistas, fighting to keep the Nicaraguan revolution alive, could offer only a few crates of munitions to the FMLN. The Reagan administration seized on this connection to announce that communism was spreading by contagion from Cuba to Nicaragua to El Salvador. Starving Salvadorans, in this view, would never think of rebelling otherwise. Critics of Reagan's policy, meanwhile, spoke as though the FSLN would, for some reason, never contemplate aiding the FMLN. Neither version captured the truth exactly. The military murders of four nuns from the United States

**SALVADORAN GUERRILLA.** An FMLN fighter, one of many women in the guerrilla ranks, stands guard in 1983. On the wall behind her is one of the revolutionary slogans that covered walls all over Latin America from the 1960s through the 1980s. *Photograph by Ivan Montecino; image by Bettmann/CORBIS.*

brought Central American issues home to observers of US foreign policy. Were our tax dollars paying for these bullets that cut down priests and nuns in the name of democracy? Massive public opposition to US policy in Latin America, led especially by religious groups, arose now for the only time in the Cold War.

Through the 1980s, FMLN guerrillas held large portions of the Salvadoran countryside. They had strong backing, especially among the country people of remote, mountainous areas along the Honduran border. The FMLN blew up bridges and power lines and levied "war taxes" on vehicles traveling through their territory. But they could not defeat the army. The Salvadoran military, for its part, had US training and equipment. Its troops rode helicopters into guerrilla territory on search-and-destroy missions. They clambered up the sides of volcanoes seeking FMLN units near to the capital city. Sometimes, when they thought no one was looking, the army conducted mass executions of peasants whom they suspected of aiding the guerrillas. One day in 1981, for example, an elite US-trained battalion entered the tiny village of El Mozote and systematically slaughtered almost everybody there, hundreds of unarmed, unresisting men, women, and children. Ironically, their military intelligence was not very good: El Mozote, it turned out, was not a guerrilla base at all. In fact, many of the families at El Mozote had recently converted to US-oriented evangelical Protestantism, and they probably favored the government over the guerrillas. El Mozote illustrates the grisly, indiscriminate violence of military anticommunism in Central America. Understandably, Salvadorans fled their country by the tens and then hundreds of thousands, many to the United States.

Because the FMLN refused to participate in elections, wary of fraudulent "management," the anticommunists invariably won, assuring US aid for the elected government. As the war dragged on and the death toll mounted—forty, fifty, sixty thousand—anticommunist electoral strength grew. The country was sick of war, and by 1990, the war was a stalemate. The stubborn optimism that had sustained the revolutionary vision now drained away day by day. The Nicaraguan election of 1990 ended the Sandinista revolution. In Europe, the dramatically rapid crumbling of the Soviet bloc had begun. An FMLN victory seemed further away than ever. And, even if achieved, an FMLN victory would not bring peace; the Nicaraguan experience showed that. So, in 1992, the FMLN signed a peace treaty and laid down its arms. Meanwhile, the Guatemalan insurgents, too, were running out of steam. A peace born of exhaustion settled over Central America.

The Cold War was over. But in Latin America, nobody had won; there were only losers. Across the hemisphere, the revolutionary fervor of the 1950s and 1960s had burned itself out in the 1970s and 1980s. In a few places, such as Uruguay, guerrilla movements had led to the collapse of democratic governments. In many other places, such as Brazil and Chile, generals inspired by national security doctrine had precipitated the terror. Either way, bright hopes of finally undoing Latin America's original sin of social injustice had drowned in blood and disillusionment. Latin America had been thoroughly militarized, occupied by its own armed forces. During the 1990s, guerrilla movements remained active in spots—Colombia, Peru, southern Mexico—but the sense of a continental revolutionary tide had evaporated totally. As in the rest of the world, the end of the Cold War clearly marked the end of an epoch. A new period of history was about to begin.

# La Violencia, Pablo Escobar, and Colombia's Long Torment

Colombia's population surpassed Argentina's in the 1990s, making it the third most populous Latin American country after Brazil and Mexico. Despite its size and importance, Colombia has not figured frequently in our story because of its often exceptional politics. For example, conservatives, rather than liberals, ruled Colombia in the neocolonial period. During the stormy years of the Cold War, the Colombian military never took over the country directly. While debt and inflation ravaged Latin America in the 1980s, a so-called Lost Decade for hopes of economic growth, Colombia's economy stayed robust. And Colombia's contrary tendencies continued into the new millennium. With the Cold War over and revolutionaries in retreat everywhere else in the hemisphere, the guerrilla armies of Colombia expanded their operations.

An unusual level of violence has plagued Colombia since the 1940s, when conflicts erupted across the Colombian countryside after the assassination of Jorge Eliécer Gaitán, the famous populist leader. This period, accurately called *La Violencia*, lasted well into the 1950s. Although channeled by Colombia's traditional parties, the liberals and the conservatives, *La Violencia* was less about politics than about socioeconomic conflict in the countryside. Terrified people flocked into the cities, abandoning their rural property or selling out cheaply. Others stayed and bought up the land at bargain prices. The use of violence increased in petty street crime, which rose to astounding intensity in the major cities. Middle-class women began to remove their earrings and men their wristwatches before setting foot downtown. In the late 1970s, the rate of violent death in Colombia began to set world records for a country not at war.

It was in this context of lawlessness that Pablo Escobar pioneered a new business, smuggling marijuana and then cocaine to the United States. Escobar created a mafia empire and became a powerful figure of organized crime, much like Al Capone in an earlier period of US history. Recall that the mafia business of Capone likewise centered on an illegal drug, prohibition-era alcohol. Escobar's version of Capone's Chicago was the Colombian city of Medellín, and his mafia became known as the Medellín cartel. The terrible scourge of easy money now lent new energy to the violence rampant in Colombian life. US consumers of illegal drugs were able to pay huge sums for the Colombian product. Colombian-grown marijuana, which dominated the trade in the 1970s, was of higher quality than the Mexican marijuana formerly consumed in the United States. Cocaine, which came from coca leaves grown in Peru or Bolivia, then refined in and exported from Colombia, dominated the trade in the 1980s. It was a new drug to most US consumers, made available in large quantities for the first time by Escobar's organization. The great wealth of the drug traffickers translated, as great wealth will do, into power and influence.

Meanwhile, Colombia suffered its own version of the Cold War. Rural guerrilla armies with their roots in *La Violencia* of the 1950s, especially the FARC, were now seen, and saw themselves, as Marxist revolutionaries. A daring group of urban guerrillas called the Nineteenth of April Movement— M-19, for short—raised the sword of Simón Bolívar, taken from a museum display case, to symbolize the new revolution. Like the Tupamaros in Uruguay, Colombia's M-19 carried out spectacular strikes with high public-relations value. In 1980, they took over the embassy of the Dominican Republic in Bogotá during a party, when it was full of diplomats, including the US ambassador, and held them hostage for two months before escaping to Cuba. In 1985, M-19 seized the Colombian Supreme Court building. The government refused to negotiate and, after ten hours of ultimatums, it sent a tank in through the front door, followed by troops with guns blazing. Ninety-five civilians—among them, all the country's Supreme Court justices—died in the crossfire.

Then things got even worse. The FARC and a second army of rural guerrillas, the ELN, forced landowners to pay "war taxes," and the landowners began to create their own paramilitary forces to help the army fight the guerrillas. Country people found themselves caught in the middle. If they helped the guerrillas, they risked death at the hands of the paramilitaries or the army. But the guerrillas might kill those who refused to help them. Meanwhile, the guerrillas, who had turned kidnapping into one of their principal fund-raising activities, had the bad idea of abducting members of rich mafia families. The drug traffickers struck back with massive violence. Medellín became a war zone where teenage boys were enlisted by the hundreds as hit men. Under pressure from Colombian police and courts, the drug traffickers escaped prosecution by slaughtering any judge willing to sign a warrant against them.

When threatened with extradition to the United States, Escobar and his associates reacted with "narco-terrorism." Truck bombs carrying tons of dynamite exploded on the streets of Colombian cities, and the Medellín cartel collectively resisted arrest and extradition. Journalists and politicians who spoke for extradition were murdered or kidnapped. Escobar and others offered to surrender in return for a guarantee of non-extradition. In 1991, that deal finally went through. Escobar surrendered and moved into a jail especially constructed near Medellín, ironically in a former drug-treatment facility. Although he was in custody, the lax conditions of his imprisonment—in which he gradually surrounded himself with luxury furnishings in mafia-style poor taste—allowed Escobar to continue to supervise his illegal business interests by remote control. Within a year, he had flown the coop. But now, despite the estimated $3 billion that Escobar had amassed, he led a miserable existence, permanently on the run. Finally, in 1993, Colombian police found Escobar by tracing his son's telephone. Escobar was still on the phone when the police arrived at his door. The world's most famous criminal died ingloriously as he fled across a Medellín rooftop.

Meanwhile, the drug trade that he initiated had become a source of income for the guerrillas too. The entry of the guerrilla armies into the drug trade threatened a further escalation of conflict in Colombia at the close of the millennium. For a while at least, the Colombian government became the world's third largest recipient of US aid. Meanwhile, a number of failed attempts to negotiate with the guerrillas led to the election of Alvaro Uribe, a hard-line president determined to win a military victory. Penniless people displaced from the war zones flooded into Colombian cities already swollen by two generations of rapid growth. Colombia's long torment was still far from over.

**The pleasures of Globalization.** At the dawn of the new millennium, consumer culture is everywhere in Latin America. For the well-off minority, the new accessibility of imported goods brings long-awaited satisfactions. But for the poor majority, like the residents of this poor Guatemala City neighborhood, where people can afford to consume little, the lure of consumer culture produces mostly anger and frustration. *Photograph by Jean-Marie Simon.*

| 1990s | 1992 | 1994 | 2001 | 2006 |
|---|---|---|---|---|
| Neoliberal reforms throughout region | Indigenous leaders meet in La Paz | NAFTA takes effect; Zapatistas rebel | Argentina defaults on its external debts | Lula reelected president of Brazil |

# IO.

# NEOLIBERALISM

In the 1990s, the political pendulum swung decisively away from nationalism in Latin America. Marxist revolutionaries were, in general, strongly nationalist, and the reactionary dictators who crushed them were often nationalists, too—though of a different kind. In the end, both revolutionary violence and the reactionaries' bloody Cold War victory against the left discredited nationalism. Already by 1990, nationalism seemed the wave of the past in Latin America, something from the sixties generation. And now, after many decades out of favor—boosted by its association with the one remaining superpower, the United States—liberalism has returned to fill the ideological vacuum. The new generation of liberals are called *neoliberals*. For better or worse, neoliberalism—with a familiar emphasis on free trade, export production, and the doctrine of comparative advantage—reigned supreme in Latin America at the turn of the third millennium.

By the mid-1990s, it already seemed that every president in the region was a neoliberal. Take Fernando Henrique Cardoso, a formerly Marxist sociology professor, a famous dependency theorist who had inspired a generation of radical social scientists throughout Latin America and the United States during the 1970s and 1980s. By the time he was elected president of

Brazil in 1994, Cardoso was a neoliberal. Even the Peronist leader twice elected president of Argentina, Carlos Menem, was a neoliberal. Even the PRI presidents of Mexico, supposed heirs of another great nationalist tradition, were now neoliberals. In fact, Carlos Salinas and Ernesto Zedillo, who led the embattled Institutional Revolutionary Party in the 1990s, both had professional training in neoliberal economics at US Ivy League universities. Neoliberals got the encouragement of the US government, and they put up sails to catch turn-of-the-century winds of globalization.

Neoliberals jettisoned all trappings of economic nationalism and embraced the basic liberal faith in the free market. So they sold off, or *privatized*, the state-run corporations and public services that nationalists had created all over Latin America as declarations of "economic independence." State bureaucracy is notoriously inefficient around the world, and state-run telephone and oil companies had proved fiascoes in Latin America. Free-trading neoliberals slashed the import tariffs that nationalists had raised to protect Latin American industries. They deregulated capital flows, for example, removing nationalist-inspired limits on profit that multinational corporations could freely take out of a country each year. They reduced or removed the nationalist-inspired subsidies that made basic foodstuffs and public services affordable for the poor. Neoliberals also initiated all-out assaults on inflation, which substantially undermines the functioning of the market.

Neoliberals had few new ideas. Everything they recommended had already been tried in Latin America before 1930. So where did they get their impressive momentum? To begin with, the ordeal of recent years had dimmed the glamour of nationalism, as we have seen. In addition, 1990s neoliberals could take credit for taming the debt crisis of the 1980s.

During the 1980s, many Latin American countries had struggled to keep up payments on foreign debts. These debts had grown huge suddenly, thanks to high world oil prices and heavy short-term borrowing in the 1970s. Overwhelmed, Mexico and Brazil temporarily stopped payments in 1982. As world interest rates rose steeply in the 1980s, large short-term loans had to be refinanced at much higher rates. The national debts of Latin America mushroomed, much as the US national debt was doing at the same time. The difference: Latin American debts were "external," owed mostly to foreign banks. The external debts of the region as a whole rose from $105 billion (1976) to $397 billion (1986), with Mexico and Brazil owing the most. Countries that defaulted on their external debts would find themselves internationally bankrupt and isolated.

Foreign lenders, such as those of the influential International Monetary Fund (IMF), believed that the solution to Latin American insolvency lay in free-market policies. So they enthusiastically promoted neoliberal policies. To encourage neoliberalism in Latin America, foreign lenders gradually "rolled over" the external debts of one country after another into long-term bonds. These debts continued to increase in the 1990s, but now the borrowing countries could make the payments. The IMF typically insisted on reductions in social spending, and Latin America's poor felt the pinch of this "belt-tightening." Still, the crisis was over, and the region seemed to have turned a corner.

Neoliberalism acquired a strong cachet of success in the 1990s. The hyperinflation that had plagued both Brazil and Argentina for decades was halted rather spectacularly for a while by neoliberal policies. For a few years, Latin America was heralded among US investors as a great emerging market, offering vast investment opportunities. Neoliberal policies encouraged foreign capital in Latin America—and in it came, billions of dollars' worth. US fast-food franchises sprang up in major cities from Chile to Mexico. In 1994, the creation of the North American Free Trade Agreement (NAFTA), the linchpin of Mexican neoliberalism in the 1990s, seemed portentous to people on both sides of the border. One year later, Brazil, Argentina, Paraguay, and Uruguay inaugurated their own free-trade zone, called MERCOSUR. The freer trade of the 1990s allowed middle-class apartment dwellers from Mexico City to Santiago to access the Internet, tune in via satellite to US or European television, and become avid consumers in a transnational economy. Neoliberal reductions in tariff barriers brought lower prices and greater variety in everything imported, from cars to VCRs to cellular telephones.

The neoliberals also attracted new transnational corporations to Latin America, but the impact of that strategy has been mixed. One of the most common transnational operations was and is the *maquiladora*, an assembly plant using lots of cheap labor, most often women's labor, to put together imported parts. Low tariffs facilitate maquiladora production. For example, maquiladoras on the Mexican side of the US border may receive parts from Asia, assemble them, then send the finished products across the border for sale in the United States. Maquiladora workers mean little to the companies that employ them. Women who become pregnant, for example, are quickly fired in most cases. Low labor costs constitute the maquiladoras' main reason for being in Latin America. So neoliberal governments try to hold wages down, even as food and transportation subsidies are withdrawn from the poor.

Chile stood out as the neoliberal success story of the 1990s. Chile's neoliberal economic reforms began during the years of dictatorship, famously advised by economists from the University of Chicago, the so-called Chicago Boys. By the 1990s, Chile boasted low inflation, good credit, steady growth, and diversified exports, going roughly equally to European, Asian, and American countries. The expansion of the Chilean economy had been so steady and vigorous that it benefited all Chileans to some extent—but, as elsewhere, the middle classes benefited

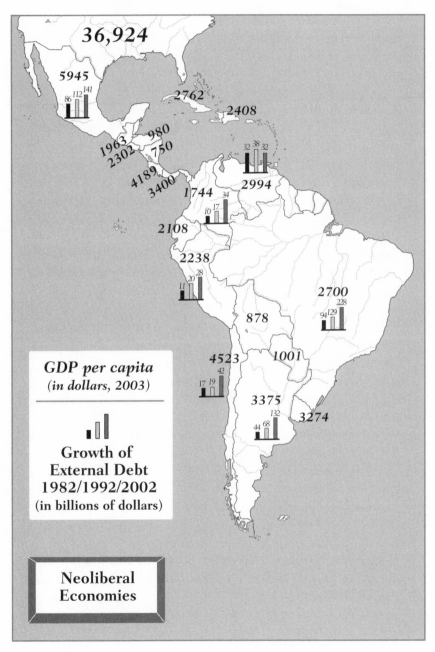

36,924

5945

86 112 141

2762

2408

980

1963

2302 750

4189

3400

1744

10 17 34

2108

2994

32 38 32

2238

11 20 28

2700

94 129 228

878

4523

17 19 42

1001

3375

44 68 132

3274

GDP *per capita*
(*in dollars, 2003*)

Growth of
External Debt
1982/1992/2002
(in billions of dollars)

Neoliberal
Economies

most. Meanwhile, Chile's distribution of wealth remained among the most unequal in Latin America. The best-case scenario of neoliberalism, in other words, still promised least to the neediest.

In a nutshell, consumers, mostly middle-class people, have benefited most from neoliberalism. To "shop the world," without trade barriers, is obviously an advantage for those with sufficient spending money. On the other hand, most producers have lost out—at least so far. Of course, producers are also consumers, but in greatly varying degrees. Poor Latin Americans consume relatively little, and many more Latin Americans are poor by US standards than are middle-class. Measured in dollars, the US economy generates over $46,000 per person, but the Brazilian, Mexican, and Argentine economies only around $8,000, the Colombian economy something like $5,000, and the Bolivian and Honduran economies less than $2,000, according to 2009 statistics.

Under neoliberalism, the gains made by Latin Americans as small-time consumers have been overwhelmed by their loss as producers. The region's impoverished majority buys inexpensive clothing sold in bins, toiletries arrayed on the edge of the sidewalk, a plastic bucket this week, a cheap digital watch the next. Most of the pitiful wages earned by Latin America's poor majority goes for the bare essentials such as rice and bus fare, day after day, month after month. Meanwhile, as Latin American industries collapse across the region, devastated by foreign competition that the nationalists had kept out, millions of workers face unemployment or long-term underemployment in the so-called "informal" service sector. They sell Chiclets at bus stops, wash windshields at intersections, and collect recyclables in rickety carts. Some are glad to find work in maquiladoras, but how happy can a maquiladora job make anyone in the long run?

Neoliberal reforms have reduced government spending, a step toward balancing national budgets and reducing debt, but at a bitter social cost. The subsidies, protected industries, state-run corporations, and large bureaucracies that the nationalists had created in Latin America were inefficient, true enough. But they also provided a living for millions whom the neoliberals have left unemployed. Similarly, state-run services lost money partly because they provided electricity or running water to the very poor. Privatized telephone companies, for another example, improved telecommunications for those who could afford a phone, but affording a phone became more difficult for many.

Sound familiar? In many ways, the impact of neoliberal reforms resembled the impact of liberal reforms in 1870–1930. Latin America became more "modern" in the technological sense. Foreign capital and foreign products poured in. Better-off people benefited, but less fortunate Latin Americans suffered. Familiar winners, familiar losers. A glance back at the 1890s puts present-day neoliberal "innovations" in historical perspective. The PRI technocrats of the 1990s seem reminiscent of the technocratic Científicos who advised Porfirio Díaz on the eve of the Mexican Revolution. Not by accident did the PRI begin to revise Mexican history textbooks to rehabilitate the image of Díaz, long painted as a villain by the nationalists.

The new textbooks also downplayed revolutionary heroes like Emiliano Zapata. But on the very day that NAFTA took effect in 1994, indigenous rebels calling themselves Zapatistas declared their opposition to the new trade arrangement. These new Zapatistas were Mayas from villages near the Guatemalan border, an area of Mexico remote from Zapata's old stomping ground. They had immediate demands relating to agricultural land, but they also had a broader vision. They took Zapata's name to remind Mexico of its nationalist heritage. Subcomandante Marcos, the mysterious ski-mask-wearing, pipe-smoking Zapatista spokesperson, soon appeared on T-shirts all over the country. The new Zapatista uprising was a fly in the neoliberal ointment. It could not threaten the PRI militarily, but it tarnished the country's open-for-business image. The new Zapatista movement showed a certain media savvy. It had a Web site. It could mobilize sympathizers in Europe and the United States. Thousands of them went to Chiapas, the state where the rebellion was occurring, as international human rights observers. There they observed government armed forces wreaking havoc in Mayan villages suspected of supporting the rebels. Although it made a show of negotiating, the Mexican government devoted itself mostly to deporting the observers and crushing the rebellion. To do so, it used all the tried-and-true techniques of "low-intensity" warfare, including widespread arming of village anti-insurgent militias, which have shown a repeated tendency to run amok, as in Colombia.

The new Zapatistas never had a prayer of defeating the Mexican army. Or rather, prayers they *did* have. The cause of indigenous people was still the cause of the Catholic Church in Chiapas, where Friar Bartolomé de las Casas had been bishop himself for a few years in the 1500s. Like Las Casas four hundred years earlier, the indigenous Zapatistas haunted the conscience of a whole society. They represented a potent moral force.

Another challenge to neoliberalism came from the Shining Path insurgency that arose in the Peruvian highlands. The Shining Path's campaign of terror owed more to the mystical vision of its charismatic leader, Abimael Guzmán, than to its old-style Marxist ideological roots. It drew strongly on the long Peruvian tradition of indigenismo, seeking inspiration in the imagery of a sort of Inca revival. Shining Path militants possessed a rare esprit de corps that maintained its potency even during years of imprisonment. Unfortunately, their courage and dedication were harnessed to a quasi-religious spirit that condoned cataclysmic violence. Shining Path made striking gains in the heavily indigenous Andes, where more orthodox Marxist insurgencies had never found many followers. And it flowed, along with the enormous internal migration of indigenous people from the highlands, to Lima. At the same time, it spread from its highland strongholds in the opposite direction, down the eastern Andean slopes toward the Amazon basin, into areas of coca production along the Huallaga valley. There Shining Path began to support and protect coca growing to finance its operations throughout Peru. However, Shining Path lost momentum after the capture of its visionary leader in 1992.

The new Zapatistas, and, in a way, the Shining Path too, advanced claims that indigenous people were making all over Latin America. In some ways, the list of grievances was five hundred years old. In 1992, the five-hundredth anniversary of Columbus's first voyage became the specific occasion of indigenous meetings and declarations. Understandably, the mood was one of mourning rather than happy commemoration. At an international meeting in La Paz, Bolivia, representatives of widely scattered indigenous peoples—Maya, Ñañú-Otomí, Kuna, Cherokee, Quechua, Tarahumara, Aymara, Guaymí, and Nahua, among others—declared, on the subject of the glorious Discovery of America: "Our wise men were persecuted, tortured, massacred. Our sacred books and symbols were destroyed. Our gold and silver, stolen. Our territory, usurped." They had a point. And it was a point that few Latin Americans could fail to recognize.

Whether gathering in Mexico or Ecuador or Bolivia, indigenous leaders demanded sufficient land to farm and a fair share of government benefits. But above all, they asked to be allowed to remain themselves, preserving their language, their lifeways, and aspects of their political autonomy. These demands reflected the multiculturalist intellectual mood of the 1990s in the West generally, but they collided with one of the strongest legacies of twentieth-century nationalism, still widely influential despite the neoliberal onslaught.

By the first decade of the twenty-first century, generations of nationalist teaching had instilled in most Latin Americans a strong respect for symbols of their mixed-race origins. Mestizo nationalism, with its emphasis on racial and cultural amalgamation, remained the emotional bedrock of national identities wherever people of indigenous descent carried demographic weight—especially Mexico, Guatemala, El Salvador, Nicaragua, Colombia, Ecuador, Peru, and Bolivia. After five centuries of struggle, Latin American race relations still left much to be desired. Many proclaimed that racism no longer existed, but that was definitely not true. Dark skin color, whether indigenous or African, remained a social disadvantage. At its worst, mestizo nationalism sometimes functioned in practice as a denial or cover-up of the problem it was meant to solve.

While mestizo nationalism redeemed a previously scorned racial status, it led to its own kind of oppression too. After all, there are as many differences *within* countries as *between* them. Whose accent, whose music, whose cuisine, whose skin tone gets to represent the whole nation? According to Mexican nationalist ideology, a mestizo is now considered somehow more Mexican than others born in Mexico. Many other Latin American nations have instituted this quasi-official mestizo self-image. The mestizo image does describe many, perhaps most, Latin Americans, but it marginalizes others. In the Dominican Republic, for example, the mixed-race image excludes people of strong African descent, especially immigrants from Haiti, who appear "too black to be Dominican." In Mexico, Central America, and the Andes, it excludes indigenous people, pushing them to "stop being Indians," adopt a mestizo identity, and enter the national mainstream.

The Zapatistas and other indigenous leaders of the new millennium resisted this pressure more vocally than in the past. In Latin America overall, however, people who maintained an indigenous identity in 2010 constituted a small percentage of the population. Despite its symbolic power, indigenous resistance did not fundamentally undercut the homogenizing pressures of mestizo nationalism. Brazil's movement for black advancement and civil rights encountered similar nationalist resistance when trying to mobilize Brazilians of African descent around a specifically black political agenda.

Nearly half of all Brazilians are of pure or mixed African descent. They tend, overall, to be the poorest half of the country, and the darker they are, the poorer. Brazil's Unified Black Movement (MNU) was formed in 1978 to mobilize these people around an awareness of their shared identity as victims of racism. But the Brazilian poor have never shown much interest in the MNU. Partly, they are skeptical about all political movements; partly they still respond to Brazil's version of mestizo nationalism. Since the 1930s, the vision of a Brazilian "racial democracy" has been the widely popular keystone of the country's national identity. The idea was so welcome, after centuries of official white supremacy, that it took root powerfully among Brazilians of all colors. The slogan "racial democracy" incorrectly suggests an absence of racism, and even though Brazilians used the occasion of the hundredth anniversary of abolition (1988) to denounce the massive presence of racism with near unanimity, they have not given up the idea that racial and cultural mixing lies at the heart of Brazilian identity.

Whatever its drawbacks, mestizo nationalism is much more democratic and inclusive than white supremacy. It constituted a popular step forward in Latin American racial politics during the 1930s, and it retains a powerful appeal today among Latin Americans, rich and poor, black and white, indigenous as well as mestizo. Latin American societies have not transcended racism by embracing indigenous American and African elements in their national mix, but they have gotten further than many other multiracial societies, including, many believe, the United States. This remains the proudest and most potent aspect of Latin American nationalism.

History repeats itself, but it never repeats itself exactly. Neoliberalism may be the old liberalism déjà vu, but Latin America has changed since liberalism's last time around. The original sin of social exploitation has not been undone in Latin America. The hegemony of European culture remains intact. But in 2010, thanks to the nationalist tide of the mid-twentieth century, the great majority of Latin Americans, including the middle classes and even some of the very rich, now honor their indigenous and African heritage, at least theoretically. Transculturation, that dynamic engine of Latin American identities, has continued. For example, *capoeira*, an Afro-Brazilian combination of dance and martial art, now has adherents worldwide. Meanwhile, in Bahia, a principal center of capoeira's development, black Brazilian youth have adopted both Jamaican reggae and US soul music as their own.

New Latin American variants of West African religion, including Brazilian *Candomblé* and its first cousin, Cuban *Santería*, have acquired many new believers since the late twentieth century. These religions include a pantheon of gods, each associated with particular qualities, somewhat as in ancient Greek religion. For example, teenage surfers in Bahia, Brazil, now commonly put themselves in the hand of Iemanjá, goddess of the sea, as they paddle into the breakers. Another rapidly growing religion, *Umbanda*, freely combines African and European elements to produce something uniquely Brazilian. Candomblé and Umbanda ceremonies include moments of spirit possession, when worshipers feel possessed by invisible forces. In traditional Candomblé, these forces are interpreted as West African gods. In Umbanda, however, most are Brazilian spirits, including the spirits of indigenous people and African slaves. Many new converts, especially to Umbanda, are middle-class and white.

Another tide of religious change transforming Latin America in 2010 is the rise of Protestantism, notably in Brazil but also elsewhere, from Chile to Guatemala. Among the fastest-growing Protestant groups are the Pentecostals and other evangelical Christian faiths originating in the United States. The Mormon Church sends out probably the most consistent and persistent waves of young, clean-cut missionaries. After four centuries in which virtually everyone in Latin America was at least nominally Catholic, some countries will soon be one quarter or more Protestant. In others, like Mexico and Colombia, however, Protestants still constitute only a small percentage of the population. Liberation theology has continued to recede, but there is no sign of an end to the religious energies of Latin American Catholics, who make informal saints of deceased pop-culture idols and leave offerings of headlights at roadside shrines.

If understanding Latin America has always challenged us in the United States, perhaps the challenge is getting easier. After all, increasingly the Latin Americans are *us*. In a United States more heavily immigrant than anytime since the early 1900s, Latin Americans are the most numerous immigrants. People of Latin American descent now compose the country's biggest minority group, representing over a seventh of our total population. Mexicans and Mexican Americans in the southwest, Puerto Ricans and Dominicans in New York, and Cubans in Florida form large, influential communities. Well over half of all US Latinos are of Mexican descent, but Latin Americans of many other countries can now be found throughout the United States. It is important to recognize that US Latinos are divided along national, racial, and ethnic lines. In fact, the umbrella term "Latino" means little outside the United States. Only here do Mexicans, Puerto Ricans, and Bolivians, brought together by the Spanish language, begin to see each other as Latinos. And Brazilians generally do not identify as Latinos, even in the United States.

Immigration from Latin America is changing US culture. Spanish-language publications abound. There are Spanish-language television networks. Supermarkets all over the country carry tortillas, cilantro, and plantains. Small *tiendas mexicanas*, frequented by farm workers, dot the rural South. Everybody's tastes are changing. Sales of spicy salsa have surpassed sales of an older American favorite, ketchup. Another kind of salsa, the fabulously polyrhythmic dance music, was born of Cuban parentage in New York and was disseminated from there throughout the Caribbean basin. Salsa remains beyond the ability of most US dancers; fortunately, the strong Dominican immigration of the 1980s brought merengue, a more rhythmically straightforward music, easier for gringo dancers to learn.

Large-scale immigration also brings challenges. As tens of thousands of people make the perilous desert crossing in search of work and a better life for themselves and their families in the United States, all sorts of issues arise en route and at their destination. Much of the current wave of migrants is going to places that formerly received few immigrants, especially southeastern states like North and South Carolina, dramatically transforming the cultural picture of many a depopulated small town. In a conflictive world of large uncertainties, the transformations created by rapid immigration are sure to produce fearful reactions; and, just as surely, political opportunists of various stripes will exploit those fears. The result is not pretty. It involves calls for a forbidding border wall of gargantuan length to keep the migrants out. It involves laws mandating the systematic deportation of those who are already here. At worst, it involves scapegoating the migrants (as if they were personally responsible for the

**CHICAGO, MAY 2006.** Mass pro-immigration demonstrations occurred in many US cities as a response to anti-immigrant initiatives in the first decade of the twenty-first century. *Photograph by Steve Schapiro/Corbis.*

global economic realities that drive their migration) and attempt-
ing to limit the health care and education available to them and
their children. Zealots volunteer to patrol the border themselves
and to maintain watch via remote surveillance cameras that can
be monitored on the Internet from the comfort of their living
rooms. It all seems un-American. But, of course, it isn't. What
could be more American, after all, than being an immigrant and
then, after a few decades, fearing immigration and reacting
against it? It is a troubled process, but no place can make it
work, in the end, like the United States of America.

Meanwhile, other challenges loom on the Latin American
horizon, particularly environmental ones. Environmental devastation is worse in developing countries than in developed ones,
because avoiding or fixing it is expensive. In addition, letting
factories pollute is one way of attracting multinational corporations to Latin America. The area of maquiladora production
along Mexico's border with the United States constitutes a
well-known example. Undoubtedly, however, Latin America's
best-known, largest-scale environmental issues concern the
Amazonian rainforest.

A significant fraction of the Amazonian rainforest has already
been destroyed, but it still occupies roughly a third of Brazil's
national territory, as well as parts of Venezuela, Colombia, Ecuador, Peru, and Bolivia. It remains, by far, the largest tropical
forest in the world. Human activity hardly made a scratch on
the Amazonian forest until the 1960s. It remained the home of
indigenous people living in relatively undisturbed tribal cultures, with a sprinkling of settlers along the major rivers, many
of them descendants of rubber tappers who arrived around 1900.
Then, in the 1960s and 1970s, the Brazilian military government
launched one major World Bank–funded development project
after another in the Amazonian rainforest, logging it, cutting
highways into it, promoting massive mining projects (iron, gold,
manganese, nickel, copper, bauxite) that stripped and tore it,

**SETTLER IN BRAZILIAN AMAZONIA.** Burning the rainforest is a way of clearing it for agriculture. Cleared land in the Amazon basin is unlikely to retain its fertility for more than a few years, yet the burning continues because of demand for land. *Photograph by Michael Harvey/Panos.*

and building gargantuan hydroelectric dams that flooded thousands of square miles of it. Highly poisonous mercury pollution, a by-product of gold mining, entered Amazonian waterways by hundreds of thousands of tons. Brazil's military government was especially eager to populate the country's remote Amazonian borders, which it regarded as a security risk, with "real Brazilians" rather than indigenous people. In Ecuadorian Amazonia, oil drilling wrought devastation. The forest tribes were decimated by disease. Some melted away to nothing in only a few years.

Still, the Brazilian and Ecuadorian governments were determined to exploit the resources of Amazonia. After all, as they pointed out, the rich farmlands of the Midwestern United States had once been mostly forested and inhabited by indigenous people, too. But tropical rainforest is not like other woodlands.

One of the world's oldest habitats, rainforests have developed a biodiversity unequaled anywhere else on the planet. Even more than elsewhere, pervasive webs of symbiotic relationships make rainforest organisms superspecialized and intricately interdependent. That interdependence, in turn, makes rainforest ecologies uniquely fragile. When large areas of the forest are cut down, a few species of trees grow back, but the original biodiversity is permanently lost. Another kind of fragility comes from the thin Amazonian soil, which is quickly washed away by torrential rains when shorn of protective tree cover. As a result, cleared land quickly erodes and becomes almost useless.

In the 1980s, when something like six thousand square miles of the forest were disappearing each year in clouds of smoke the size of Belgium, the disastrous consequences of Amazonian development became obvious. Rondônia, a western state bordering on Bolivia, had become the Brazilian government's great model of agricultural colonization, its much ballyhooed "Northwest Pole." But even when the land was allotted to poor settlers from other parts of Brazil, arriving by the hundred thousand each year, Amazonian colonization rarely worked. The would-be colonists had high hopes but little preparation, and less than a tenth of Rondônia turned out to be suitable farmland anyway. Most settlers gave up after only two or three years. Their plots were often bought by wealthy ranchers.

Ranching, which uses a lot of land and employs few people, accounts for much of the deforestation in Amazonia. The ranchers are often large-scale speculators for whom ranching is a business venture rather than a way of life. Commonly, they live in cities, work in air-conditioned offices, and leave the ranching itself to hired administrators. They buy enormous tracts of land, clear them with bulldozers, put cattle on them until the degraded soil and scrubby vegetation will no longer support even cattle, then sell the land and move on. After all, they are in business to make money. Curbing the natural profit motive that drives free markets is not exactly a neoliberal strong point.

It's time to revisit the "political pendulum" metaphor that began this chapter. The pendulum metaphor helps us visualize decisive reversals of political trends. But it also suggests alternating swings of equal length, and that may be misleading. The neoliberal model is already giving clear signs of exhaustion as we enter the second decade of the twenty-first century, and nationalism is making a comeback.

The blush was off the neoliberal rose already by September 11, 2001, when a terrorist attack brought down the twin towers of New York's World Trade Center. Mexico's neoliberal president, Carlos Salinas, had already earned universal disgrace for the massive corruption of his administration, and 1994–95 saw the worst economic crisis to occur in Mexico in decades. Urban delinquency was reaching new heights in the Mexican capital and many of the region's other largest cities, provoking some of the most massive protest demonstrations ever seen anywhere. The optimism of the 1990s evaporated in most of Latin America, despite the new cars and computers enjoyed by the middle class, as globalization failed notably to produce universal prosperity. Argentina, a country that had implemented all of the rigorous recommendations of the International Monetary Fund, imploded economically in December 2001, defaulting on its foreign debts. Indigence and homelessness reached heights not witnessed in Buenos Aires during the whole of the twentieth century.

Gradually, in country after country across Latin America, voters began to reject the neoliberal vision of free-market supremacy by electing presidents of a markedly nationalist bent. In the US media, these presidents were often characterized as leftist, but few of them turned decisively toward socialist economic policies. Rather, they revived the nationalist vision of anti-imperialism and activist government. They did not reject the entire concept of capitalist globalization, but they declared their determination to mitigate its impact within the borders of their countries. And they stood together in international forums, forcefully dramatizing their refusal to toe any policy line laid down by the United States. By 2010, presidents who more or less matched this description governed most of the countries of the region.

In 2002, Brazilians elected Luiz Inácio da Silva, "Lula," a former metalworker and union leader, to govern Latin America's largest, most populous, and most economically dynamic nation. Before becoming president, Lula had spent twenty years forging a cohesive and democratic grassroots labor party, the PT, running unsuccessfully for president over and over. He finally won on his fourth try. Lula's most urgent goal was to ensure that no Brazilian go to bed hungry, yet this "zero hunger" initiative proved difficult to achieve, given Brazil's enormous debt obligations. Lula vowed to meet those obligations and advanced toward his social goals with a caution that disappointed many of his more radical supporters. However, the "family scholarship" instituted by the PT government, providing income support for poor families as long as they kept their children in school, began to reduce poverty and encouraged poorer voters to reelect Lula in 2006. The Brazilian economy forged ahead, showing remarkable resilience during the global recession that began in 2008. Over all, Brazil's new nationalist government offered a steady and substantive counterexample to neoliberal governance along the lines promoted by the United States and the World Trade Organization.

Venezuela's president Hugo Chávez, a former army officer, offered a different sort of nationalist alternative. Flamboyant, reckless, and outspoken, Chávez contrasted with Lula in all sorts of ways. His first bid to take over Venezuela, back in 1992, had been a coup attempt. Then, in 2002, he survived an attempted coup against his own elected presidency and entrenched himself in power for the rest of the decade. Chávez has channeled resources to poor Venezuelans largely in the form of patronage in exchange for their support for his political initiatives. This approach is admittedly less than desirable, but the resulting largesse is more than the Venezuelan poor have gotten from their governments in the past, and they have rewarded Chávez with powerful loyalty. On the other hand, Chávez's furious rhetoric and domineering use of government authority against his political adversaries have won him the implacable hostility of the Venezuelan middle class. In addition, Chávez has been the most high-profile of Latin America's new nationalist presidents internationally, active in a number of projects for regional integration. In 2009, he won a referendum eliminating term limits and allowing him to be reelected indefinitely.

A third notable new nationalist president, Bolivia's Evo Morales, took office in 2006. Morales is an indigenous Aymara, the first to rule this largely indigenous country since the time of the Spanish Conquest. As a boy he herded llamas, and as a young man he headed a union of coca growers, producers of the leaves consumed by Bolivia's indigenous people since time immemorial—but also consumed as a raw material by refiners of cocaine. Morales thus began his political career by resisting US-inspired efforts to eradicate the crop that provided his followers' livelihood. As president, Morales has his base of support in the heavily indigenous Andean highlands, and he has been systematically opposed in the lowland eastern region around Santa Cruz, the country's principal pole of economic growth. The opposition is founded not only on regional economics, but also on the antagonism expressed around Santa Cruz toward the bid for political empowerment by the Aymara and Quechua supporters of Morales. Despite that opposition, Morales has called a constituent assembly and managed to oversee the creation of a new constitution that significantly improves the situation of

Bolivia's long-oppressed indigenous majority. The constitution took effect in 2009.

Mexico and Colombia, the second and third most populous Latin American countries, remained exceptions to the nationalist comeback of 2001–9. During those years both countries were governed by presidents of a strongly neoliberal orientation, closely associated with US interests. In Chile, a leftist president was elected in 2006 but replaced in 2010 by a neoliberal businessman. So much for too-tidy pendulum metaphors.

Will globalization solve Latin America's basic problems of social inequity? There is very little sign of that happening, and Latin American voters have strongly registered their reservations about the power of a totally unfettered free market. Still, they have not entirely rejected free-market capitalism, and the election of Barack Obama as US president has softened the attitude of many Latin Americans toward the United States. Perhaps the sudden eclipse of nationalism since the 1980s will prove to be just that—an eclipse, remarkable but temporary. The recent global economic crisis has reminded everyone that the explosive growth of unregulated markets can be destructive as well as beneficial. Neither liberalism nor nationalism, in a pure form, has allowed Latin American societies to escape the lingering consequences of their "original sin," their birth in blood and fire half a millennium ago. What will the future bring? No history book can answer that question, so watch the news, but be prepared for surprises.

# GLOSSARY
## of Foreign Language Terms and Key Concepts

*Americanos* (Spa. and Port.): the nativist term used during the wars of independence to suggest a natural alliance among all people born in America against the Spaniards and Portuguese.

*Bandeirantes* (Port.): the wandering frontier raiders of colonial Brazil, based mostly in São Paulo. Their chief activity was slave hunting.

*Cabildo* (Spa., equivalent to *câmara* in Portuguese): the city council, one of the most important institutions of colonial government. Around 1810, at the outset of Spanish America's wars of independence, open city council meetings (*cabildos abiertos*) constituted early steps toward independent authority.

*caste system*: a social hierarchy encoded in law and based on inherited characteristics, real or imagined. Latin America's colonial caste system corresponded more or less to what we call *race*. Caste can be usefully contrasted to *class*, which is based more on socio-economic factors.

*caudillo* (Spa.): a strong political leader who commands the personal loyalty of many followers. The mid-1800s was the heyday of *caudillismo*. Although Brazil has also seen strong leaders, caudillismo has operated more powerfully in Spanish America.

*Científicos*: see *Porfiriato*.

*clients*: in political terms, *clients* receive benefits (such as protection or government employment) from a *patrón* in return for their loyalty (in civil wars or elections, for example).

*comparative advantage*: a concept promoted by free-market liberal economists. If each producer specializes in what it produces with *comparative advantage*, free trade then theoretically creates maximum benefits for all involved. Nationalist economists had a counterstrategy, ISI.

*core/fringe*: an analytical concept used to assess the geography of large social systems. The core areas of the Spanish and Portuguese colonies (e.g., Mexico, Peru, and northeastern Brazil) were defined by their large populations and profitable export products. The fringe areas were poorer and attracted fewer colonists. An analogous concept, *center/periphery*, is applied to the geography of international economic relationships.

*costumbrismo* (Spa.): an artistic and literary form dedicated to depicting (and thereby defining) national customs and lifeways during the middle 1800s.

*Creole* (equivalent of *criollo*, Spa.): a person of Spanish descent born in the New World. Brazilians of Portuguese descent tended to be called simply *brasileiros*. See also *Peninsular*.

*decent people*: the phrase *gente decente* (Spa.) was used especially in the 1800s to separate prosperous families of European blood and culture from the poor majority of indigenous, African, or mixed heritage people (collectively called the *pueblo* in Spanish America and the *povo* in Brazil).

*dirty war*: the *guerra sucia* (Spa.) was a campaign of terror waged by the Argentine military against left-wing guerrillas and their sympathizers (real and imagined) in the 1970s. Similar but smaller campaigns were carried out simultaneously by the Chilean, Uruguayan, and Brazilian militaries.

*ejido* (Spa.): common lands belonging to a town or village. The Mexican Revolution famously restored and created ejidos during its land reform of the 1920s and 1930s.

*enclave*: an area sealed off, in some way, from its surroundings. In Latin American history, the most famous *enclaves* were created by outside economic interests, such as mining and banana companies.

*encomienda* (Spa.): an institution whereby groups of indigenous people were legally "entrusted" to a Spanish conqueror with the duty of paying him labor and/or tribute. In return, the holder of the encomienda (the *encomendero*) was to provide instruction in the Christian religion.

*Estado Novo* (Port. for "New State"): the Brazilian regime created by Getúlio Vargas, 1937–45. The Estado Novo's industrialization program and general expansion of government activities were typical of mid-1900s nationalist movements.

*focos*: focal points of guerrilla activity intended to create revolutionary conditions in adjacent areas. Che Guevara was the principal exponent of this strategy (called *foquismo*) in Latin America.

*GNP, GDP*: two similar measures of total national economic activity: Gross National Product and Gross Domestic Product. The former is a more inclusive measure, which includes the profits of companies operating abroad.

*hacienda* (Spa.): a large property owned by one family, generally of Spanish descent. In contrast to *plantations* (such as Brazilian sugar plantations, for example), many haciendas did not produce lucrative export crops.

*hegemony*: a basic principle of social control, in which a ruling class dominates others ideologically, with a minimum of physical force, by making its dominance seem natural and inevitable. Hegemony usually involves some degree of negotiation.

*Iberia*: the peninsula defining the southwestern extreme of Europe, separated from France by the Pyrenees Mountains. Both the Spanish and Portuguese are *Iberians*, so that term is often used to discuss their combined colonial presence in America.

*Indigenismo* (Spa.): a literary, artistic, and political movement beginning in the late 1800s, but most characteristic of twentieth-century nationalism, that honored the indigenous heritage but focused on assimilating indigenous people into national life.

*ISI, import-substitution industrialization*: the creation of domestic industry to provide products previously imported. ISI occurred in Latin America mostly during the mid-1900s, encouraged by interruptions of international trade and by nationalist economic policies.

*legitimacy*: a quality of governments generally recognized as proper and legal by those whom they rule.

*liberalism*: a cluster of political ideas, emphasizing *liberties* of various civil, political, and economic kinds. Latin American liberalism focused on European and, later, US models.

*liberation theology*: a small but influential grassroots movement within the Latin American Catholic Church beginning in the late 1960s. In accord with liberation theology, consciousness raising and social organizing among the poor became central missions.

*managed elections*: elections at least partly manipulated by the government to influence the outcome. Such elections were a standard element of rural life throughout Latin America until the middle of the 1900s. Managing urban elections is more difficult and requires an especially powerful government (such as Mexico's PRI).

*Manifest Destiny*: a vision of US territorial growth in the mid-1800s. According to this vision, it was "manifest" (totally obvious) that according to the laws of history, the United States would (and should) expand to the Pacific Ocean, occupying Native American and Mexican lands by force, if necessary.

*Mestizo* (Spa.): of mixed race, especially indigenous American and European. The Portuguese equivalent, *mestiço*, just as often refers to an African-European mix. (For simplicity, only the Spanish version is used in the text. *Mestizaje*, the noun form, means "race mixture.")

*mita*: a labor draft exacted by the Inca Empire and, after the conquest, by the Spanish colonial rulers of the Andes. Colonial mita workers traveled to work, above all, in the silver mines, the most famous of which was Potosí.

*Monroe Doctrine*: a foreign policy (first announced by US President James Monroe in 1823) by which the United States proclaimed European "hands off" the Western Hemisphere, reserving it for US influence. The doctrine was rarely invoked until the expansion of US naval power in the 1890s.

*Roosevelt Corollary to the Monroe Doctrine*: a sort of rider added by Theodore Roosevelt in 1905, whereby the US military would function as a hemispheric policeman in protection of European and US economic interests.

*nationalism*: a political movement (dominant in the mid-1900s) espousing a strong state, national pride, and economic development. Latin American nationalists oppose "imperialist" outside influence. Often, but not always, they show a real commitment to defending the poor majority.

> *Mestizo nationalism*: a common definition of Latin American national identities founded on the notion of race mixture. This became an official definition of national identity in many Latin American countries during the mid-1900s.

*nativism*: a political attitude pitting all those of native birth against those born elsewhere. Nativist attitudes, promoted by the patriots during the independence wars, were part of the early development of nationalism. Nativism can also be an attitude of prejudice against poor immigrants, as in Argentine and US history.

*neocolonialism*: an informal sort of "colonization" by outside powers, associated in Latin America with the 1880–1930 period. Although politically independent during these years, Latin American countries experienced occasional military intervention as well as overpowering economic and cultural influence from Great Britain, France, and the United States. See *postcolonialism*.

*neoliberalism*: an updated version of liberalism that swept Latin America in the 1990s, following the period of cold war reaction and military rule.

*oligarchy* (from Greek, "rule by the few"): a cluster of powerful families able to dominate a local, state, or national government because of their social and economic influence. In Latin America, oligarchies of large landowners held sway in many countries between 1880 and 1930 when the most common alternative was *dictatorship*.

*patronage*: the granting of benefits by a wealthier or more powerful person, a patron (*patrón* in Spanish, *patrão* in Portuguese), to a person further down the social hierarchy. Patronage is repaid by loyalty and various services. See *clients*.

*Peninsular* (Spa.): a Spaniard resident in the New World during the Independence period. The conflict between Peninsulars and native-born Creoles became important at that time.

*peon*: an agricultural worker who lives and works on a large estate, such as a Spanish American hacienda. Peons were not slaves, but they commonly lacked freedom of movement, being tied to the hacienda, at times by debt. The peon's situation is called *peonage*.

*populism*: a style of politics aimed at the urban working and middle classes, who, together, composed the *populist coalition*. Most vigorous in the years following 1945, populism generally employed nationalist themes and promoted ISI.

*Porfiriato* (Spa.): the long period of rule by Mexico's Porfirio Díaz, 1876–1911, often cited as a prime example of neocolonialism in Latin America. Díaz imposed strict political control, encouraged European and US investment, and gave special influence to a group of positivist thinkers called Científicos.

*positivism*: a social philosophy (associated especially with the French thinker Auguste Comte) of great influence in neocolonial Latin America. *Positivists* cultivated a "science of society," with "Progress" as its centerpiece. In practice, positivism defined its supposedly scientific principles in highly Eurocentric terms. One element of positivist thought, for example, was "scientific racism."

*postcolonialism*: the lingering effect of previous colonization on nations that have gained their formal independence. In Latin America, the language, laws, religion, and social norms implanted by Spanish and Portuguese colonizers carried over almost entirely between 1825 and 1850, making the new, politically independent countries *postcolonial* in cultural terms. See *neocolonialism*.

*Progress*: in the meaning common in the 1800s and 1900s (signaled in the text by capitalization), *Progress* was any application of advanced technology, any importation of European or US material culture, or any transformation that made Latin American societies more like their European or US models. Especially before 1930, Progress was equated with Civilization, the opposite of Barbarism (a term used to brand African and indigenous American cultures as primitive).

*proxy force*: a military force representing the interests of a country not formally involved in the fight. The *Contras* who attacked

Nicaragua in the 1980s are a famous example of a US proxy force in Latin America.

*quilombo* (Port.): a settlement where escaped slaves lived out of Brazilian slave owners' control. Brazil's largest and most famous quilombo was Palmares. Such settlements existed also in the Caribbean region, where they were called *palenques* (Spa.).

*royal fifth*: a 20 percent tax that the Spanish Crown placed on mining.

*sedentary* patterns of indigenous life occurred most often in highland environments. Sedentary people had fully sustainable agriculture, allowing the creation of cities and large, complex social organizations. In a few cases—the Aztecs, Incas, and Mayas—sedentary people built large empires.

*semisedentary* patterns of indigenous life were typical of forest environments. Semisedentary people practiced shifting agriculture and moved their villages every few years. They organized themselves in tribes and clans that rarely numbered more than a few thousand. Example: the Tupian people of Brazil (also Paraguay).

*nonsedentary* patterns of indigenous life were typical of grasslands, especially arid ones. Nonsedentary people depended on gathering and hunting for food. They moved constantly, and their social organizations were therefore simple. Examples: the Chichimecas of Mexico, the Pampas of Argentina.

*senhor de engenho* (Port.): literally, "lord of a mill," referring to a mill for processing sugarcane. The senhores de engenho, who also owned sugar plantations, were dominant figures in the society of colonial Brazil.

*state*: in political analysis, a collective name for the institutions of government power, including courts, schools, bureaucracy, police, and armed forces. The *state* can be usefully contrasted to the *nation*, the shared identity (ideally, but not always) felt by people who live within a state.

*transculturation*: the creative interaction between two cultures, resulting in a new culture. Transculturation among Europeans, Africans, and indigenous Americans created distinctive Latin American cultures.

*ultramontanism*: an orientation within the Catholic clergy that stressed loyalty to the pope above loyalty to royal or national authorities. The Jesuit order was famous for its *ultramontane* loyalty.

*viceroyalty*: the largest administrative subdivision of the Spanish and Portuguese empires in America, ruled by a *viceroy* who acted in the place of the king.

# Further Acknowledgments

From its original conception to the final selection of its title and cover art, W. W. Norton editor Jon Durbin had an active intellectual involvement in the first edition of this project at every stage. He is, quite simply, this book's co-creator. Karl Bakeman had a similar role in the second edition. Jon Durban rejoined the team for this third edition. He convinced me of the need for a companion reader, and he helped shape the vision of it. I am also grateful for the efforts of Jason Spears, who helped manage the manuscript, and Trish Marx, who handled photo research. In addition, thirteen reviewers commissioned by W. W. Norton contributed very substantially to the manuscript, thanks both to their specialized professional expertise and to their general understanding of what makes a good introduction to Latin American history for US readers. Let me, therefore, hereby acknowledge my debt of gratitude to Jonathan Ablard of the State University of West Georgia; Suzanne Austin Alchon of the University of Delaware; Sarah Cline of the University of California, Santa Barbara; Paul Dosal of the University of South Florida; Leo Hernandez of Oswego University; Andrew Kirkendall of Texas A & M University; Erick Langer of Georgetown University; Daniel Lewis of California State Polytechnic University, Pomona; Thomas

A9

Pearcy of Slippery Rock State University; William Summerhill of UCLA; Kathy Wells of the Wayneflete School; Thomas Whigham of the University of Georgia; and Molly Wood of Wittenberg University. I am also grateful to all the reviewers who helped shape the third edition and its new companion reader, *Born in Blood and Fire: Latin American Voices*: Carlos Aguirre of the University of Oregon; Eve Buckley of the University of Delaware; Jurgen Buchenau of the University of North Carolina, Charlotte; Patricia Juarez-Dappe of California State University, Northridge; Neil Dhingra of Carroll Community College; Paul Dosal of the University of South Florida; Mark Healey of the University of California, Berkeley; Andrew Hurley of the University of Missouri, St. Louis; Andrew Kirkendall of Texas A & M University; Erick Langer of Georgetown University; Jane Mangan of Davidson College; Kathryn Maguire of Napa Valley College; Rosa Maria Pegueros of the University of Rhode Island; Donald Ramos of Cleveland State University; Michael Scardaville of the University of South Carolina; William Skuban of California State University, Fresno; Susan Socolow of Emory University; José O. Solá of Cleveland State University; Allen Wells of Bowdoin College; and Bruce Wilson of the University of Central Florida.

# INDEX